D0290170

ALSO BY JENNIFER POTTER

The Rose: A True History

*Strange Blooms: The Curious Lives and
Adventures of John Tradescants*

Lost Gardens

Secret Gardens

SEVEN

FLOWERS

AND HOW THEY SHAPED OUR WORLD

JENNIFER POTTER

The Overlook Press
NEW YORK, NY

This edition first published in paperback in the United States in 2015 by

The Overlook Press, Peter Mayer Publishers, Inc.
141 Wooster Street
New York, NY 10012
www.overlookpress.com

For bulk and special sales, please contact sales@overlookny.com,
or write us at the above address.

Copyright © Jennifer Potter, 2013

All rights reserved. No part of this publication may be reproduced or
transmitted in any form or by any means, electronic or mechanical,
including photocopy, recording, or any information storage and
retrieval system now known or to be invented, without permission
in writing from the publisher, except by a reviewer who wishes to
quote brief passages in connection with a review written for
inclusion in a magazine, newspaper, or broadcast.

The author and publisher wish to thank the following for permission to reproduce
copyright material: Excerpt from *The Big Sleep* by Raymond Chandler, copyright © 1939 by Raymond
Chandler and renewed 1967 by Helga Greene, Executrix of the Estate of Raymond Chandler. Used by
permission of Alfred A. Knopf, an imprint of the Knopf Doubleday Publishing Group, a division of Random House LLC. All rights reserved; Six line excerpt ['We're not our skin of grime…/…'.] from 'Sunflower Sutra' from Collected Poems 1947–1980 by Allen Ginsberg. Copyright © 1955 by Allen Ginsberg.
Reprinted by permission of HarperCollins Publishers; 'Still Life with a Bridle: Essays and Apocryphas
by Zbigniew Herbert, translated by John and Bogdana Carpenter. Copyright © 1991 by Zbigniew Herbert
and John and Bogdana Carpenter. Reprinted by permission of HarperCollins Publishers; Approximately
60 words from *Wide Sargasso Sea* by Jean Rhys (First published by Andre Deutsch 1966, Penguin Books
1968, Penguin Classics 2000). Copyright © Jean Rhys, 1966. Reproduced by permission of Penguin
Books Ltd; Rainer Maria Rilke, excerpt from 'The Roses: II' from *The Complete French Poems of
Rainer Maria Rilke*, translated by A. Poulin. Translation copyright © 1979, 1982, 1984, 1986 by A. Poulin
Jr. Reprinted with the permission of The Permissions Company, Inc. on behalf of Graywolf Press,
Minneapolis, Minnesota, www.graywolfpress.org; 'Rosa Sancta' taken from *Tender Taxes*
© Jo Shapcott, 2001, and reprinted by permission of Faber and Faber Ltd.

Every effort has been made to trace or contact all copyright holders.
The publishers will be pleased to make good any omissions or rectify any mistakes
brought to their attention at the earliest opportunity.

Library of Congress Cataloging-in-Publication Data
Potter, Jennifer, 1949-
Seven flowers and how they shaped our world / Jennifer Potter.
pages cm
Includes bibliographical references and index.
ISBN 978-1-4683-0817-4 (alk. paper)
1. Flowers. 2. Flowers--History. 3. Plants and civilization. I. Title.
SB404.5.P68 2014
635.9--dc23
2013045707

Manufactured in the United States of America
ISBN 978-1-4683-1009-2
2 4 6 8 10 9 7 5 3 1

For Ros

To see a World in a Grain of Sand
And a Heaven in a Wild Flower,
Hold Infinity in the palm of your hand
And Eternity in an hour.

WILLIAM BLAKE, 'Auguries of Innocence'

Contents

Foreword

ALL MY LIFE, flowers have been creeping up on me.
My early childhood was oddly flower-free, aside from memories of threading daisy chains in the Silverdale garden of my maternal grandfather, and the lemony sweetness of *Philadelphus* flowers pinned to the fairy costume I wore to a local show. The flowers of Malaya, where we moved when I was eight, naturally came as a shock: frangipani, flaming cannas, hibiscus, the night-blooming Keng-hwa cactus, Spider orchids and Flame of the forest trees. These were flowers bold as brass but I took them entirely for granted. They were simply there, part of the given, like the bad-feet smell of the durian fruit and the flickering lights of the Hindu Diwali festival; I cannot claim foreknowledge of the way flowers would come to govern my life.

Returning to the English Lake District, I began to pay flowers more attention. My mother had turned into an assiduous gardener, determined to reclaim a derelict garden high above the town of Ambleside, on a hillside that had also sheltered the émigré artist Kurt Schwitters at the end of the war. Springtime is the time I remember best, when the garden filled with the flowers that still remind me of my Cumbrian home: tiny wild daffodils, Himalayan rhododendrons and, in late summer, banks of the saffron-coloured South African import montbretia (*Crocosmia*), which have escaped into the wild.

Everything changed when I went to university in the late sixties. Flowers became my emblem and the power of flowers my mantra. Like many of my contemporaries, I was drawn to eastern religions, and after graduating travelled westwards around the world, paying an obligatory visit to Haight Ashbury in San Francisco, which still functioned as the faintly beating heart of the Flower Power generation. While I never wore flowers in my hair, I slept on somebody's floor, ate a macrobiotic diet of brown rice and adzuki beans, and imagined – like everyone else – that I was changing the world. It is easy with hindsight to deride such facile optimism, but the flowers we embraced represented a sincerely held belief that peace would prevail if we could only disinherit the past, counter guns with guerrilla theatre and let a thousand flowers bloom.

Ten years after leaving university, I acquired a garden of my own. Seeking refuge above all, I created a lushly green urban jungle where I could pretend to be somewhere else and where the sole flowers I allowed were white lilies and tobacco plants, because of their heavenly fragrance after dark. The space was small, no more than ten metres by ten, and its illusion of other worlds persisted until a neighbour chopped through the stems of my rampant Russian vine, exposing the fragility of my gimcrack Eden.

After jungles, my interest turned to landscapes, imaginatively re-created in fiction and later studied at London's Architectural Association, then to books about gardens, secret and lost. These were followed by a biography of Britain's first celebrity gardeners and plantsmen, the John Tradescants, and most recently a cultural history of the rose, which reminded me once again of the power of flowers to express our inner selves.

For five long years I tracked the rose's evolution as a flower and as an idea, struck by how central it has been to so many cultures around the world. My conclusions were disarmingly simple: that who you are dictates how you see the rose; and that each age and each society has reinvented the rose in its own image. Through the rose we tell our stories, both personal and collective, and I wondered: if the rose can do this, what about other flowers? Can they also tell us something about who we are and where we have come from? Can they codify our aspirations, help to diffuse our fears? Can they speak to us, in other words, about things other than themselves?

Out of such questions came this book. While it cannot emulate

The Rose's breadth of enquiry undertaken for a single flower, it uses the same approach to interrogate seven flowers that have exerted power or influence of one kind or another, whether religious, spiritual, political, social, economic, aesthetic or pharmacological. I have chosen my flowers carefully; they are the lotus, lily, sunflower, opium poppy, rose, tulip and the orchid. Each has shaped our lives in some way, for better or worse, and each has some connection with my life, from the stylized lotuses of a Tibetan monastery in the Scottish Borders to the Spider orchids of a tropical childhood. I want to know where my flowers originated, when and how they gained their powers, what use men made of them in gardens, and how – or more truly why – their powers transmuted into art.

Although the book was conceived and written in Europe, I have looked further afield wherever possible, tracking the 'Aztec' and 'Inca' sunflowers through Central and South America, for instance, and tulip fever into the flower's Turkish heartlands where its consequences were particularly brutal. Some flowers are inevitably missing; had space permitted, I would like to have included western carnations, eastern peonies and chrysanthemums, and plants endemic to the southern hemisphere, such as banksias, proteas and the waratah.

As in *The Rose*, I wanted to look beyond the usual stories to untangle the flowers' botanical and cultural evolution. Writing for me is a form of detection; I like to be taken by surprise. One of my least favourite flowers – the orchid – beguiled me the most, but all seven took me to unexpected places. Here are the flowers of healing, delirium and death; of purity and passion; of greed, envy and virtue; of hope and consolation; of the beauty that drives men wild. All seven demonstrate the power of flowers to speak metaphorically, if we would only care to listen. It isn't enough to let the flowers bloom; we must also decode what they have to say.

Jennifer Potter, London, 2013

'The Summer Garden', drawn and engraved by
Crispin de Passe the Younger, *Hortus Floridus* (1614).

— 1 —

Lotus

Om mani padme hum
Tibetan Buddhist mantra, traditionally translated as
'the jewel in the heart of the lotus'

O F ALL THE flowers that have inflamed human societies, the lotus has to come first. Natives of the tropics and subtropics, true lotuses (*Nelumbo nucifera*) do not flower outdoors in Britain and my first sight of them was a revelation. I had driven from Pennsylvania into New York State to look at gardens along the Hudson Valley and stopped at the Chinese-inspired Innisfree Garden at Millbrook, north of New York City. I remember climbing the low hill from the entrance and catching sight of these remarkable flowers stretching far into the lake like airborne water lilies, their fat pink buds and star-shaped flowers poking stiffly out of upturned skirts of leaves held high above the water.

Until then, the lotus had been for me a flower of Buddhist contemplation, familiar from youthful visits to a Tibetan monastery near Lockerbie in the Scottish Borders, but so abstracted that I scarcely thought of it as a flower at all. Here were lotuses in the landscape, thousands of them, and I wanted to know more about them. Where had they come from, these perfectly formed flowers that develop strange, triffid-like seed pods, and what were they doing in this ornamental landscape created in the 1930s by the American painter Walter Beck and his wife Marion, daughter of a nineteenth-century iron baron?

My search took me first to ancient Egypt, since the pink lotuses I had seen flowering in the lake at Innisfree are not the only flowers to bear the name 'lotus'. Egyptologists call the water lilies of ancient Egypt 'lotuses', although they belong to a very different plant family: the tropical blue water lily (*Nymphaea caerulea*) and the white water lily (*Nymphaea lotus*), native to Central and North Africa. Both sorts of lotus made their mark at roughly the same time, nearly five thousand years ago, and both demonstrate the fundamental power of flowers in helping early civilizations to grasp and express the world around them.

I MAGINE THE STILL waters of the Nile at dawn. The surface is covered with the shiny egg-shaped leaves of the blue lotus (*Nymphaea caerulea*) from which rise conical buds, held some twenty to thirty centimetres above the water. As the sun climbs into the sky, the buds open into sharp-pointed stars, their petals – up to twenty in number – a startling violet blue at the tips fading to white near the cluster of bright yellow stamens at the base. The opening flowers release a delicate fragrance that lingers until the flowers close at noon, when they sink back into the water. They will open and close on two more days, flowering for a little longer than they did on their first day. The fruit, too, will be held above the water until it ripens and disappears into the Nile. The flowers of the night-blooming white lotus (*Nymphaea lotus*), by contrast, open around dusk and close mid- to late morning on four successive days. Also delicately scented, the white has rougher-edged leaves and rounder petals – details that the decorators of ancient tombs captured more than three and a half thousand years ago.*

Like all the flowers of this book, Egyptian lotuses are of a rare beauty – the blue lotus in particular – but beauty on its own does not account for their enduring fascination. Linked by their Nile habitat to ancient Egypt's extraordinary fertility, attributable to the river's annual flooding, they were adopted as the insignia of Upper Egypt in contrast to the papyrus reed of Lower Egypt's Nile delta, whose simplified shape it resembled. Lotus and papyrus came together around 3000 BCE, when the two kingdoms were united, a political union celebrated in the intertwined lotus and papyrus plants carved into King Khafre's massive black funerary throne in his valley temple near the Great Sphinx. Even greater than its political power was the lotus's close association

---

* Principal sources appear at the end of the book, on pages 239–7.

with two of ancient Egypt's most powerful deities, the sun god Ra and Osiris, lord of the afterlife, which gave the flower a leading role in the very mystery of creation.

In the early cosmogonies of ancient Egypt, it was naturally the day-blooming blue lotus that appeared at the beginning of creation, arising from the dark, watery chaos (Nu or Nun) on the morning of the first day to produce the sun god, Ra or Atum. As Ra travelled across the sky by day, he brought life to the people on earth, experiencing a symbolic death at sunset and journeying back through the netherworld to re-emerge from the horizon at dawn – just like the blue lotus.

The beginnings of Egypt's dynastic period brought another of the gods into prominence: Horus the falcon, god of the sky and the infant sun in early cosmogonies, who is shown emerging from an opening lotus flower with the sun disc balanced on his head. Later accounts made Horus the son of Isis and her husband-brother Osiris, first-born son of Geb (earth) and Nut (the overarching sky). Osiris ruled on earth but was treacherously killed by his brother Set, who cast his dismembered body into the Nile. Briefly brought back to life through Isis's knowledge of magic spells, he was able to beget Horus before returning to rule over the netherworld. Just so did the blue water lily flare briefly in the calm waters of the Nile before setting seed and returning to the deep, Osiris incarnate.

Blue lotuses were naturally included in propitiatory offerings to Osiris as lord of the afterlife, and they later blossomed in the collections of spells known as Egyptian Books of the Dead, commissioned by the wealthy elite to empower, protect and guide them on the perilous journey to the afterlife. Surviving Books of the Dead contain tantalizing glimpses of the many lotuses you might encounter on your journey through the afterlife – in offerings laid before Osiris and other deities; as lotus stands displaying the four sons of Horus; as hair adornments for women and sometimes for men. You might even choose to turn yourself into a lotus – or a falcon, heron, swallow, snake, crocodile, god or mythical being – through one of the transformative spells empowering you to move freely about the universe and return, like Osiris,

A funerary banquet of offerings topped with Nile lotus flowers, from an Egyptian Book of the Dead, *c.*1070-945 BCE.

from the underworld. The lotus's associations with rebirth and regeneration made it especially apt.

Among those choosing to transform themselves into a lotus was Nu, an official of the eighteenth dynasty (*c.*1400 BCE), who opted also for a mythical *benu*-bird and a snake; and the scribe Ani, whose lotus spell shows a human head emerging from an open blue lotus flower flanked by buds. 'I am this pure lotus which went forth from the sunshine, which is at the nose of Re,' reads the accompanying text. 'I have descended that I may seek it for Horus, for I am the pure one who issued from the fen.'

The Egyptian elite also took lotus flowers with them into their burial chambers, which they crammed with objects intended to sweeten their journey into the afterlife. Among the most celebrated was Tutankhamun's burial chamber in the Valley of the Kings, west of Thebes, discovered by the English Egyptologist Howard Carter and his team in November 1922 and renowned ever since as the best preserved and most intact of all the pharaonic tombs. Piled around gilt couches carved into monstrous animals and life-sized figures of the king was a jumble of exquisitely painted inlaid caskets, alabaster vases, strange black shrines, bouquets of leaves, beds, staves, chairs, overturned chariots. There, in the doorway to the burial chamber, stood a beautiful cup of pure semi-translucent alabaster, carved with the rounded petals of the night-blooming white lotus, its lotus-flower handles supporting the kneeling figures that represent eternal life.

An avid lotus lover, Tutankhamun had blue lotuses and chamomile flowers embroidered on his sandals. He took with him into the grave an exquisitely carved alabaster lamp combining the rounded petals of the white lotus with the smooth leaves of the blue, and two extraordinary silver trumpets, fashioned into long-stemmed lotus flowers like Victorian post-horns. They were still in working order when played by a military bandsman in Cairo's Egyptian Museum more than three and a half thousand years later, although reputedly mellower in tone.

More lotus petals – real ones, this time, dried to a crisp – adorned the boy king's funeral wreath laid on his golden mummiform casket, along with olive leaves and cornflowers, and the great floral collar draped around Tutankhamun's face on the innermost casket. Tied together with papyrus and date palm strips, its nine rows of ornaments included blue-green pottery beads, berries of Indian ginseng, willow and pomegranate leaves, blue water-lily petals, cornflowers, bristly ox-tongue and persea fruits, a gorgeous combination of colours that must have glowed brightly in the flickering torches held by the priests.

Daily and princely life was equally resplendent with lotuses, both white and blue. The garden pond of the granary scribe Nebamun supported fish and geese as well as floating lotuses, while King Thutmose

III included double- and triple-flowering *Nymphaea* among the botanical curiosities of his famous 'Botanical Garden' at Karnak, a carved relief created in the fifteenth century BCE that celebrated the exotic plants and animals brought back from his campaigns in Syria and Palestine. Thutmose's vizier Rekhmire placed a lotus pool at the heart of his orchard; and at Deir el-Medina on the Nile's west bank at Luxor, the sculptor Ipuy filled the water tank beside his shrine with white and blue lotuses, shown flowering together in the morning before the white flowers closed for the day, beside clumps of papyrus and shade-giving fruit trees. Lotus buds similarly adorn the capitals to the shrine's entrance columns, an early example of flowers turned into stone.

Lotus flowers were also an essential feature of Egyptian entertaining. Servants washed the feet and hands of each arriving guest, anointing their heads with oil and giving each one a lotus flower to hold and enjoy, as well as offering them lotus necklaces and garlands, or a single lotus flower for the head. Supplies were constantly replenished from the garden, and fresh flowers kept in jars of water until required.

Such carefully recorded details come from tomb paintings; sometimes the lotuses are blue, suggesting morning entertainments, and sometimes white. Although the night-flowering white lotus was generally used to decorate drinking vessels and the day-flowering blue lotus preferred for ritualistic use, the distinction was not absolute. In tomb paintings of Prince Tehuti-hetep's daughters at El-Bersheh, for instance, one daughter wears a crown of white lotuses and another a crown of blue. The long-stemmed lotus flower each daughter holds to her face is clearly the sharp-petalled blue lotus of ritual, leading some ethno-botanists to give it a shamanistic power akin to the water lily of the Maya, *Nymphaea ampla*. This seems unlikely, however, as no alkaloids have been identified in analyses performed on the blue lotus. But while not chemically defined as a hallucinogenic, the blue lotus contains flavonoids in concentrations similar to those found in *Ginkgo biloba*, a plant used in Chinese medicine for thousands of years to ward off old age, improve mental alertness and enhance sexual potency. Sniffed or added to wine, the blue lotus would undoubtedly have increased the pleasures of life for the Egyptian elite, even if its precise effect remains uncertain.

MIDWAY THROUGH THE first millennium BCE, the story of the lotus in Egypt becomes confused by the arrival of the true lotus of the East, *Nelumbo nucifera*, also known as the sacred lotus, and – to the ancient Greeks and Romans – as the Egyptian bean. Credit for its introduction usually goes to the Persians, who may have brought it with them when they conquered Egypt in 525 BCE. Nearly a century later, the Greek historian Herodotus described both sorts of 'lotus' growing in the marshes of Egypt. The first were the indigenous water lilies, 'which grow in great abundance when the river is full and floods the neighbouring flats'. The people would dry the harvested plants in the sun, then pick out from each blossom a fruiting head resembling a poppy's, which they would grind and bake into loaves. The roots were also edible, according to Herodotus, round and sweet-tasting, 'about as big as an apple'. He then sketched a second sort of lotus found in the Nile: 'This resembles a rose, and its fruit is formed on a separate stalk from that which bears the blossom, and has very much the look of a wasps' comb. The fruit contains a number of seeds, about the size of an olive-stone, which are good to eat either fresh or dried.'

Herodotus could not have seen the sacred lotus for himself, as the fruit develops from the flower, not alongside it. But Alexander the Great would certainly have encountered it on his conquest of Egypt when he founded his great city of Alexandria in the fourth century BCE. It made such a strong impression on him that after he had continued his victorious journey eastwards across Syria, Mesopotamia and the great Persian Empire, up the Hindu Kush and into the Indus Valley of the Punjab, the presence of crocodiles in the River Jelum and of 'Egyptian beans' in the River Chenab disoriented him completely. According to Strabo, the great geographer of the ancient world, 'he thought he had discovered the sources of the Nile, and was about to equip a fleet with the intention of sailing by this river to Egypt; but he found out shortly afterwards that his design could not be

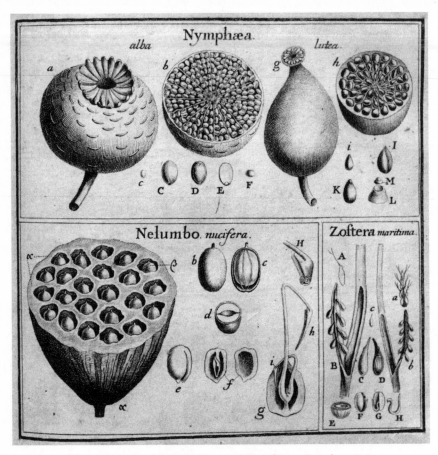

The curious seed-head of water lilies (*Nymphaea*) and the
eastern lotus (*Nelumbo nucifera*), from Joseph Gaertner, *De fructibus et
seminibus plantarum* (Stuttgart, 1788).

accomplished, "for in midway were vast rivers, fearful waters, and first
the ocean".'

Theophrastus, father of botany to the ancient Greeks and inheritor
of the mantle of Alexander's tutor Aristotle, made no such mistake
in his meticulous accounts of both sorts of lotus, which he included
in the ancient world's oldest surviving treatise on plants. Taking the
Indian lotus first, he followed Herodotus in calling it the Egyptian

bean and located it primarily in the marshes and lakes of Lower Egypt. His descriptions show the botanist at work. 'Thick as a man's finger', he recorded, the longest stalks were four cubits in length (roughly two metres) and resembled a pliant reed without joints; each contained distinct tubes 'like a honey-comb', holding aloft the fruiting head 'like a round wasps' nest', with up to thirty 'beans' protruding from individual cells. The flower was twice as large as a poppy's 'and the colour is like a rose, of a deep shade; the "head" is above the water. Large leaves grow at the side of each plant, equal in size to a Thessalian hat.'

Clearly established by this time as an economic staple, the Indian lotus was harvested for its roots, which the people of the marshes ate raw, boiled and roasted. While it grew mostly of its own accord, it was also sown in prepared bean fields, 'and if the plant once takes hold it is permanent. For the root is strong and not unlike that of reeds, except that it is prickly on the surface. Wherefore the crocodile avoids it, lest it may strike his eye on it, since he has not sharp sight.' Theophrastus reported that this lotus grew also in Syria and parts of Cilicia (the coastal stretch of south-eastern Turkey), where its fruit was unable to ripen, and also in a small lake in central Macedonia, where it ripened to perfection.

Theophrastus then went on to describe the Nile water lily, which he called '*lotos*' and which he located primarily in the Nile flood plains of Lower Egypt. Its stalk and leaves he likened to those of the Egyptian bean, although smaller and slimmer, but his description of the flowers is a curious amalgam of white and blue lotuses, as if his informants had ascribed the day-blooming habits of *Nymphaea caerulea* to the white flowers of *N. lotus*:

The flower is white, resembling in the narrowness of its petals those of the lily, but there are many petals growing close one upon another. When the sun sets, these close and cover up the "head," but with sunrise they open and appear above the water. This the plant does until the "head" is matured and the flowers have fallen off ... In the Euphrates they say that the "head" and the flowers sink and go under water in the evening till midnight, and sink to a

considerable depth; for one can not even reach them by plunging one's hand
in; and that after this, when dawn comes round, they rise and go on rising
towards day-break, being visible above the water when the sun appears; and
that then the plant opens its flower, and, after it is open, it still rises; and that
it is a considerable part which projects above the water.

Despite linking the flower's habits to the sun, Theophrastus stops
short of drawing any religious or mythical parallels, concentrating
instead on the water lily's contribution to the Egyptian diet. After
harvesting, he explained, the heads were left to decay in heaps by the
water, the fruit removed and dried, then pounded to make a kind of
bread. The round roots called 'korsion' were also edible – either raw or
(better) boiled or roasted, when the white insides turned the colour of
egg yolk and were 'sweet to taste'.

Rome's renowned natural philosopher Pliny the Elder gets his
facts even more muddled when compiling his great encyclopedia of
Natural History in the first century CE, as if he had made notes from
Theophrastus and was then unable to recall which lotus he was actually describing. To his description of a marsh-dwelling lotus he added
the 'singular fact' – from hearsay – that 'when the sun sets, these
poppy-heads shut and cover themselves in the leaves, and at sun-rise
they open again; an alternation which continues until the fruit is perfectly ripe, and the flower, which is white, falls off'. Such sensitivity to
the sun was even more marked in the Euphrates lotus, he claimed, describing it almost as a separate species; and in a later book dealing with
leguminous plants, he transferred the crocodile-repelling prickles of
Theophrastus' Egyptian bean from the roots to the stalk.

Despite the confusion in the texts, it is clear what was happen-
ing on the ground. Of the two different sorts of 'lotus' growing in
Egypt by Roman times, it was the eastern import, *Nelumbo nucifera*,
that had gained the ascendancy and travelled northwards across the
Mediterranean, literally into gardens as well as metaphorically as a
signifier of Egyptian exotica. The Roman garden writer Columella,
who was roughly a contemporary of Pliny, recommended that farm-

ers should plant thickets of Egyptian bean in the middle of their duck ponds – not as an ornament, but rather to shade the ducks. They should nonetheless keep the outer edges of their ponds plant-free so that on sunny days 'the water fowl may vie with one another to see which swims the fastest'.

In two famous Roman mosaics portraying exotic scenes from the Nile – the Nile mosaic of Palestrina (ancient Praeneste) and the floor mosaic from the House of the Faun in Pompeii – the sacred lotus of the East has again usurped Egypt's true native water lilies. In both mosaics, the lotus flowers, buds, seed-heads and leaves are faithfully and similarly reproduced, suggesting that they may have been executed by itinerant craftsmen from the same workshop, who surely saw the original plants for themselves. The Palestrina mosaic almost certainly came first, created between 120 and 110 BCE for an underground grotto-nymphaeum. Lotuses are especially evident in the party scenes taking place in a lattice-work pergola curved like a vault and overgrown with vines. Beyond the pergola, two large crocodiles and a hippopotamus lurk among the reeds.

No people appear in the floor mosaic of a Nile scene created c.90 BCE at Pompeii's luxurious House of the Faun, but there is abundant wildlife: a crocodile, a snake, a hippopotamus, a sharp-nosed mongoose, plus assorted ducks and small birds. The sacred lotus is beautifully portrayed in all stages of flowering and fruiting and a fat frog sits on two water-lily leaves, suggesting that Egypt's native 'lotus' was not entirely absent. The smooth-edged leaves indicate that this was the blue rather than the white water lily, but the lack of a flower makes identification uncertain.

UNTIL A RESURGENCE of interest in Egypt's ancient civilization, encouraged by Napoleon Bonaparte's expedition to Egypt at the end of the eighteenth century, the water-lily lotuses of the Nile slipped quietly out of view. Native to northern and tropical Africa and unable to survive outdoors in more northerly climates, they were not intrinsically different from European water lilies. It is only natural, therefore, that *Nelumbo nucifera* proved the hardier survivor in the European imagination, as travellers' tales and herbarium specimens began to inflame the curiosity of early plantsmen and scholars such as Carolus Clusius, the great sixteenth-century Flemish botanist and one-time gardener to the Holy Roman Emperor, Maximilian II.

In Britain, the strange fruits of the true pink lotus from the East caught the eye of royal apothecary John Parkinson in his herbal of 1640, *Theatrum Botanicum*, dedicated to King Charles I. After first dismissing the presentation of the 'Egyptian bean' by the Italian botanist Matthiolus as 'moulded from his owne imagination', Parkinson recounted Clusius's careful description in his 'booke of *exotickes* or strange things'. The fruit, presumably dried, had been brought to Amsterdam by Dutch mariners; its origin was unknown although it was later established to have come from the island of Java in the East Indies. Clearly conversant with earlier descriptions by Theophrastus and Herodotus, Clusius had nonetheless observed the fruit for himself, commenting that it resembled 'a very large Poppy head, cut off at the toppe: and consisted of a rough or wrinckled skinny substance; of a brownish colour somewhat light, whose circumference at the top was nine inches, and growing lesser and lesser by degrees, unto the stalkes'. The fruit had twenty-four holes or cells, added Parkinson, 'placed in a certaine order, like unto the combe of waspes', each containing one nut, which he compared to an acorn.

Parkinson then included eyewitness accounts: the first from two good friends, the Huguenot Dr Daniel Heringhooke and Dr William Parkins, who had seen a book of Javanese plants sent over to Holland from the Dutch factory there by 'a certain Dr Justus Heurnius, physician and divine'. The book was kept under glass at Leiden's University Library, open at the lotus page, where you could read that it grew in 'Moorish places, and by river banckes: the leaves are wondrous great and like unto those of the Water Lilly, and so is the flower also of a very strong smell like unto the oyl of Aneseedes'. Parkinson's second eyewitness account came from *Purchas his Pilgrimes*, a collection of travel stories put together by the English traveller Samuel Purchas, in a report by the English merchant Mr William Finch or Fincham, who had seen lotuses growing in a great lake to the north-west of Fetipore (Fatehpur Sikri), near Agra in northern India.

Parkinson reported that the pink lotus had not been seen growing in Egypt 'for many ages past', although he thought optimistically that industrious and knowledgeable men might still find it growing there. By the time Napoleon Bonaparte mounted his Egyptian campaign in 1798, trailing a second army of scientists, scholars and artists (including Henri-Joseph Redouté, younger brother of the more famous flower painter, Pierre-Joseph), the sacred lotus had quite disappeared, its tender roots eventually unable to withstand the Nile's cycles of drought and flooding. At least Napoleon's scientists correctly identified its homeland as Asia, not Africa, and were able to examine the flowers and leaves of specimens brought back from the East Indies by the French naturalist Jacques-Julien Labillardière and a drawing executed in China that included the roots.

Napoleon's scientists found the indigenous water-lily lotuses still flourishing in the rivers, ditches and canals of Lower Egypt, and their cooked roots on sale in the markets of Damietta. The blue water lily in fact received its Latin name of *Nymphaea caerulea* only in 1803 from a member of Napoleon's expedition, the French naturalist M. J. C. L. Savigny; it makes a fine appearance in Pierre-Joseph Redouté's *Choix des Plus Belles Fleurs*, a work of images without supporting text, which he undertook late in life when he was short of funds.

Both *Nelumbo* and *Nymphaea* lotuses play starring roles in Robert John Thornton's grandiose *Temple of Flora*, whose pompous, sugary text gleefully recounts that while Napoleon listened to Savigny expounding on sacred water lilies, the British fleet was annihilating the French at the Battle of the Nile. As stage-managed by Thornton himself, the *Temple of Flora*'s illustration of the eastern lotus (by artist Peter Henderson) makes botanical nonsense, marrying its pink flower to the yellow of a North American variety and laying claim to varieties in all three primary colours: 'an azure *blue*, or blushing *red*, or pale

Brahama, the Hindu god of creation, emerges from a lotus
flower emanating from the navel of Vishnu, the Vedic Supreme Being;
massaging Vishnu's legs and feet is his consort Lakshmi.

yellow . . . and also of a dazzling *white*, all which majestically (different
from our humble aquatics), rise with their foliage above the surface of
the flood, and present their luxuriant leaves to the vaulted heavens'.
He was a little more accurate with the blue lotus, which he planted in
the Nile against a backdrop of Aboukir, where the Battle of the Nile was
waged, but here, too, he was using flowers to recast history in a patriotic glow. For all his posturing ambition, the enterprise was a financial
disaster, which even a botanical lottery of the original artworks could
not salvage, and he was 'ever afterwards a beggared man'.

THE TRUE STORY of the sacred lotus, *Nelumbo nucifera*, resides not
in the overheated brains of men like Robert John Thornton but far
away to the east, in the Indus Valley of the Punjab, which Alexander

the Great mistakenly yet prophetically linked to ancient Egypt. Now considered a native of much of eastern and south-eastern Asia, northern Australia and the Volga River delta at the Caspian Sea,* the genus *Nelumbo* is thought to have originated in India, and in China where its cultivation has a long history. Reports suggest that it was widely grown along China's two longest rivers, the Chang Jiang and the Huanghe, before 7000 BCE, and Neolithic sites in China have yielded carbonized lotus seeds that are 5,000 years old.

But the flower's mythological power belongs originally to India, where it developed in ways strikingly similar to the blue Nile lotus of ancient Egypt. This eastern lotus, too, was present at the very beginning of creation in the ancient canonical texts of Hinduism, the Veda, which some scholars date back as far as 1400 BCE. One set of texts, the *Taittiriya Brahmana*, links the lotus to Brahma, part of the trinity of Hindu gods concerned with creation (Brahma), preservation (Vishnu) and destruction (Shiva). Desiring to bring forth the universe from the cosmic waters, Brahma willed a lotus leaf to emerge from the ocean, which unfurled a thousand-petalled lotus of pure gold, radiant as the sun, and a portal to the very nucleus of the universe. In some versions of the creation story, the lotus opened to reveal Brahma himself; in others, Brahma is born from a lotus that emerges from the navel of Vishnu.

Vishnu's consort is also closely associated with the lotus. Known as Shri, Lakshmi and even Padma, one of the Sanskrit words for lotus, she appeared relatively late in Vedic scriptures in a hymn attached to a later version of the Rig Veda. But already she springs to life with her lotus credentials fully formed, praised as 'lotus-born', 'lotus-coloured', 'lotus-thighed', 'lotus-eyed', 'abounding in lotuses' and 'decked with lotus garlands'. An archetypical mother goddess, bestower of health, long life, prosperity, fecundity and fame, she is almost invariably

---

*A plant sometimes known as the Indian blue lotus is, confusingly, another water lily, the day-blooming *Nymphaea nouchali*, native to southern and eastern Asia, Borneo, the Philippines, Sri Lanka and Australia.

represented sitting or standing in a lotus flower and holding a lotus in each hand.

However late this lotus goddess came to the Veda, she reigned supreme in the Indian subcontinent long before the strictly patriarchal Aryan warrior-herdsmen arrived from the north and displaced the highly developed civilization of the Indus Valley. At sites such as Harappa and Mohenjo-daro in the Punjab, which reached their peak about 2500 BCE, archaeology has unearthed a treasury of seals, inscriptions and objects of worship, including the phallus, representing the generative male energy of the universe, and a bare-breasted goddess with lotuses in her hair. After the Indus civilization collapsed, the ancient goddess lingered on, reappearing as Lajja Gauri or Aditi, a strange, lotus-headed deity who is always shown with her knees drawn up and her legs spread apart in the posture of birthing or sexual receptivity. From the second to the eleventh centuries, her cult spread across central India and stone statues proliferated; several icons of the goddess are still worshipped today.

Lajja Gauri coexists with more spiritual lotuses in other texts sacred to Hindus, among them the early Upanisads, thought to date from the seventh or sixth centuries BCE, a century or so before Buddhism emerged as another of India's great religions. In the *Brihadaranyaka Upanisad*, the visible appearance of the universal spirit, *brahman*, is likened to 'a golden cloth, or white wool, or a red bug, or a flame, or a white lotus, or a sudden flash of lightning'. A man wishing to attain greatness is advised to collect every type of herb and fruit into a bowl, follow a ritual of offerings and incantations, then lie beside the fire with his head to the east. In the morning, he should worship the sun, saying, 'You are the one lotus among the quarters! May I become the one lotus among men!' And when the woman he has created is about to give birth, he should sprinkle her with water and repeat these words:

> As from all sides the wind churns a lotus pond,
> so may your foetus stir and
> come out with the afterbirth.

In another pre-Buddhist Upanisad, the *Chandogya Upanisad*, the lotus appears as the meditative centre, the space within the heart that contains all things.

Now, here in this fort of *brahman* there is a small lotus, a dwelling-place, and within it, a small space. In that space there is something – and that's what you should try to discover, that's what you should seek to perceive . . .

As vast as the space here around us is this space within the heart, and within it are contained both the earth and the sky, both fire and wind, both the sun and the moon, both lightning and stars. What belongs here to this space around us, as well as what does not – all that is contained within it.

This same lotus would soon blossom into the central metaphor of Buddhism, which developed out of the teachings of the historical Buddha, Prince Siddharta Gautama, who lived and taught in the sixth or fifth centuries BCE. According to Buddhism's basic philosophy, we are trapped in a cycle of suffering and rebirth caused by craving and an attachment to self. The path to enlightenment involves breaking this cycle by denying the self and the material world, aided by enlightened beings known as Bodhisattvas, whose compassion has led them to help all sentient beings towards enlightenment.

Whereas the blue Nile lotus gained its power from its intimations of rebirth and transformation, and its connection to the sun god Ra, the Buddhist lotus speaks of purity and spiritual growth. Each culture has fashioned the flower in its own image, but each has looked closely at the real flower, developing metaphors that express and reflect its nature. Putting down roots deep into the slime of lake beds, the day-blooming *Nelumbo nucifera* flourishes in muddy water that is often disturbed by sheltering wildlife, yet it thrusts its leaves and then its buds high above the surface, where they open into supremely scented pink flowers, pure and unsullied. The fragrance is especially strong on the first and second days.

Living lotuses are absent from the sacred garden of Lumbini in Nepal, which commemorates the birthplace of Prince Siddharta, but

legend links them to his birth and early childhood, as told in the fant-
astical biography of the Buddha, the *Lalavistara*, written originally in
Sanskrit and later translated into Chinese and Tibetan. The Buddha's
birth is foretold in a dream recounted by his mother, Queen Maya,
to her husband, King Suddhodhana of Kapilvattu in the Himalayan
foothills. In the dream, a noble white elephant entered her belly (in
one commentary, bearing a white lotus in its trunk). On the night the
Buddha-to-be entered the womb of his mother, 'a stalk arose from the
water below the earth, and, penetrating through sixty-eight hundreds
of thousands of yojanas* of the great earth, bore a lotus high up in the
region of Brahmá.' More lotuses attended the Buddha's miraculous
birth, appearing as he alighted on earth and as he made his first steps,
'and where he set his foot there sprouted forth lotuses'.

   In Buddhist iconography, the lotus is one of eight auspicious symbols, and every important deity is shown sitting on a lotus, standing
on a lotus, or holding a lotus in each or either hand in the form
known as Padmapani, the lotus bearer. Some paintings and figurines
combine all three poses, as in a tiny bronze statuette of the Bodhisattva
Avalokitesvara, from eastern India, who sits in an open lotus flanked
by two more, one held loosely in his left hand while his right foot
rests on another small lotus attached to the statue's rim. Tibetan
art similarly teems with lotuses, floating above the muddy waters of
attachment to signify the primordial purity of body, speech and mind.
In Tibetan Buddhism, the colour of the lotus is also significant: the
white lotus represents spiritual purity; red is the lotus of love, compassion, passion, and all qualities of the heart; blue signifies the victory of
the spirit over the senses; while the pink lotus reigns supreme and is
generally reserved for the highest deity.

As LOTUSES WERE indigenous to China, the country had no need
to wait for Buddhism's arrival in the first century (some scholars place it much earlier) to recognize their beauty. The lotus was in

---

* A Vedic measure of how far an ox cart can travel in a day, some eight to ten miles.

any case revered by the old philosophical and ethical traditions of Taoism and Confucianism. It was the flower beloved by He Xiangu (Ho Hsien-ku), the only woman among Taoism's Eight Immortals who is commemorated by the tai chi movement, 'The fair lady works the shuttles'; and it stood as the model for the 'superior man' in Confucian thought — a reputation that continued well into the twentieth century. Before China's revolution, every schoolchild was expected to memorize these lines by the celebrated eleventh-century philosopher and cosmologist, Zhou Dunyi (Chou Tun-i):

[The lotus] emerges from muddy dirt but is not contaminated; it reposes modestly above the clear water; hollow inside and straight outside, its stems do not struggle or branch. Its subtle perfume pervades the air far and wide. Resting there with its radiant purity, the lotus is something to be appreciated from a distance, not profaned by intimate approach.

The lotus appears often in Chinese poetry, for example in the (imaginary) pleasure gardens of a poem from the southern state of Ch'u, written some time around the fourth century BCE. In the poem, lotuses belong to the pleasures of nature and of life, which the shamans hope will tempt a dying king's soul to return to his body, together with the light-footed princesses who wait for him in his garden pavilion, where the galleries catch the scent of orchids on the breeze and the view looks down on a winding pool. 'Its lotuses have just opened; among them grow water chestnuts, and purple-stemmed water-mallows enamel the green wave's surface.'

The tone is wistful, as in much early Chinese poetry, evoking the beauties of nature without comment. Nature goes its own way; man alone changes and suffers. In 'Plucking Willows' by Xiao Yi (Hsiao I), written during the chaotic northern dynasties of the fifth and sixth centuries, the sight of a weeping willow reminds the traveller of his home and his beloved, and of the willow branch he received on parting. But the willow that 'joins hearts together' also breaks like a heart — a play on the homonym for 'lien', 'lotus', which sounds like the word to sympathize, or to love.

The mountain is as charming as lotus blossoms,
The flowing water glitters like the bright moon.
In the cold night, the gibbons' cries pierce his heart;
The wanderer's tears soak his clothes.

Yet for all nature's changelessness in poetry, the lotus is responsible for one of the great seasonal transformations in Chinese gardens:
it is 'the flower of summer lassitude, just as the peony is the flower of
early summer plenty'. Winter skating lakes turn in summer into 'vast
seas of lotus, over which pass strange and baffling blue-green shadows
when breezes stir the great cupped leaves'. On a visit to Beijing's lakes
in the 1930s, the American garden writer Loraine Kuck was entranced.
'To cross this jungle of water plants,' she wrote, 'a small boat must wind
through dim green waterways which have been purposely kept clear, or
the boat could not move at all. It is quite impossible to see out over the
forest of tall leaves and stems on either side.' In the old China, every
home with a courtyard had one or two large porcelain bowls filled in season with exquisite lotus flowers, 'bringing to the mind of the beholder
all the thoughts of exaltation of which this flower is emblematic'.

Although plants rarely featured in Chinese ornament before the
First Emperor unified China in 221 BCE, the lotus gradually spread
into every corner of Chinese life and art, 'painted on porcelain, carved
in jade, ivory, wood or stone, cast in bronze, embroidered on silk,
and in a highly conventionalized form … a very common motif in
the decorative borders of wooden or lacquered panels'. Enhanced by
the prestige of Buddhism, lotus petals were used to decorate Chinese
ceramics, and for a time during the Northern Song dynasty (960–
1127 CE) and again in the fourteenth century, the lotus displaced the
peony as a central motif in porcelain decoration. In textile art, the peony
and again the chrysanthemum took precedence, except during the
Ming dynasty, when the lotus outshone them. At about the same time,
the stylized motif of the lotus palmette, thought to have originated in
the seventh century BCE in the carved stone floor panels and cover-
ings of the Assyrian royal palaces of Nimrud and Nineveh, travelled

back from China with the Mughals to the great carpet-making centres of Persia, reappearing in the 'Shah 'Abbasi palmettes', named after Persia's great Safavid ruler of the late sixteenth and early seventeenth centuries. The lotus's travels clearly illustrate how flowers are carried from continent to continent by conquest and migration, undergoing subtle transformations as they adapt to new cultures and civilizations.

A much darker sign of the lotus's emblematic influence can be seen in the ancient custom of footbinding, prevalent in China from the twelfth century and eradicated only in the twentieth, which sought to constrict women's feet from girlhood into tiny 'golden lotuses', considered a sign of affluence and erotic appeal. The American historian Howard S. Levy has traced the practice to the dynastic rule of the sovereign-poet Li Yü, who controlled part of a divided China towards the end of the tenth century. Li Yü's favourite concubine was a gifted dancer named Lovely Maiden, for whom he had built a six-foot-high golden lotus with a carmine carpel at its heart. Instructed to bind her feet with white silk cloth, which turned her toes into the points of a sickle moon, Lovely Maiden then danced in the centre of the lotus, 'whirling about like a rising cloud'. As Lovely Maiden was still able to dance, her bindings cannot have been too constricting, but after the practice spread slowly southwards into the rest of China, they became ever more severe, and women's distorted feet ever smaller. Songs, poems and plays of China in the Mongol era refer to 'lotus blossom' feet of just three inches.

I T I S H A R D to equate the lotus of female containment with the gentler mantra of eastern meditation, the jewel in the heart of the lotus, *om mani padme hum*, which travelled westwards alongside a more general interest in eastern religions, resurfacing in the work of Carl Jung, one of the twentieth century's great pioneers of psychoanalysis. Jung provided a foreword to the sinologist Richard Wilhelm's translation of *The Secret of the Golden Flower: A Chinese Book of Life*, which contains a guide to meditation that was originally transmitted orally and later written down by a monk from the monastery of the Double Lotus Flower in the

eastern Chinese province of Anhui. This lotus, too, unlocks the shimmering heart of the meditative experience: 'The thousand-petalled
lotus flower opens, transformed through breath-energy. Because of
the crystallization of the spirit, a hundred-fold splendour shines forth.'

For Jung, the 'Golden Flower' of ancient Chinese thought was a
mandala symbol representing the universe, one he likened to drawings
brought to him by his patients in the form of a geometric ornament,
like a lotus-rosette, or a blossom growing from a plant. While he would
increasingly visualize the mandala symbol as the rose of a Christianized western tradition (see Chapter 5), he recognized its roots in the
eastern lotus. As he said in *Psychology and Alchemy*,

The centre of the mandala corresponds to the calyx of the Indian lotus, seat
and birthplace of the gods. This is called the *padma*, and has a feminine significance. In alchemy the *vas* [the alchemical vessel] is often understood
as the uterus where the 'child' is gestated. In the Litany of Loreto, Mary is
spoken of three times as the 'vas' ('vas spirituale,' 'honorabile,' and 'insigne
devotionis') and in medieval poetry she is called the 'flower of the sea' which
shelters the Christ.

Another remarkable lotus survives in popular culture, *Avatar*'s
Order of the White Lotus in the popular animated television series
developed in the United States, which traces its ancestry back through
the martial arts monk-heroes of the Shaolin monastery in Hunan
to Buddhism's White Lotus Society, forced underground when the
Mongols took control of China in the late thirteenth century. The lotus
may focus minds on the still centre of the turning world but it can also
foment rebellion and change, or transform itself into a highly innovative racing and sports car marque, such is the power of its accumulated associations.

IN THE EARLY twentieth century, one of the best places to view the
lotus was undoubtedly Japan in the damp hot days of August, when
the cicadas sang from earliest dawn and the true lotus lover got very

little sleep, anxious to hear the buds open 'with the sudden touch of dawn'. Enthusiastic portraits of the opening lotus come to us from the well-travelled Du Cane sisters in a book about the flowers and gardens of Japan, its watercolours by Ella and breathy descriptions by Florence, who wrote of the great buds opening with a noise that was 'indescribable to one who has not heard it', noting

how quickly the delicate pink or white petals unfurl, as though hastening to make the most of their short life, for before the overpowering heat of the August noonday the flower closes, to open once more on the morrow and then die a graceful death; the petals dropping one by one, but still retaining all the freshness of their colour, and then nothing will be left but the great seed pod, very beautiful in itself, but not as beautiful as the great bluish-green leaves studded with dewdrops, which seem to reflect every passing cloud.

Although not generally considered a Japanese native, the lotus had arrived early in Japan – perhaps as early as 2000 BCE, along with apricots and flowering peaches. More lotuses came with Buddhism around the mid-sixth century, and records tell of a lotus festival borrowed from the Chinese and celebrated by the aristocrats of Nara in the Heian period (794–1192 CE). The number of lotus varieties was also steadily increasing, from twenty-two in 1688 to thirty a little over a century later, reaching almost a hundred by the mid-nineteenth century. Most parts of the lotus were popular as food, and the leaves used to wrap other foods as well; by extension, a 'lotus leaf' came to mean a fickle woman. The lotus was also prized by the samurai class and by connoisseurs, so that by the late Edo period Japan had overtaken China in the number of ornamental varieties grown.

Later chapters in this book tell the story of how Japan – a relatively closed society – was forced to open its doors to the West, starting with the mission in 1853 of the American navy's Commodore Matthew Perry. But while the lotus's popularity within Japan began to wane in the sweeping changes of the Meiji Restoration, the lotus caught the eye of western visitors who had come to help modernize Japanese society, or simply to admire its exotic otherness. In a curious convergence of our eastern and Egyptian lotuses, the designer Christopher Dresser marvelled in the early 1880s at the many echoes of ancient Egypt he detected in Japan's art, architecture and artefacts. Singling out the carved stem and flower of a Buddhist lotus on the altar of a Tokyo temple, he discovered in its rigidity 'that simplicity, yet dignity, in its treatment, and that stern conventionality in the drawing of the flower, which would almost lead us to believe that it was produced under the Pharaohs'. He marvelled, too, at the Japanese love of flowers, especially those that required you to look upwards, such as flowering cherries. For Dresser, the almond reigned as the flower of spring, the lotus as the flower of summer, and the chrysanthemum – Japan's imperial flower, which bears the same relation to Japan as the rose does to England – as the flower of autumn.

Another westerner who wrote admiringly of Japan was the young British architect Josiah Conder, hired in the 1870s by the Meiji government to help modernize its architecture. Conder's books fanned a craze in the West for Japanese gardens, which used few flowers beyond marginal plantings of flag and other irises by streams and marshy beds, summer lotuses grown in some garden lakes, and a few choice flowers and grasses of late summer. Conder is remembered as one of the first westerners to write about the art of Japanese flower arranging, in which the lotus was among the featured flowers of summer, although its spiritual and religious associations precluded its use on more secular festive occasions.

He wrote of the lotus:

Growing out of the muddiest and most stagnant water, its leaves and flowers are always fresh and clean; although it is particularly sensitive, and quickly withers if brought into contact with any of the foul fertilizers by which other plants are nourished. This purity which the Lotus maintains amid surrounding filth, is mentioned as the reason for associating it with a religious life, and in a well-known book of Buddhist precepts, it is written:- 'If thou be born in the poor man's hovel, but hast wisdom, then art thou like the Lotus flower growing out of the mud!'

Of the lotuses Conder recommended for flower arranging, the sweetest and most powerfully scented was the white lotus, while the more handsome red had little scent, he said. Other varieties included a 'Gold-thread-lotus', its red blossoms marked with yellow lines; a fine deep-crimson variety; and sometimes the Indian lotus, whose large red blossoms never closed (ordinary lotus blossoms generally close around noon) but dropped off after five or six days. Almost as esteemed as the flowers, lotus leaves were selected according to Conder to represent the Buddhist divisions of time into past, present and future: past time signified by a partly decayed or worm-eaten leaf; present time by a handsome open leaf, also known as a 'Mirror Leaf'; and future time by a leaf about to uncurl.

Not all Europeans viewed the changing lotus with such serenity. Visiting Japan in the early 1890s, the Victorian artist and garden designer Alfred Parsons found painting Japanese flowers extremely irksome as 'the buds of yesterday are flowers to-day, and tomorrow nothing is left but the ruin of a past beauty'. Lotuses — which he spied first near the railway on his way to Tokyo — he found especially troublesome, branding them 'one of the most difficult plants which it has ever been my lot to try and paint; the flowers are at their best only in the early morning, and each blossom after it has opened closes again before noon the first day, and on the second day its petals drop.' The large glaucous leaves were no easier, reflecting every passing shade of the sky and being 'so full of modelling that it is impossible to generalize them as a mass; each one has to be carefully studied, and every breath of wind disturbs their delicate balance, and completely alters their forms'.

Parsons had installed his easel by the lotus beds beside the little temple of Benten at Shiba (the Shinobazu pond in Ueno Park, Tokyo), where he was jostled from morning to night by curious onlookers, mostly children with babies tied to their backs. Despite the best efforts of a patrolling policeman to disperse the crowd, their ranks were quickly refilled. 'The spectators are almost always polite,' remarked Parsons, 'and take care not to put themselves between you and your subject; but they squeeze up very close to your elbow, and trample on your nerves, if not on your materials.'

Although adopted by the Buddhists, said Parsons, the lotus excited no animosity among the followers of Shinto, and lotus ponds were left unscathed when Buddhist shrines were pulled down. The largest ponds he saw were connected to the great Hachiman shrine at Kamakura, where white, bright-rose and shell-pink lotuses grew freely. The white lotus was particularly favoured by adherents of Nichiren, 'a noisy sect which beats a drum during the long hours of prayer'; the same variety was also grown in rice fields as a food crop. They tasted of very little, except of the sugar with which they were boiled, 'but they are crisp in texture and pleasant to munch'. The seed-heads, which Theophrastus had compared to a Thessalian hat, Parsons described as 'very like the rose of a watering pot'.

While Parsons remained ambivalent about the lotus, associating its evident beauty with the discomforts of a Japanese summer, other western writers and artists welcomed the lotus as a way of projecting the exotic 'otherness' of Japan. The fashion for all things Japanese, fanned in Britain by the American-born artist James McNeill Whistler, lured to Japan a select band of western visitors, among them the 'Glasgow Boy' painters, George Henry and his friend Edward Atkinson Hornel. In *The Lotus Flower*, painted in 1894, Hornel brings huge pink and white lotuses to the foreground while above them floats a gorgeously dressed *oiran* or courtesan having her hair arranged in traditional style. Hornel surely intended such a head-on collision between an exotic contemporary sensuality and Buddhism's sacred flower.

The soft 'but rather cloying' scent of late lotus blossoms also pervades the final pages of Pierre Loti's *Madame Chrysanthème*, which lent its oriental atmosphere and part of its plot to Puccini's opera, *Madame Butterfly*. Widely read in its day, *Madame Chrysanthème* is tainted for today's readers by the cultural arrogance of its hero, a 'superior'

foreigner who acquires a *mousmé* or temporary wife in a purely commercial transaction. Often irritated by her, he nonetheless admires her
Japanese flower arrangements and especially her lotus flowers, 'great
sacred flowers of a tender, veined rose-colour, the milky rose-colour
seen on porcelain; they resemble, when in full bloom, great waterlilies, and when only in bud, might be taken for long pale tulips'. As
he prepares to leave Japan, he gives a farewell tea party at which the
burning lamps and the damp breath of the *mousmés* bring out the perfume of the lotus, which blends in the heavy-laden atmosphere with
the camellia oil the women use in their hair; and as his ship sails away
from Nagasaki, he throws his last, faded lotus blooms into the sea,
making his 'best excuses for giving to them, natives of Japan, a grave so
solemn and so vast'.

THE LOTUS IN late nineteenth-century art and literature demonstrates how flowers can accrue meanings that turn them into metaphors. The exotic lure of the East is one such lotus abstraction. Another
is the connection between lotuses and dreams, an idea already present
in the 'lotos' of the ancient Greeks, a name given by Theophrastus to
at least six different plants: the two Nile water-lily lotuses (*Nymphaea
caerulea* and *N. lotus*); the Lote or Nettle tree of the Mediterranean
(*Celtis australis*); a perennial clover (*Trifolium fragiferum*); fenugreek
(*Trigonella foenum-graecum*); and North African jujube (*Ziziphus lotus*).
This last is traditionally assumed to bear the mesmeric fruit that
Odysseus encountered on the island of the Lotophagoi as he made
his way home from Troy. As sweet as dates and the size of a lentisk-
berry, according to Herodotus, the fruit of this lotus could be made
into a wildly intoxicating wine; in Homer, any crewman who ate the
'honey-sweet fruit' lost all desire to return home,

> their only wish to linger there with the Lotus-eaters,
> grazing on lotus, all memory of the journey home
> dissolved forever.

Although this strange North African fruit bears no botanical rela-tion to either ancient Egypt's Nile water lilies or the sacred lotuses of the East, its 'languor and honeyed bliss' have infected the lotus story, reappearing virtually unchanged some two and a half millennia later in the drowsy rhythms of Alfred Lord Tennyson's poem, *The Lotos-Eaters*, where

> The Lotos blooms below the barren peak;
> The Lotos blows by every winding creek.

Other flowers contribute to Tennyson's enchanted atmosphere: the myrrh bush (probably a kind of acacia), amaranth, moly, acanthus, poppy and beds of asphodel, and in the opening verse of the choral incantation:

> There is sweet music here that softer falls
> Than petals from blown roses on the grass.

But the lotus is the flower that lingers in the memory.

The same drowsily decadent lotus resurfaced in the French poet Charles Baudelaire's 'Le Voyage', which closed the second edition of *Les Fleurs du Mal* published in 1861. Now, however, the traveller will almost certainly eat the perfumed lotus, these 'miraculous fruits for which your heart hungers', and thus succumb to the 'strange gentleness of this afternoon which shall never end'. Only by drinking death's poison can the traveller plumb the depths of the abyss, reaching beyond the unknown to encounter the new.

Such finality infuses John William Waterhouse's dreamily bewitch-ing painting *Hylas and the Nymphs*, which captures the moment when the Argonaut Hylas falls for the imploring eyes and gentle caresses of the Naiades as they lure him into their watery abode, tangled with sinuous water lilies. They are worlds apart from the serene, sunlit wa-ter lilies that Claude Monet painted in his water garden at Giverny, when his eyesight was fading. After a lifetime of trying to capture atmosphere filtered through light, he was now trying to capture light filtered through water, which presented an even greater challenge; his lilies appear to float on clouds reflected in the surface of this 'trick mirror'.

The Indian lotus has left a fainter impression in western art and poetry than either water lilies or Japanese lotuses, but one that lingers nonetheless. Particularly memorable are Howard Hodgkin's water-colour lotuses dating from the 1980s when he stayed as a guest of the Sarabai family, mill owners from Ahmedabad, living in a small white bungalow at the centre of their Douanier Rousseau garden. Long fascinated by Indian art, Hodgkin painted the everyday sights around him: a concrete wall with a flower garland hanging from it; vistas of horizon and sky; a train crossing a distant landscape. Occasionally his hosts would eye him through the bungalow windows, 'rather like eighteenth-century gentry in England would look at their pet hermit'. In Hodgkin's own arrangement of his watercolours, he placed the larger lotus last in the sequence, an image of 'fulfilment or perfect pleasure when all struggle is ended'.

A similar 'lotos' arises from the once-dry pool in 'Burnt Norton', the opening poem of T. S. Eliot's *Four Quartets*, its flower rising quietly from roots embedded in the slime and breaking through the surface of the water to attain enlightenment. Thus does the American-born poet bring the eastern lotus into a poem redolent of western roses, and half-rembered moments in the rose-garden where time stops still.

TODAY, YOU CAN order the tropical blue Nile water lily *Nymphaea caerulea* from specialist growers, including Latour-Marliac in France, who supplied Monet with his water lilies and whose recent catalogues boast nine *Nelumbium* in white, red, pink and rosy lilac. Many more true lotuses are available in Japan, some 300 at least, of which two-thirds are preserved at the University of Tokyo's Exper-imental Station for Landscape Plants. To see the Nile water lilies in flower, you will almost certainly have to visit a botanical garden with a tropical water-lily house, but many gardens in warmer regions of the United States can show you fine beds of the sacred lotus, *Nelumbo nucifera*: at California's Huntington Botanical Gardens, for instance, where the lotuses bloom from mid-July; and at Walter and Marion Beck's Innisfree Garden in the Hudson Valley, where my lotus quest began.

Like Eliot, the Becks brought eastern ideas into a western setting, inspired by references to a Chinese garden created in the eighth century by the poet, painter and garden-maker Wang Wei, which they discovered on a research visit to London. As interpreted by Walter Beck, Wang Wei sculpted his country estate in a series of 'cups' or three-dimensional pictures, centred on a large lake with gently enclosing hills. Innisfree's original lotus pool, planted in 1945 with white varieties of lotus, has since been abandoned and a new pool excavated east of Tiptoe Rock. Now lotuses are part of the large bog garden that begins in the meadow and moves ever northwards, while white and pink lotuses creep into the lake, appearing in midsummer and flowering for a month or more.

Their appeal is timeless. Nearly thirteen centuries ago, Wang Wei wrote about the lotus in a series of poems inspired by his country retreat:

> A light boat greets the arriving guest,
> Coming over the lake from far away,
> Across the gallery we raise our cups;
> On every side the lotus is in bloom.

Innisfree's lotuses take me back to the abstracted lotuses of Samye Ling, the Tibetan monastery in a gentle Scottish valley where the lotus mantra and its intimations of other realities once formed part of my everyday habits. As simile, metaphor, idea, fragrance, garden flower, medicine or simply as food, the lotus finds echoes in all the other stories that follow but the lotus is – for this writer at least – where the power of flowers began.

— **2** —

Lily

I see a lily on thy brow,
With anguish moist and fever dew,
And on thy cheeks a fading rose
Fast withereth too.

JOHN KEATS, 'La Belle Dame sans Merci'

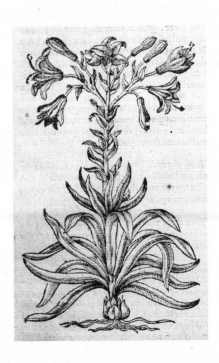

THE WHITE MADONNA lily (*Lilium candidum*) is Europe's answer to the lotus. Grown in gardens for more than 3,500 years, it surpassed even the all-powerful King Solomon in its 'beauty and braverie'. So wrote the Elizabethan herbalist John Gerard, doubtless seduced by the white lily's association with the Virgin Mary, which turned it into one of Christendom's most potent symbols. But the lily's sacred associations stretch back far beyond biblical times, to the Minoans of Crete and the eastern Mediterranean, who painted its earthly and symbolic beauty onto their walls and artefacts, leaving us strange hints of its potency, even then.

Gardeners today are far more likely to plant the larger, showier Asiatic species and hybrids, so when you chance upon a bed of Madonna lilies, their white flower clusters appear smaller than you might imagine, the flower trumpets not so pronounced. I have never grown them myself, although lilies were among the very few flowers I allowed into the urban jungle of my first garden: white Regal lilies (*Lilium regale*), introduced into Europe by Ernest 'Chinese' Wilson. I loved them for their ethereal night-time fragrance and for their fleeting reference to Rimbaud, one of my flawed heroes, who slipped shivery white lilies into the surreal and scurrilous verses he dedicated to the Parnassian poet, Théodore de Banville, 'What one says to the poet on the subject of flowers'. (He also included roses, a blue lotus and a sunflower, among many others.)

In common with all the flowers in this book, the lily has a complex and contrary history. Adopted as the badge of Mary's purity, it

gradually ceded ground to the rose in Christian iconography, just as
the garden lily lost out to American and Asiatic varieties, reinventing
itself eventually as the languid flower of late nineteenth- and early
twentieth-century art movements, which elevated art to the status of
religion. In the West, the white lily *Lilium longiflorum* from southern
Japan and Taiwan is celebrated as the flower of funerals and of Easter,
while the great British plantswoman Gertrude Jekyll so cherished the
Asiatic Tiger lily (*L. lancifolium*) that she looked on it as an old English
native. Flowers are forever crossing boundaries of one kind or another,
as the lily's story so clearly shows.

UNLIKE THE ROSE, which took centuries – millennia, even – to
evolve into a garden beauty, the lily sprang fully formed into the
public eye. First to record its beauty were the Bronze-Age Minoans
of Crete and Thera (Santorini) in the eastern Mediterranean, whose
civilization came to a catastrophic end around the middle of the
second millennium BCE. Among the mementos they left behind are
some spectacular lily frescoes found in the Cretan palace complex of
Knossos and its eastern port of Amnisos. Cruder perhaps but equally
full of life and charm, the lily paintings of Thera confirm the Minoans'
delight in this most fragrant of cultivated flowers, which joined the
saffron crocus in the pantheon of flowers the Minoans revered most.

Crete's painted lilies owe their discovery to the wealthy British
archaeologist Sir Arthur Evans, who bought the entire archaeological
site of Knossos in 1900 and whose invasive excavations and 'restor-
ations' have laid false trails ever since. One fresco irreparably dam-
aged by his excavations showed a fine group of white lilies with orange
anthers and green foliage against a dark red background, dated at
between 1700 and 1600 BCE. In a naturalistic touch, the petals of one
of the flowers had become detached as if by the passing breeze, a detail
that went far beyond 'mere decorative art' in Evans's view, which he
likened to a Minoan seal of about the same time showing trees swayed
by the wind.

More formal in a garden sense are the frescoes from the 'House of the Lilies' at Amnisos, in which tall, white-petalled lilies bearing a dozen flowers each stand before a stepped frieze – a garden wall, perhaps. They look like *Lilium candidum*, which may once have grown wild in the vicinity, although the garden variety is typically sterile and the type is usually assumed to have originated further east. Another townhouse fresco from Amnisos portrays clusters of tall lilies growing beside a formal garden feature, which reminded Evans of the fountains at Versailles; and he naturally enthused about the many lily decorations found on Minoan vases, jugs, and another naturalistic wall painting found at the little palace of Hagia Triada in south-central Crete.

Beloved in gardens and as ornament, the lily also appears to have played a more obviously sacramental role in Minoan iconography, at least if we accept the evidence of one of Evans's most trumpeted finds at Knossos. This is a painted relief he dubbed the 'Priest-King', discovered among the rubble of a ceremonial corridor abutting the Central Court and 'restored' by Émile Gilliéron *fils*, one of a pair of Swiss artists, father and son, who helped Evans with his reconstructions. While not exactly forgers, the Gilliérons executed brash and overconfident reconstructions from the flimsiest of evidence, frequently obliterating the very fragments they sought to conserve.

In Gilliéron's reconstructed scene, a muscular young man strides through a field of stylized lilies (Evans identified them as irises), wearing nothing but a loincloth, a plumed lily crown and a red lily collar. Thrusting his right shoulder forwards, the youth appears to be leading an animal, which Evans interpreted as a sacred griffin. Here, said Evans, with breathless assurance, was the earthly representative and adopted son of the Minoan mother goddess, 'a Priest-King after the order of Minos' and nothing less than 'Minos himself in one of his mortal incarnations'.

Provoking an immediate furore, the painted figure and its interpretation remain disputed to this day. Is it a man or a woman? A theocratic king or a female leaper? One person or two, facing left or right? And what are we to make of the lily emblems on the crown and necklace: do they really support Evans's views about the figure's status? As

Evans himself described, the stylized lilies in fact combine two flowers in one: the fan-shaped papyrus or *waz*, borrowed from the snake goddess of the Egyptian delta, grafted onto a Minoan lily. Convinced that the crown represented a mystic Egyptian element, Evans proclaimed the lily as 'pre-eminently the Minoan sacred flower'. Ritual dances before the goddess took place in a field of lilies, he claimed, relying on the evidence of signet rings from Candia and especially Mycenae, which linked the goddess to offerings of lilies.

While scholars today are far more cautious in their interpretation, Evans's pronouncements on the 'Priest-King' are regaining partial favour, and expert opinion grants at least some religious significance to the Minoan lily. But without supporting texts, we cannot know exactly what the Minoans intended when they painted lilies on the walls of their houses and sacred spaces.

A similar mystery surrounds the red lilies discovered in other Bronze-Age wall paintings at Akrotiri on the island of Thera, ironically preserved by the volcano's catastrophic eruption midway through the second millennium BCE. Painted around three walls of a ground-floor room to an Akrotiri town house, small clumps of red lily flowers protrude from a rocky Aegean landscape that looks almost Japanese in its boldly delineated blocks of red, yellow, black and shades of blue. Swallows, flying either alone or in pairs, swoop close to the blooms, but in contrast to the nearby fresco of the saffron-gatherers, people are entirely absent. Like a theatrical backdrop, the 'Spring Fresco' of lilies and swallows looks as if it is waiting for something to happen. Perhaps this is why virtually all scholars have accorded the room a ritual function, despite the absence of any real evidence. Whatever its original purpose, by the time of Thera's eruption it was little more than a storeroom for domestic clutter. No text has yet elucidated the mystery, but equally no 'restorer' has imposed a modern view on these lilies, which some experts believe were painted before 1759 BCE. And what of the lilies themselves? Did Thera's artists paint what they saw, adding the bright red of the endemic Scarlet turkscap lily (*Lilium chalcedonicum*) to their stylized lilies based more closely on the form of the white lily,

Bronze-Age Minoan wall painting of red lilies and swallows from a
townhouse at Akrotiri on the Aegean island of Thera.

L. candidum? Or did they – the more usual explanation – simply paint
white lilies red to make them stand out against the white background?

The same red lilies, with blue rather than yellow stems, appear in
another house at Akrotiri in elegant two-handled vases, displayed
in trompe-l'oeil open windows close to a room containing friezes in
miniature of exploration and perhaps conquest. While the friezes tell
us nothing specific about the lily, they map a context for its gradual dispersal, as the most prized flowers spread slowly outwards from
their native lands, whether seized as booty, passed from conqueror
to conquered, or simply bought and sold in the marketplaces of the
civilized world and handed eagerly from one delighted plant collector
to another.

After the Minoan catastrophe, the lily lost for a time its religious
associations but it was undoubtedly colonizing the lands of the
Mediterranean. By the early seventh century BCE, graceful and clearly

recognizable trumpet lilies had reached the northern palace of the
Assyrian King Ashurbanipal at Nineveh (modern-day Mosul in Iraq),
carved into a stone relief. Another tomb relief of Egyptians gathering
cultivated white lilies for perfume shows that lilies had reached Egypt
by the twenty-sixth dynasty, the last to rule Egypt before the Persian
conquest of 525 BCE. The vast quantities of flowers required to make
perfumes imply cultivation on a commercial scale; as the lily is not indigenous to Egypt, it may have travelled there with the Greeks, who
established a trading colony around this time at Naucratis on the Nile
delta. Lilies were woven into the wreaths and bouquets left by mourn-
ers in the tombs of pharaonic Egypt, along with their 'lotuses' and
many other flowers.

Lilies were in any case gaining a foothold in the ordinary garden
plots of the early Greeks, who loved the lily for its sweetness even if
they gave it no central role in the complicated genealogies of their
gods. In Hesiod's *Theogony*, for instance, lilies appear only fleetingly in
the 'lily-like' voices of the Muses that sweeten the ears of their father,
Zeus. And in the epic pre-*Iliad* cycle of poems known as the *Cypria*,
perfumed garlands to adorn the goddess Aphrodite contained seasonal flowers such as 'crocus and hyacinth and flourishing violet and
the rose's lovely bloom, so sweet and delicious, and heavenly buds, the
flowers of the narcissus and lily'.

The lily comes into clearer focus in the works of the Greek botanist
Theophrastus. While the detail in Theophrastus' *Enquiry into Plants*
does not permit a reliable taxonomy of Greek lilies, he knew of at least
two different types that accord with two of Europe's native species.
These were the white Madonna lily, *Lilium candidum*, believed to have
originated in the Balkans before it was taken into cultivation by the
Cretans and carried into western Mediterranean countries by the
Phoenicians and others; and the Scarlet turkscap lily, *L. chalcedonicum*
from the mountains of Thessaly, the Ionic isles and much of Greece,
which Theophrastus seems to have known only through hearsay. He
refers also to planting the seeds of Martagon lilies, possibly a form of
L. martagon, which is native to much of Europe.

Theophrastus classed his lilies with other coronary plants grown principally for garlands. He described them – as he described all his plants – dryly and methodically, noting the lily's colour variation and its manner of flowering, generally on a single stem that divided occasionally into two, perhaps due to differences in position and climate. There was ample root, he said, fleshy and round, and although the fruits were able to germinate, they produced smaller plants. The plant – presumably he meant the bulb and underground stems – also produced 'a sort of tear-like exudation, which men also plant'.

Like the Egyptians before them, the Greeks used lily flowers in their perfumes. Because of its lightness, lily was recommended for men along with other light perfumes such as rose and *kypros*, a compound perfume steeped in sweet wine, while women were thought to require a perfume that would linger, such as myrrh oil, sweet marjoram and spikenard. The clearest guidance on how to make lily ointment comes from the Greek-born herbalist, Pedanius Dioscorides, writing in the first century CE, who reveals just how messy the ancient business of perfumery could be. First you had to thicken the oil by boiling it in fragrant wine, with aromatics such as sweet flag or myrtle sedge and myrrh, adding bruised cardamom steeped in rainwater to the strained oil. After more straining came lily flowers in vast quantities:

Take three and a half pounds of this thickened oil and a thousand (counted) lilies, and having stripped off their leaves, put them in a broad but not deep jar. Pour in the oil, stir it around with your hands (that have been previously rubbed with honey) and let it stand for a day and a night. The next morning pour it into a cupped strainer and presently (when it is strained) separate the oil on top from the water that is strained out with it . . . Pour it out again into other jars smeared with honey, first sprinkling a little salt in there and taking away the filth carefully as it gathers together.

And so the process continued with ever more steepings, strainings and pressings, adding more cardamom and more fresh lily flowers, a thousand at a time.

Finally when it seems to you that you have enough, mix with every preparation seventy-two teaspoons of the best myrrh, ten teaspoons of crocus and seventy-five teaspoons of cinnamon. Some take the same amount of crocus and cinnamon (having pounded and sifted it), put it into a jar with water, and pour on it the ointment from the first pressing: afterwards (leaving it alone a little while) they put it into little dry jars (first smeared around with gum or myrrh and saffron and honey diluted with water). Do the very same things to the second and third pressings.

As for the lily's healing virtues, Dioscorides judged it warming and softening, an effective cure for all female ailments and especially for reducing inflammation around the vulva. It was also good, he said, in cases of scaly scalp, varicose veins, dandruff and fever marks on the skin, while the leaves were used for snakebites, burns, ulcers and soothing old wounds. Although generally very purifying, expelling bile through the bowels and inducing the flow of urine, he warned that it could also damage the stomach and cause nausea.

Writing about the same time as Dioscorides was Rome's Pliny the Elder, who completed his vast compendium of *Natural History* just before scientific curiosity lured him to his death in the volcanic eruption of Mount Vesuvius, which destroyed the nearby towns of Pompeii and Herculaneum. Pliny and Dioscorides almost certainly never met, or Pliny would have cannibalized the other's work for his own writings. Yet however widely he borrowed, or stole, from other authors, Pliny lets us see the lily through Roman eyes.

Like Theophrastus before him, Pliny writes of the lily as a garland or chaplet flower, ranking it second after the rose. 'No flower grows taller,' he declared, entranced; 'sometimes it reaches three cubits, its neck always drooping under the weight of a head too heavy for it. The flower is of an exceeding whiteness, fluted on the outside, narrow at the bottom and gradually expanding in width after the fashion of a basket. The lips curve outwards and upwards all around'; standing upright at its heart were saffron-coloured stamens and a slender pistil. The lily's perfume was twofold, he said, exuded by

petals and stamens alike; both were used in making lily oils and
unguents.

Such pure white lily trumpets add their sweetness to the garden
frescoes of Pompeii, preserved for centuries like Thera's wall paintings under a coating of volcanic debris. Pompeiian lilies include a
stylized flower in the House of Cornelius; a lily bearing five or more
blossoms in the House of Adonis; four lily blooms in different stages of
opening at the House of the Fruit Orchard; a couple of Madonna lilies
in a badly preserved tomb painting of a young man's funeral banquet
by the Vesuvius Gate; and, most resplendent of all, the white lilies
in Pompeii's House of the Gold Bracelet, thrown together with wild
morning glories, a young date palm, camomile and opium poppies in
an orgy of early summer.

The frescoes catch echoes of the lilies in Virgil, who placed them
in the garden of an old Cilician smallholder from southern Anatolia,
always the first to welcome the bees to his plot of cabbages, brambles,
roses, apples and 'white lilies in a ring, with vervain, and with frail
poppy'. The Spanish-born Columella, another Roman writer on agriculture, also urged the spring planting of lilies and other flowers:

> Now. In all hues, paint the flowers – they are earth's own stars:
> Snowdrops in shimmering white. Burnished marigold-en eyes.
> Sprays of narcissus. Wild lion's raging mouth gaping wide
> miming snap dragon. Lilies putting their strength in white cups.

Throughout this time, the number of lily varieties in cultivation
was slowly increasing. Pliny counted four but his text is confused,
proposing a red lily known as 'crinon' (the usual Greek name for a
white lily) and called by some 'cynorrodon' (the usual Greek name for a
Dog rose). He also included a new medical use for lily bulbs, suggesting that they could be boiled in wine and applied to corns on the feet,
'not being taken off before the end of three days'. As the Latin word
for lily spread into the languages of northern Europe many centuries
before Linnaeus codified its use in plant names, is it too far-fetched to

suppose that Rome's conquering armies took lily bulbs with them to cure the corns and aching feet of their foot soldiers?

L IKE THE ANCIENT Greeks before them, the Romans gave the lily only an incidental role in their mythology. It was said to be the flower of Jupiter's wife Juno, queen of the Roman pantheon, who was celebrated as the goddess of women, of childbirth and as the patron goddess of Rome. But Juno's principal feast day, the Matronalia, was celebrated in March, long before the lily comes into flower; and although the goddess was believed to delight in flowers, it is hard to find contemporary evidence of the lily's role in her cult. One suspects that the lily came later, added as an origin myth like those created by the Babylonian *Epic of Gilgamesh*. The Elizabethan herbalist John Gerard recounts his version of the lily's birth from milk spilled from Juno's breast, saying that the lily was sometimes called '*Rosa Junonis*, or *Junos* rose, bicause as it is reported, it came up of hir milke that fell upon the ground'. According to Gerard, the child Hercules, born of Jupiter and Alcmene, was put to Juno's breast while she was sleeping, and after he had suckled, a quantity of milk fell away – one part to earth, and 'of this sprang the Lillie', and the other to the heavens, where it formed the Milky Way.

The story does not feature among the Roman poet Ovid's *Metamorphoses*, whose one possible lily appears in his retelling of the death of Hyacinth, inadvertently slain by a discus thrown by Apollo and commemorated with a new flower that bore the signs of Apollo's lament: 'Gorgeous as Tyrian dye, in form a lily'. But in Ovid, the lily's silvery petals had turned into the 'richest purple', marked with the letters 'AI AI'; if the poet really did have a lily in mind, he may have intended the red-flowered *L. chalcedonicum*.

A ruder story explains how the lily gained its prominent sexual organs, when the goddess Venus – the Greek Aphrodite – experienced a wave of jealousy at the sight of the flower's ethereal whiteness. Like the wicked fairy in *Sleeping Beauty*, she turned her spite into a malevolent gift, making a giant pistil emerge like a donkey's penis from its heart. These are just the kind of lilies to appeal to Des Esseintes, the decadent anti-hero of Joris-Karl Huysmans's late nineteenth-century novel, *Against Nature* (*À Rebours*). Venturing into his garden, Des Esseintes spied a row of white lilies, immobile in the heavy air, and his lips 'curled up in a smile' as he remembered the ancient writings on toxicology of Nicander of Colophon, who 'likened the pistil of a lily to the testicles of an ass'.

G IVEN THAT THE lily had such a scurrilous heritage, it is hardly surprising that the early Christian Church tried to ban the flower, like the rose, from its rituals. The wearing of floral crowns or chaplets was particularly condemned as a lingering pagan practice that smacked of idolatry. Christians, wrote the early Church father Minucius Felix, 'do not crown our heads; we are accustomed to receive the scent of a sweet flower in our nostrils, not to inhale it with the back of our head or with our hair'. Garlands wither, too, in contrast to the everlasting flowers of heaven.

Yet despite the Church's disapproval, lilies (and roses – see Chapter 5) regained their place in Christian hearts, just as they became an essential feature of Church gardens. The sixth-century historian and bishop Gregory of Tours speaks of the priest, Severus, who gathered lily flowers (*flores liliorum*) to decorate the walls of his church – but were they yellow flag iris from boggy fields, or white Madonna lilies from a garden? White lilies and little red roses adorned the monk's cell at Tours of the scholarly Alcuin of York, adviser to Emperor Charlemagne. The lily also led the list of herbs, fruits and nuts that an imperial decree of the time ordered to be planted in all royal estates. A bed was naturally kept for lilies in the *herbularius* or infirmary garden in the roughly contemporary plan of an idealized monastery preserved at the great abbey of St Gall in Switzerland. (The other beds contained kidney bean, savory, rose, horse mint, cumin, lovage, fennel, tansy or costmary, sage, rue, flag iris, pennyroyal, fenugreek, mint and rosemary.) The lily's 'white of glistening snow' and 'scent of sweetest frankincense' gladdened the heart of Germany's great gardening

monk, Walahfrid Strabo, abbot of Reichenau, who ended his gardening poem musing on the respective virtues of the lily and the rose, both
intimately linked with Christ's fate:

> By His holy word and life He sanctified
> The pleasant lily; dying,
> He gave its colour to the rose.

WHILE THE LILY was undoubtedly useful in early monastic life
– Walahfrid recommended crushed lilies boiled in wine as an
antidote to snakebites – even more critical to its pre-eminence in
medieval times was its growing power in Christian iconography as it
underwent a subtle transformation from simple flower of Paradise,
to an emblem of the Virgin Mary, to the crucified Christ – sometimes
combining all three associations (and more) at the same time.

First came the lilies of Paradise, which appear at their loveliest in
the apse mosaic of the Transfiguration in the Church of St Apollinaris
at Classe, Ravenna. A gem of Byzantine art created in the mid-sixth
century, the mosaic concentrates on the moment when Christ revealed
his divinity to the apostles Peter, James and John. In the lower part,
St Apollinaris, whose relics originally lay under the altar, intercedes
for his flock, portrayed as twelve white lambs, separated by clumps of
white lilies, completing the paradisiacal landscape of a green meadow
filled with pine trees, rocks, bushes and flowers – a landscape bathed
in the light of Christ's glory.

In the Christian hierarchy of flowers, *Lilium candidum* derived
its most enduring power from its affinity with the Virgin Mary. The
bloom's astonishing whiteness and all-pervading sweetness make
this lily the perfect emblem of spiritual and physical purity; and so –
despite the asceticism of the early Christian fathers – the white lily of
the ancients became the 'Madonna lily' of Christianity.

By the eighth century, the Benedictine Paul the Deacon was painting
the lily in words that better describe the lotus, suggesting that just as
virginity yearns for a higher realm, so the lily raises herself up from

the earth and looks towards the sky – the fact that the lily often hangs
her head is not allowed to spoil his argument. And just as the flower is
white on the outside and flame-coloured on the inside, 'so the purity of virginal flesh shows white on the outside while burning inwardly
with the burning heat of clarity'.

The lily's sweetness also bolstered its growing influence. In a
twelfth-century manuscript written in the Byzantine Greek of the
Orthodox Church, begun perhaps in the previous century by a Greek
monk who loved the solitude of his walled plot, the lily of poverty grew
inside a deeply symbolic garden, alongside the lemon tree of purity,
the fig of gentleness, the vine of spiritual joy and the pomegranate
of courage.

After the sight of the lemon trees, there is the flowering of the lily bed, giving
delight and pleasure to the sight by the beauty of its colour and its rounded
shape, breathing forth the most pleasant good cheer of its perfume and fur-
nishing a pattern of greatness of soul. What is more, it is after the practice
of incorruptible, peaceful purity that the love of learning, disinterested in
money, usually blossoms. Why indeed would he who was striving for simplicity and holiness choose to amass treasure, since he has nowhere to spend it
for his own pleasure?

Throughout the Middle Ages, the lily's power seemed actually to increase as a signifier of Mary's virginity, so that by the early Renaissance
a lily frond had become an essential prop in scenes of the Annunciation, as in Sandro Botticelli's *The Annunciation* (c.1490) in which a
kneeling Angel Gabriel carries a single lily stem bearing five flowers in
place of the traditional wand or palm frond. In a nineteenth-century
reworking by the Pre-Raphaelite artist Dante Gabriel Rossetti, *Ecce
Ancilla Domini!* (*Behold the Handmaid of the Lord*), a wingless Gabriel
points a phallic three-budded lily stem at the womb of a cowering
Virgin who crouches, barely awake, on her pallet bed. Nearby hangs
a lily embroidery from *The Girlhood of Mary Virgin*, which Rossetti had
painted the previous year. Rossetti's lily stem has two opened buds,

representing God and the Holy Spirit, and an unopened bud that heralds the unborn Christ.

Even more complex in their web of Christian allusions are the strange 'lily crucifixions' that appeared in England and Wales between the fourteenth and sixteenth centuries. A rare manuscript example survives in the Llanbeblig Book of Hours, dating from the late fourteenth century, which opens with scenes from the Annunciation. Bearing a palm frond in his right hand, Gabriel kneels before the Virgin, who sits under a green canopy on the opposite page. Beside her stands a large silver pot containing a tall white lily in flower, the crucified Christ nailed to its stalk and leaves.

Here is Christ as a lily flower born of the lily-like Mary, the flower's association with purity signifying at once the Virgin and the theme of Christ crucified by the virtues, a late medieval notion that emphasized how Christ, by his dying, had brought to perfection such human virtues as humility, obedience, patience and perseverance. Here, too, is a subtle allusion to the lily's role in curing women's ailments, especially those concerned with conception and childbirth. John Gerard believed that white lily flowers steeped in olive oil and set in the sun in a strong glass would soften the womb — as would roasted red lily bulbs pounded with rose oil — while distilled lily water could procure 'easie and spedie' childbirth, and rapidly expel the afterbirth.

Even after the Reformation waged war on 'papist' idolatry, the Marian lily lingered on in pockets of Catholic resistance, as in the writings of the English Jesuit Henry Hawkins, who drew on the Church's long tradition of garden symbolism for his book of meditations on the Virgin Mary, *Partheneia Sacra*, published in 1633. Hawkins gives the lily its own chapter, alongside the rose, violet, sunflower, iris, olive and palm, musing on the lily's classical associations but concentrating on the flower's connection with the Virgin Mary and with notions of purity, virginity and sweetness.

'The *Lillie* besides is always fragrant,' wrote Hawkins, 'and of a most sweet odour: and our *Lillie* was perfumed with an odiferous oyntment, which made her so fragrant and redolent, composed of three

odoriferous spices: *aromatizing as Balme, Mirrh, and Cinamon.*' Used to
adorn the bedchambers of Kings, 'that they may rest more deliciously
among them', lilies also bedecked the Virgin Mary, 'not the Chamber
only of a KING, but of GOD also'.

Hawkins ends his lily meditation with reference to the Old Testa-
ment's Song of Songs, which contains some of the loveliest biblical
references to the flower. As the Song's female voice declares: 'I am the
rose of Sharon, and the lily of the valleys./ As the lily among thorns, so
is my love among the daughters.' And later: 'My beloved is mine, and I
am his: he feedeth among the lilies.'

Think of lilies in the Bible and these are the lines you will probably
remember, together with Christ's 'lilies of the field' in the Sermon on
the Mount. But the original Hebrew word is *'sosannah'*, and neither
botanists nor Hebrew commentators can agree which flower is actually meant; lily, hyacinth, narcissus, sternbergia, even a lotus have
all been proposed. The same is true of the biblical 'rose' (in Hebrew,
'habasselet'), also called a tulip, crocus, lily or simply a wildflower. Yet
most versions opt for the lily and the rose, so resonantly joined by
W. B. Yeats in his poem, 'The White Birds':

I am haunted by numberless islands, and many a Danaan shore,
Where Time would surely forget us, and Sorrow come near us no more;
Soon far from the rose and the lily, and fret of the flames would we be,
Were we only white birds, my beloved, buoyed out on the foam of the sea!

THE GENESIS OF the heraldic fleur-de-lis reveals a similar confusion over floral identities. Literally 'flower of the lily', it is much
closer to the common flag iris, *Iris pseudacorus*, than to any true lily.
Used as a stylized emblem or motif in both the Old and New Worlds, it
is found on countless objects: Mesopotamian cylinder seals; Egyptian
bas-reliefs and Mycenaean pottery; Greek, Roman and Gallic coins;
Sassanid fabrics from the old Persian Empire; Amerindian clothing;
and Japanese arms. Its meaning shifts from culture to culture, appearing sometimes as a symbol of purity or virginity, sometimes as a mark

of fertility and fecundity, and sometimes as an insignia of power or sovereignty.

In medieval Europe, the motif acquired a Christian gloss with increasingly Marian overtones. In the eleventh and twelfth centuries, the Virgin is often portrayed surrounded by lilies and occasionally by genuinely heraldic fleurs-de-lis, a fashion that peaked in the thirteenth century when the rose usurped the lily in Christian iconography, the flower of love apparently taking precedence over the flower of virginity.

While the rose was gaining the ascendancy in matters of religion, so the fleur-de-lis was transforming itself into the heraldic emblem of the kings of France. The Valois kings of the fourteenth century seized on the device to legitimize their claim to the French throne, proclaiming the fleur-de-lis as a sign of the Trinity and reinforcing the legend that it came directly from the angel of God to Clovis, whose conversion to Christianity had made him the first Catholic king of the Franks. According to this version of the legend, the angel told Clovis to replace the three diabolical frogs on his shield with three fleurs-de-lis, whose three petals could be viewed as the three virtues of faith, wisdom and chivalry, or as an actual symbol of the Trinity.

The legend makes no historical sense, of course. Clovis reigned in the late fifth and early sixth centuries, many hundreds of years before armorial badges appeared in Europe, but the Valois kings had cleverly chosen a heraldic device that was already in royal use. Under Marian influence, two earlier Capetian kings, Louis VI and Louis VII, had introduced it into their repertory of symbols, and the upstart Valois – from a cadet branch of the Capetian clan – were well advised to capitalize on a symbol that linked them to France's ruling dynasty, and to their Mother Church.

THUS FAR, THE story of the lily has focused on European varieties. From the late sixteenth century onwards, new varieties arriving from East and West created enormous excitement among gardeners and artists.

We gain a hint already in the lilies John Gerard grew in his famous garden in Holborn, and the ones he described so admiringly in four separate chapters of his great *Herball* of 1597. He wrote about white lilies first, both the ordinary ones and the white lily of Constantinople, then wild red lilies from Italy and the Languedoc, already common in English gardens and in Germany. Among these he included a 'Gold red Lillie', not in his garden, its flowers similar to those of a white lily but coloured saffron red and speckled with black like the inkblots on 'rude unperfect draughts of certaine letters'. Next came the greater and lesser mountain lilies from Syria, Italy and hot countries beyond the borders of Greece and the Peloponnese; among these, he obtained the greater mountain lily from his 'loving friend', the London apothecary Master James Garrett.

Gerard's fourth sort was the red lily of Constantinople, which he called *Lilium Byzantinum*, shaped like a mountain lily with petals of a deep sealing-wax red. It grew wild in fields and mountains, he explained, many days' journey from Constantinople, where it was brought by 'poore pesants', to be sold for 'the decking up of gardens. From thence it was sent among many other bulbs of rare & daintie flowers, by master *Harbran* ambassador there, unto my honorable good Lord and master, the Lord Treasurer of England, who bestowed them upon me for my garden.' Gerard's 'good Lord and master' was William Cecil, Lord Burghley, Queen Elizabeth I's trusted adviser, whose gardens Gerard tended in the Strand, London, and at Theobalds Park in Hertfordshire. In the days before organized plant hunting, this is how new plant varieties arrived in Europe's gardens, carried by travelling diplomats, merchants, sea captains and ships' doctors and passed to enthusiastic collectors at home.

North America, too, was sending her first lilies to Europe, as the continent slowly opened up to European settlement. As early as 1629, the royal apothecary John Parkinson could count Canada's elegant spotted Martagon (*L. canadense*) among his lily stock, joining others from Germany, Austria, Hungary, Italy, Macedonia and Turkey; 'this strange Lilly', he called it. Gerard's red-spotted Martagon remained a

rarity, while the 'red Martagon of Constantinople is become so common every where, and so well knowne to all lovers of these delights,
that I shall seeme unto them to lose time, to bestow many lines upon
it'. Parkinson nonetheless judged it worthy of praise, 'because it is so
faire a flower, and was at first so highly esteemed'.

According to Parkinson, the white lily was still used in medicine
although quack doctors or 'Empericks' had previously used red lilies
as well. Even the white lily seemed to have experienced a loss of
potency. While only thirty years earlier John Gerard had vaunted its
efficacy for curing a string of ailments from plague sores to dropsy,
Parkinson's summary of its virtues is noticeably brief. The white lily
had, he said, a mollifying, digesting and cleansing quality, helping to
suppurate tumours, and to digest them, 'for which purpose the roote is
much used. The water of the flowers distilled, is of excellent vertue for
women in travell of childe bearing, to procure an easie delivery . . . It
is used also of divers women outwardly, for their faces to cleanse the
skin, and make it white and fresh.'

Were the lily's powers generally beginning to fade? In contrast to
the rose, it played only a muted role in Shakespeare's floral imagination, usually as a stock referent for elegance and beauty without any
real focus on the flower. Only rarely does the dramatist give it real
power, condemning as 'wasteful and ridiculous excess' any attempt 'To
gild refined gold, to paint the lily'; and proposing, in his lovely Sonnet
94, that the gift of beauty confers an obligation to behave virtuously:

> For sweetest things turn sourest by their deeds;
> Lilies that fester smell far worse than weeds.

IF THE SYMBOLIC lily was losing ground, garden lilies were
multiplying fast, as new varieties from North America continued
to dazzle European eyes. Travelling to New England in the 1630s and
again in the 1660s, Kentish gentleman John Josselyn found red lilies
growing all over the country, 'innumerably amongst the small Bushes',
as well as the later-flowering mountain lilies, 'bearing many yellow

Flowers, turning up their Leaves like the *Martigon*, or *Turks Cap*, spotted with small spots as deep as Safforn [saffron]'.

Josselyn noted no medicinal uses by Native Americans of true lilies, although they ate the roots of yellow-flowered water lilies, 'which are long a boiling', he said, adding that 'they tast like the Liver of a Sheep'. America's great apologist of outdoor living, Henry David Thoreau, would later describe the taste of what he thought were *L. superbum* bulbs as being 'somewhat like raw green corn on the ear'; according to his native guide, they were used for thickening soups and stews.

This same Virginian swamp lily (*L. superbum*) had reached Britain by the mid-seventeenth century – 'yet scarce to bee had' – where it was painted by gentleman-gardener Alexander Marshal for his fine florilegium, the only English flower book to survive from this time. Another early arrival from further north was the red-spotted Flame lily, also known as the 'dwarf lily of Acadie', eventually named by Linnaeus as *L. philadelphicum*. Acadie was in fact a French colony in Nova Scotia, hundreds of miles north of Philadelphia, but Linnaeus was better at botany than he was at geography. It was later sent by the indefatigable plant collector, John Bartram of Philadelphia, to his Quaker English contact, Peter Collinson of Mill Hill, and to the gardener Philip Miller, who grew it in the Society of Apothecaries' garden at Chelsea.

Many other North American lilies commemorate the great names in American plant exploration. Described as a 'rare beauty' with spotted, spidery, pinkish-orange flowers and a golden throat, *L. catesbaei* honours Mark Catesby, the English naturalist who described it first in *The Natural History of Carolina, Florida and the Bahama Islands* under the name 'L. carolinianum'. What we now call the Carolina lily, *L. michauxii*, commemorates another naturalist, the Frenchman André Michaux, who compiled North America's first flora. This tall spotted Turkscap lily received its name posthumously in 1813 from a fellow French botanist, Jean Louis Marie Poiret.

When the Rockies were finally conquered, surprisingly late in America's slow push west, the Pacific coast offered up many fine lilies. These included *L. humboldtii*, the Tiger lily of the west coast, named to commemorate the centenary of the birth of the German explorer and naturalist Baron Alexander von Humboldt; and *L. parryi*, the Lemon lily from the San Bernardino Mountains in southern California, discovered growing in the boggy soil of a settler's potato patch in 1876 but slow in reaching Britain.

WHILE GARDEN LOVERS throughout Europe continued to welcome new lilies from North America, real excitement was reserved for the Asiatic lilies from China, Japan and Korea, which began to arrive in the early nineteenth century to immediate acclaim. The two great centres of Asiatic lilies — China and Japan — had virtually closed their doors to the West for hundreds of years, leaving gardeners ill prepared for the astonishing beauty of their many lily varieties.

The Chinese are known to have grown three sorts of lily since ancient times: the dainty Morning star lily (*Lilium concolor*); the sweet-scented Musk lily (*L. brownii*), considered by many gardeners as 'the perfection of lily form'; and the Tiger lily (*L. lancifolium*), the oldest of them all and in cultivation for at least two thousand years. Yet despite their beauty, these lilies were valued by the Chinese not as ornamental plants but for their contribution to medicine and diet. Lily bulbs first appeared in a classic of Chinese medicine, the *Divine Husbandman's Materia Medica*, believed to date from the first century and so roughly contemporary with Dioscorides; the bulbs were said to moisten the lungs, stop dry coughs, clear the heart and calm the spirits. One of the lilies used has been named as *L. brownii* var. *colchesteri*, which was still employed in the 1970s, according to a herbal pharmacology of the People's Republic of China. Known collectively as Pai Ho (Hundred Together), lily bulbs are considered a purifying tonic; peeled and cooked with water and sugar, they are eaten in large quantities in the summer.

Early reports of Chinese lilies filtered back to Europe with one of the first dedicated plant collectors to visit China, ship's surgeon Dr James Cunningham, who was appointed resident surgeon at Amoy (Xiamen) in Fujian in the late 1690s. Travelling on to Chusan Island, he found white-flowered lilies smelling of jasmine and woodland roses, although it would be a hundred years or more before living lily plants reached Britain. Two came in the first consignments of plants despatched to London by William Kerr, Kew's first resident plant collector in Canton, sent out by Sir Joseph Banks in 1803. One of these, Chinese medicine's *L. brownii* var. *colchesteri*, struggled into flower in 1812 and then died out, only to be reintroduced a few years later. But the second of Kerr's lilies was the much loved Tiger lily, *L. lancifolium*, which was propagated so successfully at Kew that within six years some ten thousand plants had entered cultivation. As Gertrude Jekyll commented a century later, the Tiger lily became cherished as an old English garden flower, 'so familiar is it, not only in our gardens, but in old pictures and in the samplers and embroideries of our great-grandmothers'. Much used by American lily breeders to develop new lily hybrids, it also played a starring role in Lewis Carroll's garden of live flowers in *Through the Looking-glass, And What Alice Found There*:

John Tenniel's engraving of Alice's encounter with the Tiger-lily in Lewis Carroll's *Through the Looking-glass* (1872), his sequel to *Alice's Adventures in Wonderland*.

'O Tiger-lily,' said Alice, addressing herself to one that was waving gracefully about in the wind, 'I *wish* you could talk!'

'We *can* talk,' said the Tiger-lily: 'when there's anybody worth talking to.'

The third of the early China arrivals was the little Morning star lily from central China, *L. concolor*, introduced in 1805 by the Hon. Charles Greville, a friend of Sir Joseph Banks and one of the founders of the Horticultural Society of London. A spotted variety – sometimes called *L. concolor* var. *pulchellum* – is the more usual form from northern China; this was the variety brought back by plant collector Robert Fortune in 1850, after the first of the Opium Wars had forced China to open more ports to foreign trade (see Chapter 4).

One of the finest Chinese lilies of all arrived in Britain some fifty years later with another of the great plant hunters, Ernest 'Chinese' Wilson, after an earlier sighting by the French missionary and assiduous plant explorer Père Jean Marie Delavay. This was *Lilium regale*, the lily in my first London garden, which Wilson found in the valleys squeezed between the borders of Szechuan and Tibet, a 'barren and desert-like' terrain inhabited by monkeys, rock pigeons and green parrots, where the plant collector had broken his leg in a landslide. Finding the beautiful *L. regale* in such an inhospitable place must have offered some compensation for all the hardships he had endured. In summer the heat was terrific, Wilson tells us, in winter the cold intense, and at all times sudden and violent windstorms made progress difficult. But in June, in rock crevices beside raging torrents and high up the precipitous mountainside, the Regal lily in full bloom greeted the weary wayfarer, not in 'twos and threes but in hundreds, in thousands, aye in tens of thousands'.

His find was clearly no ordinary lily. Wilson wrote glowingly of its large trumpet-shaped flowers,

more or less wine-coloured without, pure white and lustrous on the face, clear canary-yellow within the tube and each stamen filament tipped with a golden anther. The air in the cool of the morning and in the evening is laden with a delicious perfume exhaled from each bloom. For a brief season this lonely, semi-desert region is transformed by this Lily into a veritable fairy-land.

Japanese lilies caused a similar stir when they finally reached Europe after Japan's self-imposed isolation from the West. Ever since expelling the Portuguese and the Spanish in 1603, Japan allowed only the Dutch and the Chinese to trade, under rigorous conditions that made freedom of movement impossible. The few Dutch nationals allowed into the country were penned into the tiny artificial island of Deshima in Nagasaki Bay. Fan-shaped, it measured just 233 metres on the outer side, 191 on the inner, and 70 on the west and east. Although it was undoubtedly beautiful – a later plant collector, Reginald Farrar, described his impression of 'looking upon a transfigured landscape through a middle distance of perfectly calm, clear water, which gives each mass of azure or violet a redoubled opulence of soft colour' – life on Deshima must have been intensely frustrating for foreigners. Kept under constant surveillance, the Dutch were required to make two annual journeys, later reduced to one, to pay costly homage to the ruling shogun in the capital, Edo (Tokyo). Yet despite all these restrictions, information about Japanese plants – and then the plants themselves – reached the West through the efforts of three remarkable Europeans who combined their medical training with a passion for botany. And each added to Europe's stock of knowledge about Japanese lilies.

The first to pass through Deshima, towards the end of the seventeenth century, was the German naturalist and physician, Engelbert Kaempfer, who stayed for two years and twice visited Edo, taking with him a box in which he kept the plants he had collected. Drawings made from these would prove useful in his descriptions of four hundred or so Japanese plants for the book he wrote about his travels, *Amoenitatum exoticarum*. Among these are eight lilies identified by pre-Linnaean Latin names, which surely included the crimson Japan lily (*L. speciosum*). When this last lily finally came to Europe, courtesy of Dr Philipp Franz Balthasar von Siebold, the magazine *Botanical Register* was fulsome in its praise:

Not only is it handsome beyond all we before knew in gardens, on account of the clear, deep rose-colour of its flowers, which seem all rugged with rubies and garnets, and sparkling with crystal points, but it has the sweet fragrance of a Petunia. Well might Kaempfer speak of it as 'flos magnificae pulchritudinis,' for surely if there is any thing not human, which is magnificent in beauty, it is this plant.

After Kaempfer came the Swedish botanist and pupil of the great Linnaeus, Karl Pehr Thunberg, who arrived in Deshima in 1775 via Leiden, Amsterdam and a spell in South Africa, where he had learned Dutch and joined forces with the Scottish plant hunter, Francis Masson. Described as 'an enthusiastic if somewhat careless botanist', Thunberg gave the 'japonica' tag to plants that in fact originated in China and put together a hotchpotch of seven lilies for his *Flora Japonica*, mistaking several genuine Japanese lilies for their European cousins. He was right about Japan's Bamboo lily, however, a beautiful pink trumpet lily, which he was the first to collect and to which he correctly gave the name *L. japonicum*.

The most successful plant collector at Deshima was another German, the Bavarian Philipp von Siebold, who was introduced to the Japanese as a 'mountain Dutchman' to explain why his spoken Dutch was far less fluent than that of his Japanese interpreters. Capitalizing on a growing interest in western sciences, von Siebold gave science lessons to his interpreters, who in return taught him Japanese and a little written Chinese, as well as helping him to procure specimens for his botanical researches; the many successful cataract operations he undertook using European techniques unknown in Japan also increased his popularity. But he broke the rules, and following the discovery of sensitive material in his possession, including maps, he was subjected to house arrest and then expelled from Japan in October 1829.

Despite this setback, he was able to take much of his living plant collection with him. Many of these plants went to Ghent, including more than twenty different kinds of lily. Among them were varieties of the crimson lily, *L. speciosum*, one of which he named *Lilium speciosum Kaempferi* in 'honour of the indefatigable Kaempfer . . . because it was he who gave the first account of it in Europe'. He pointedly did not name a lily after Thunberg, whose mistakes he took pains to correct, naming *L. callosum* as the mountain lily Thunberg had mistaken for *L. pomponium*.

The lily that caused the greatest stir of all, however, was *L. auratum*, the great Golden-rayed lily of Japan, collected by John Gould Veitch and first shown on 2 July 1862 at the Royal Horticultural Society's Third Great Show by his family's renowned nursery firm. Japan had by now been forced by the gunboat diplomacy of Commodore Perry to open its doors to the West, and Veitch was one of the first to take advantage of the opportunities this offered for systematic plant collecting. He had found the lily growing wild on hillsides in central Japan, where it was much sought after for food. 'They are boiled and eaten in much the same way as we do Potatoes,' he noted, 'and have an agreeable flavour resembling that of a Chestnut.'

'One of the best new plants that has been introduced for years,' trumpeted *Gardeners' Chronicle*, calling it as 'sweet as Lily of the Valley' and the focus of ten thousand eyes at the Kensington Show. Just one week later, the paper printed an even more effusive report, declaring that it stood far above all other lilies as regards size, sweetness and exquisite colouring, emitting a perfume of orange blossoms sufficient to fill a large room but 'so delicate as to respect the weakest nerves':

Imagine upon the end of a purple stem no thicker than a ramrod, and not above 2 feet high, a saucer-shaped flower at least ten inches in diameter, composed of six spreading somewhat crisp parts rolled back at their points, and having an ivory white skin thinly strewn with purple points or studs and oval or roundish prominent purple stains. To this add in the middle of each of the six parts a broad stripe of light satiny yellow losing itself gradually in the ivory skin. Place the flower in a situation where side light is cut off, and no direct light can reach it except from above, when the stripes acquire the appearance of gentle streamlets of living Australian gold, and the reader who has not seen it may form some feeble notion of what it is.

Even this fine lily was absent from formal Japanese gardens, however. Visiting Japan early in the twentieth century, the sisters Ella and Florence Du Cane noted how big buds of *L. auratum* would be fighting their way among the rank growth along the roadside, filling the air with their scent, yet no lily found its way into the hallowed company of Japan's 'seven beautiful flowers of late summer'. Tiger lilies were still grown in village gardens as prized vegetables, wrote Florence Du Cane, their flower heads cut off to strengthen the bulbs, and thousands if not millions of *L. longiflorum* bulbs were cultivated annually for export, but only humble folk grew lilies for show, 'many a giant bearing from twenty to thirty unblemished blooms, at the top of a stem some six or seven feet high, clad with equally unblemished foliage'.

GIVEN ITS GROWING popularity in the West, the lily naturally slipped from the garden into literature and art, reinventing itself with each successive 'school' until it became the most potent flower in the lexicon of late nineteenth-century art. Among Britain's early Pre-Raphaelite painters, the pale white lily started out as the ultimate floral accessory to the Annunciation scenes of Dante Gabriel Rossetti, and of Arthur Hughes, who painted a profusion of lilies at Gabriel's feet. Edward Burne-Jones similarly fell under the lily's spell, planting lilies in his gardens at Red Lion Square and Kensington Square, and including them in two Annunciation scenes he painted for *The Flower Book*, which portrayed the subjects suggested by the flowers' names, rather than the flowers themselves.

The lily was also the perfect accoutrement of Japonisme, the craze for all things Japanese ushered in by artists such as James McNeill Whistler, who never visited Japan himself but who gave his mistress Joanna Hiffernan a wan white lily to hold in the first of his three 'Symphony in White' paintings – in the later two, the lily gave way to Japanese azaleas.

And those are surely speckled varieties of *Lilium auratum* in John Singer Sargent's celebrated *Carnation, Lily, Lily, Rose*, in which two young girls, daughters of the illustrator Frederick Barnard, play with paper lanterns amid the tangled flowers of a Cotswold garden.

The lily found its echo, too, in the decadent strains of poets such as Algernon Charles Swinburne, a close associate of Rossetti, who described his lover leaning over his sad bed as

> Pale as the duskiest lily's leaf or head,
> Smooth-skinned and dark, with bare throat made to bite,
> Too wan for blushing and too warm for white.

French poets have likewise drawn the lily into their most intimate imaginings. Bewitched like many of his contemporaries by the biblical story of Herodias and her daughter Salome, the French symbolist poet Stéphane Mallarmé evoked a strange, brooding lily, which he internalized in the virgin Hérodiade – a compression of Salome and her mother – who preferred to cling to her virgin state in the face of her impending marriage. As she told her nurse:

> I pause, dreaming of exiles, and,
> as if close to a pool whose fountain welcomes me,
> I strip the petals off the pale lilies within me.

In *The Beloved* of 1865–6, by contrast, Rossetti jettisoned the wan white lily for a flaming Tiger lily to accompany the Bride from the biblical Song of Songs, advancing with her handmaidens to meet her lover, their floral offerings celebrating the sensual pleasures she will shortly enjoy. And while the painter returned to a triple-blossomed Madonna lily in *The Blessed Damozel*, painted twenty-five years after his poem of the same name, the full-blown flowers held by the dead girl reek of sexual longing for her earthly lover. Their love may well have been unconsummated, but it was hardly pure.

Later, under the influence of Japonisme, the lily was to become

decidedly more stylized. Among the most active in promoting a Japanese aesthetic was the Scottish designer Christopher Dresser, who used
the lily to teach designers how to achieve the vigorous simplicity of
Japanese drawings. 'The lily is grandly drawn,' he noted in his influential book on Japanese art, architecture and art manufactures. 'The
sweep of line, the precision of touch, and the crispness of its render-
ing, make it charming to the artist: and the little bits of grass, which
mingle with its leafage, destroy that hardness which the sketch, in
their absence, would have.'

The lily received its greatest praise from aestheticism's high priest,
Oscar Wilde, who divided his affections – as did many in the Aesthetic
Movement – between the lily and the sunflower. The art critic Henry
Currie Marillier recalled a schoolboy memory of having seen Sir Edward
Poynter's portrait of the royal mistress Lillie Langtry, the 'Jersey Lily',
in Wilde's drawing room, displayed on an easel surrounded by lilies.

Wilde took his love of lilies to America in 1882, on a lecture tour
arranged by the impresario Richard D'Oyly Carte, who had also
organized the highly successful New York run of Gilbert and Sullivan's
comic opera *Patience*, which contained a merciless parody of Wilde's
aesthetic principles. Scornfully rebutting *Patience*'s caricature of the
aesthete 'walking down Piccadilly with a poppy or a lily in your mediaeval hand', Wilde ended one of his American lectures with a tribute to
his two favourite flowers, explaining that

the reason we love the lily and the sunflower, in spite of what Mr. Gilbert may
tell you, is not for any vegetable fashion at all; it is because these two lovely
flowers are in England the two most perfect models of design, the most naturally adapted for decorative art – the gaudy leonine beauty of the one and the
precious loveliness of the other giving the artist the most entire and perfect joy.

For Wilde, there was no greater praise. 'We spend our days, each one
of us, in looking for the secret of life,' he told his American audience.
'Well, the secret of life is in art.'

The lily's apotheosis in art was almost complete. All that remained were the twisting plant forms of art nouveau, known variously as Jugendstil and even Lilienstil, which reached its popular peak at the turn of the twentieth century. Leading the field was the Czech artist Alphonse Mucha, who made his name with a last-minute commission to produce a poster for the darling of the French stage, Sarah Bernhardt, at whose feet Oscar Wilde had flung an armful of lilies when she arrived in Folkestone with the Comédie Française.

Mucha's posters and lithographs reflect a Belle Époque of women with impossibly flowing hair, wreathed with lilies or clad in elegantly jewelled and feathered headgear. He naturally included the lily in his four flower posters of 1897, which also featured an iris, a carnation and a rose. In his lily poster, a fair-haired woman stands in a sinuous pose, her head tilted backwards. Apparently growing out of a clump of giant white lilies, she holds in each hand a lily stalk whose flowers reach up to form a crown above her head. Art, it seems, had taken the lily as far as she could go.

A FTER SUCH A public crowning, lilies slipped quietly back into the garden. Gertrude Jekyll devoted one of her early books to instructing amateurs in their cultivation, believing that these 'most stately and beautiful of garden flowers' were not 'nearly so much grown in gardens as their beauty deserves'. Lilies were best grown on their own among quiet greenery, she declared, apart from her obvious favourite, the white Madonna lily, 'so old a garden flower' that it belonged with other old favourites, such as Cabbage roses (*Rosa* × *centifolia*) and the late Dutch honeysuckle. She wrote glowingly, too, of the Nankeen lily (*Lilium* × *testaceum*), then of mysterious origin but since revealed as a cross between the Madonna lily and *L. chalcedonicum*. Its name was only an approximation of its colour, she said, for in place of the 'clear though rather pale washed-out wash-leather colour, there is a tender warmth in addition that must be allowed for in thinking of the colour of this charming Lily'.

For all Jekyll's efforts, the lily remained a Cinderella of the garden, viewed as 'difficult' and 'capricious' – a condition that Jekyll blamed on the ignorance of the gardener rather than the plant. Many of the newly arrived Asiatic species were indeed better grown under glass than outdoors, among them the lovely Easter lily, *L. longiflorum* from the Liu-kiu islands off the south coast of Japan.

Until the 1940s, most new garden lilies were dug up in the wild and transplanted into the gardens of Europe and the United States, and deliberate hybrids were rare. But knowledge of the genus *Lilium* had been growing steadily since the first French monograph of the 1840s and the series of British monographs and supplements, begun in 1880 by Henry John Elwes, a wealthy Gloucestershire landowner. From the late 1930s, gardeners could turn to the increasing number of good, easy-growing lily hybrids available, starting with those produced at the Oregon Bulb Farms by Dutchman Jan de Graaff, hailed as 'the greatest grower and hybridizer of lilies of the present time, and probably of all time'. He called his first commercial lily 'Enchantment'; for a time it was the world's most widely grown lily and is still on general sale, especially as a florist's flower. Its hot-coral petals unfurl brashly from a speckled throat, and it is hard to image a lily further removed from the cool white lilies that so enchanted the Minoans more than 3,500 years ago. Even the scent is lacking.

But if you are diligent, you can still track down the original varieties, hidden away in botanic gardens and old physic gardens or massed in old-style cottage gardens. I suspect their sweetness will take you by surprise, and their beauty. In contrast to the rose and the sunflower, only the lily emerges unsullied from the poet William Blake's very particular natural history:

> The modest Rose puts forth a thorn,
> The humble Sheep a threat'ning horn,
> While the Lilly white shall in Love delight,
> Nor a thorn nor a threat stain her beauty bright.

Sunflower

We're not our skin of grime, we're not our dread bleak
dusty imageless locomotive, we're all golden sunflowers
inside, blessed by our own seed & hairy naked accomplishment-bodies
growing into mad black formal sunflowers in the sunset,
spied on by our eyes under the shadow of the mad locomotive
riverbank sunset Frisco hilly tincan evening sitdown vision.

ALLEN GINSBERG, 'Sunflower Sutra'

COMPARED WITH THE lotus or the lily, the common sunflower (*Helianthus annuus*) is a brute. These are the doodlings of a child's imagination: taller than grown-ups at full height, they carry their plate-sized flowers on giant stems, a fringe of burnished yellow petals surrounding a disc of exquisitely arranged individual florets. I remember a field of sunflowers next to my sister-in-law's house, deep in rural France. Whenever you stepped outside, you felt they were watching you. 'Do you know what faces they have?' asked the painter Edward Burne-Jones, 'how they peep and peer, and look arch and winning, or bold and a little insolent sometimes?' Some people find this creepy: 'They got Van Gogh and now they're after you . . .'

Long cultivated in the Americas before the arrival of Columbus, the sunflower burst into Europe fully formed in the first half of the sixteenth century, dazzling gardeners, courtiers, artists and collectors of botanical curiosities with its sheer size and bravura. Its celebrated ability to track the sun's daily progress from east to west was quickly harnessed for symbolic ends, and the sunflower was given both a heathen past, as a flower reputedly sacred to the ancient civilizations of South America, and a Christianized future as the perfect symbol of Marian devotion. 'Could there be devised a more noble Symbol of our Incomparable LADIE then this flower,' mused the English Jesuit Henry Hawkins, 'regarding indeed the true Sunne of Justice, whom she followed stil in the whole course of her life, unto her death?' Secular artists and writers added a variety of other 'meanings', usually dependent on the flower's uncanny ability to lock you into its stare.

The sunflower's emblematic power is based on a false premise, however. Green plants are phototropic and respond by growing towards the light, especially in their early stages. At sunrise, the unopened buds of cultivated young sunflowers are usually turned towards the east, and over the course of the day they follow the sun from east to west, returning overnight to an eastward orientation. As the stems mature, however, their tissues stiffen so that by the time the flowers appear their position is fixed, typically facing towards the east. With wild sunflowers, only the leaves exhibit some heliotropism; the flowering heads may face in any and all directions. Yet poets, painters, writers, literary and religious symbolists continue to flaunt the 'virtues' of this giant member of the daisy family. How did the sunflower gain such power, enabling it to confuse the evidence of our own eyes?

THE SUNFLOWER'S STORY begins in the Americas where the plant family of *Helianthus* first arose some 50 million years ago, in what is now the south-western United States. For thousands of years, the common annual sunflower (*H. annuus*) has been flowering and setting seed in the wild as it slowly dispersed around temperate North America. Today, colonies grow wild across much of northern America, from central Mexico in the south right up to southern Canada.

The cultivated sunflower is of much more recent origin, however. Until a decade or so ago, it was recognized as the USA's only significant New World food crop brought into cultivation, but the archaeological evidence presented something of a puzzle. While the oldest wild sunflower achenes – the individual fruits containing a single seed – were found towards the south-west, the larger cultivated achenes were all from central and eastern North America. These included two finds given an earliest date of around 1260 BCE from sites in northern Arkansas and eastern Tennessee. The most plausible explanation for this geographical discrepancy was that wild seeds gathered by Native Americans in the south-west had then migrated with their hosts as camp-following weeds, travelling west to California, south to Texas, then northwards and eastwards across the Mississippi River, where they were eventually brought into cultivation. According to the respected American economic botanist, Charles B. Heiser Jr, this new plant could thrive only in disturbed sites around native villages; and as it had larger heads and consequently larger achenes than the wild variety, it proved an even better food plant.

Heiser's theory enjoyed widespread support until early this century, when the claims of central US states such as Tennessee to have nurtured the earliest domesticated sunflowers were apparently trumped by a find at Tabasco on the Gulf coast of Mexico. Carbon dating took the oldest of these achenes back to around 2110 BCE, giving Mexico the lead role in domesticating sunflowers. Now this find, too, has been challenged, and the specimen identified as most likely the seed of a bottle gourd. As Heiser now concludes, the wild sunflower may have grown in northernmost Mexico in early times, but no convincing evidence has so far emerged to prove that sunflowers were domesticated independently in Mexico; and as yet, genetic testing has revealed little Mexican ancestry in modern North American sunflower cultivars.

The sunflower's story abounds in such confusion. Ever since it arrived in Europe – often bearing a Peruvian tag, but 'Peru' in sixteenth-century Europe was geographically vague – the flower has attracted a fabulous mythological history. The plant is variously described as sacred to the Aztecs and Mayans of Meso-America and to the Incas of Peru, and its 'discovery' by Europeans has linked it to many of the great names of the Spanish conquest, among them Hernán Cortés, who brought the Aztecs of Mexico to their knees, and Francisco Pizarro, conqueror of the Incas of Peru. Europeans saw sunflowers in the golden-rayed sun discs of the Incas and drew parallels that were never intended by their creators. It was the story of El Dorado all over again, when the Europeans' greed for gold fed the myth of 'the gilded one', always a few days' march away into the jungle. In the words of the Trinidadian-born Nobel laureate V. S. Naipaul, the legend of El Dorado became like 'the finest fiction, indistinguishable from truth'; for it was an Indian memory that the Spaniards pursued, a memory 'confused with the legend, among jungle Indians, of the Peru the Spaniards had already conquered'.

In truth, the sunflower appears to have played no role in Inca or Mayan mythology or ritual, and a very minor one among the Aztecs of Mexico. The archaeological evidence for the latter is scanty: three large sunflower achenes recovered from a dry cave associated with burials and ritual activities, carbon-dated to around 290 BCE; and a handful of much more recent (but still pre-conquest) wild *Helianthus annuus* achenes, found in an offering made at one of the principal Aztec temples, the Templo Mayor in Tenochtitlan, now Mexico City.

Other plants have played a more obvious role in Aztec ritual, notably amaranths, marigolds and maize. Amaranth grain obtained from the tassel-flowered plant *Amaranthus* was one of the basic food crops of the Aztec Empire, along with maize, beans and squash. On feast days honouring the Aztecs' principal god, Huitzilopochtli, amaranth dough moistened with honey or cactus syrup was used to make ceremonial cult images of the deity. The dough became so closely linked in European minds with perceived idolatry that the conquering Spaniards forbade the cultivation of amaranth, although the edict was largely ignored and amaranth dough slipped unnoticed into Catholic ritual as locally made rosary beads.

Marigolds and maize were similarly venerated by the Aztecs – marigolds as flowers of the dead, used even today to deck the private altars celebrating the Mexican Day of the Dead, while maize featured in many ancient superstitions. According to the early Spanish chronicler Bernardino de Sahagún, it was customary to breathe on maize before you boiled it, to overcome its fear of being cooked. The Incas in Peru went further, linking maize – the empire's prestige crop – to Inti, the principal sun deity, through protracted celebrations of sowing, harvesting and ploughing. You will even come across reports of maize plants made of gold adorning the maize garden at Inti's Temple of the Sun – the Coricancha at Cusco – during seed time, harvest and for the initiation of young Inca noblemen, although these, too, may evaporate on closer inspection like the gilded sunflowers of popular legend.

Even if sunflowers are largely absent from the earliest Aztec histories and herbals, the Aztec love of flowers is not in doubt. The rulers of ancient Mexico adored fine gardens and flowers, especially fragrant ones, and created the first botanical gardens in the Americas. Their well-developed culture of flowers has survived in the Nahuatl names used to differentiate between various sorts of gardens, whether gardens in general ('xochitla', 'flower place', or 'xoxochitla', 'place of many flowers'); walled gardens ('xochitepanyo'); pleasure gardens of the ruling class ('xochitecpancalli', 'palace of flowers'); or the humble gardens of the Indians ('xochichinancalli', 'flower place enclosed by a fence made of cane or reeds').

Indeed, Moctezuma, the last great Aztec ruler, who died in Spanish hands, gives us a vital clue to the sunflower's role in Aztec society. According to a long-lost chronicle written in 1565 by the scholarly Dr Cervantes de Salazar, Moctezuma enjoyed his many pleasances and fine gardens crossed by paths and irrigation channels. Containing only medicinal and aromatic herbs, flowers, shrubs, and trees with fragrant blossoms, these gardens gave great pleasure to all who visited them, especially in the mornings and in the evenings. Vegetables and fruit were banished on the orders of Moctezuma himself, who believed it was not 'kingly' to cultivate plants for utility or profit; rather, 'vegetable gardens and orchards were for slaves or merchants'.

The reference to merchants takes us to another early chronicle, by the Franciscan Friar Bernardino de Sahagún. Usually known as the *Florentine Codex*, it contains a book devoted solely to the customs of Aztec merchants and artisans – those who worked in gold, precious stones or feathers. Here at last we find a probable sunflower in the rituals performed at a merchant's banquet, in which seasoned warriors offered honoured guests tobacco tubes and 'shield flowers', 'chimalsuchitl', almost certainly the common sunflower, and a word still used by indigenous Nahua. Both gifts were intended symbolically: the tobacco tubes as spears and the sunflowers as shields. After the serving of food and chocolate, the sunflowers, tobacco tubes and garlands of flowers were laid as offerings before the war god,

Huitzilopochtli, and at the altars of four other temples. The ritual continued in the courtyard with much whistling, singing, the beheading of a quail, incense-burning, more chocolate, magic mushrooms, the telling of visions followed by singing and dancing until dawn, when the gifts of sunflowers and tobacco tubes were buried with the incense ash in the middle of the courtyard. It must have been quite a night.

Sahagún even gives us a cartoon of the flowers and tobacco offered to Huitzilopochtli. His tasselled sunflower looks remarkably similar to the stylized flower held by the Aztec ruler of Texcoco, Nezahualpilli, in a slightly later chronicle, the *Codex Ixtlilxochitl*, dating from the late sixteenth century. So while the sunflower may never have played a part in

The Aztec ruler Nezahualpilli (d. 1515) holding in his left hand a stylized sunflower, from the late sixteenth-century *Codex Ixtlilxochitl*.

sun worship, it had some ritual significance, and it is one of the flowers mentioned by the Spanish Jesuit priest José de Acosta, who travelled to the Spanish Americas in 1572 and wrote one of the earliest natural histories of the region on his return, some fifteen years later. 'The Indians are great lovers of flowers,' he wrote, 'and in new *Spaine* more than in any other part of the worlde, & therefore they are accustomed to make many kindes of nosegaies, which there they call *Suchilles*, with such prety varietie and art, as nothing can be more pleasing.' At their feasts and dances, Acosta tells us, the Indians carried flowers in their hands, and their kings and noblemen held flowers as a sign of their high status. 'For this reason we commonly see their ancient pictures with flowers in their hands, as we see heere with gloves.'

By the time Acosta arrived in New Spain, many of the native flowers in Indian bouquets had been replaced with Castilian imports – pinks, roses, jasmines, violets, orange flowers and the like – and it is not entirely clear whether the sunflowers and marigolds he mentions were actually bundled together with the other flowers, or whether he was merely using his train of thought to list a few native blooms: 'It is a thing well knowne,' he wrote, 'that the flower which they call of the Sunne, hath the figure of the Sunne, and turnes according to the motion thereof. There are other kindes which they call gilleflowers of the *Indies* [marigolds], the which are like to a fine orange tawnie vellet, or a violet; those have no scent of any account, but onely are faire to the eye.'

To THE SPANISH and their New World territories goes the honour of introducing the sunflower to Europe, although reports that it reached Madrid as early as 1510 are unlikely to be true. Cultivated first in Spain and Italy, it moved northwards into the rest of Europe, provoking wonder at its prodigious vitality. Men marvelled at its flower like a 'greate Platter or Dishe'; its stem thick as Hercules' club or, more prosaically, 'the bignesse of a strong mans arme'; its rapid germination in hot climates; and the height it achieved in a single growing season: as high as twenty-four *palmi* in Madrid (a massive eighteen feet or so), but only ten to eleven *palmi* (a more sober eight feet) in colder, damper Belgium.

One of the first Europeans to describe the sunflower was the Spanish physician and botanist Nicolas Monardes from Seville, who never visited the Americas himself but who wrote about this 'straunge flower', along with other medicinal plants and herbs arriving from the New World, in a series of works from the late 1560s which were later 'Englished' by John Frampton, a British merchant returning from Spain. The sunflower, Monardes tells us, had already been in Spain 'some yeres past', and he had finally received seeds for himself. It needed support when growing, he said, or it would always be falling over, and 'it showeth marveilous faire in Gardens'.

Although of interest to the medical community, the sunflower seems to have arrived in Europe without any clues about its medical or other properties, and a number of botanists and gardeners bravely experimented on themselves to see what might happen. The curator of the botanical garden at Padua, Giacomo Antonio Cortuso, recommended cooking and eating the stalks and head, rather like artichokes, declaring them to be even more palatable than mushrooms or asparagus. Eating the plant was also said to produce aphrodisiac effects, a fact the Belgian botanist Rembert Dodoens coyly conveyed in Greek rather than the more accessible Latin.

One who might have spared the Europeans much risky experimentation was the Spanish naturalist and physician to King Philip II of Spain, Francisco Hernández de Toledo, who set out for the New World in 1570 with a mission from the king to research and describe the region's natural history. His projected stay of two years stretched to seven, mostly based around what is now Mexico City; he never reached his intended destination of Peru, and it would be eighty years before the Latin text of his manuscript was published in full.

Accompanied by his son and a group of native artists who illustrated his specimens, Hernández travelled around the country in a litter carried by a retinue of bearers, plagued by insects and complaining about the food, the climate and the terrain. Yet Hernández identified more than three thousand plants previously unknown in Europe and became, to contemporary eyes, worryingly sympathetic to the native people, even going so far as to learn their language and translating some of his writings for them.

Interestingly, Hernández labelled the sunflower the 'Peruvian or large Chimalacatl', saying that it grew in Peru and everywhere in the American provinces in plains and woods, thriving best in wooded areas and in the places where it was cultivated. He compared its seeds to those of the melon, being similar in colour, temperament and nature, although a surfeit of sunflower seeds could cause headaches, he warned. 'However, they can help pains in the chest and even take away these pains and heartburn. Some people grind the seeds and roast them and make them into bread.' As Cortuso had discovered in Padua, Hernández too claimed that the sunflower might 'excite sexual appetite', implying that he knew this only from hearsay.

The sunflower's supposed heliotropic properties also gave rise to some confusion. Most authorities followed Monardes in declaring that the flower 'doth tourne it selfe continually towardes the Sunne, and for this they call it of his name'. Cortuso disagreed, moving into the realm of poetry with his observation that the sunflower responded only to the rising and setting sun. 'I maintain that it is not heliotropic but rather a worshipper of the Sun, and if I were permitted to introduce fables among records of fact, I should want to show you that this had been one of his lovers, since preserved by love and compassion in the form of this beautiful, wonderful plant.' The more prosaic and empirical Rembert Dodoens avoided any reference to the plant's apparent fixation on the sun, merely commenting that 'They call it Sol Indianus, because it seems to have rays like the Sun'.

England's John Gerard was, unusually, the most sceptical of all. In his great *Herball* of 1597, much of it 'borrowed' from Dodoens, Gerard declared that the plant's Latin name of '*Flos Solis*' (Flower of the Sun) came from reports that it turned with the sun, 'the which I coulde never observe, although I have endevored to finde out the truth of it'. Some thirty years later, the royal apothecary John Parkinson reverted to Cortuso's view that the flower could be seen 'bowing downe the head unto the Sunne', but made no mention of it tracking the sun's movements from east to west. According to Parkinson, the sunflower played no part in European medicine, although sometimes the heads were dressed and eaten 'as Hartichokers are, and are accounted of some to be good meate, but they are too strong for my taste'.

From Gerard, too, we get one of the best descriptions of the sunflower's spiral arrangement of seeds, 'set as though a cunning workeman had of purpose placed them in very good order, much like the honie combes of bees'. Here is an unwitting reference to the Fibonacci sequence of numbers, named after the Italian mathematician who discovered them early in the thirteenth century, explaining that they correspond in nature to the most efficient arrangement possible.

BY THE TIME Gerard and Parkinson were writing about sunflowers, the plant's fame had been fanned by eyewitness accounts from North America of sunflowers growing wild and in native encampments. Twenty years before the permanent settlement of Virginia by Europeans in 1607, the Englishman Thomas Hariot had visited villages and palisaded towns in what is now North Carolina, where he described having seen a great herb in the form of a marigold, about six feet in height and its flower head a span in breadth. 'Of the seedes heereof they make both a kinde of bread and broth,' he noted.

According to Hariot, the Indians used neither muck nor dung for their crops, nor did they plough or dig, but simply broke up the top soil with their mattocks and hoes (or short 'peckers' in the case of women), planting their crops of maize, peas, beans, squash, pumpkins and gourds, herbs and sunflowers, either separately or mixed together in the same ground. The Flemish engraver Theodor de Bry used these details to add garden plots and a stand of giant sunflowers to the much sparser depiction of an Algonquian village painted originally by John White, governor of Sir Walter Raleigh's failed colony of Roanoke. De Bry's sunflowers have heads that are very much larger than those of the Native Americans seen wandering about the village, or engaged in a ceremonial dance around a circle of carved wooden posts.

Thirty-five years after Hariot and White recorded sunflower crops in North Carolina, the Frenchman Samuel de Champlain sent back similar reports from New France across the border into what is now Canada. Here among Ontario's many lakes and waterways he found the land cleared of trees. 'The soil is good and the savages grow a great deal of Indian corn, which does extremely well for them, as do squash and sunflowers. Sunflowers they grow for their seeds, from which they extract an oil used in anointing the head.'

By 1640, the sunflower was so associated with the Americas, North and South, that John Parkinson used it on the title page of his herbal, *Theatrum Botanicum: The Theater of Plantes*, as one of the continent's defining plants. In a hotchpotch of habitats and traditions, a bare-breasted and allegorical female America rides a droopy-eared goat (or is it a llama?) through a desert landscape dotted with spiny cacti, a passion flower and a giant sunflower. The other continents are similarly exotic. A turbaned lady Asia sits atop a rhinoceros, while Africa rides a prick-eared zebra.

In North America particularly, as travellers and pioneers pushed ever westwards, reports continued to surface of sunflowers grown and harvested by the indigenous populations, and their many uses in food and medicine. Even today, the common sunflower finds many uses among Native Americans: for its analgesic, anti-rheumatic and disinfectant properties; as a pulmonary, dermatological and gynaecological aid; as a snakebite remedy among the White Mountain Apaches and the Zuni of New Mexico; and as a stimulant and dietary aid. Several native peoples, among them the Gros Ventre and the Ree of Montana, and the Mandan of North Dakota, report its use in ceremonial medicine, using oil from the seeds to lubricate or paint the face or body. The Navajo of Arizona, New Mexico and Utah include it as one of the ingredients in the liniment for their war dance, along with double bladderpod, sumac and mistletoe, while the Kayenta Navajo of north-eastern Arizona use it in their sun sand-painting ceremony.

In Europe, by contrast, it was the sunflower's beauty and strangeness that caught public attention, rather than its utility. From the early seventeenth century, the plant's resplendent flower head dominated the florilegia that became so popular across Europe, combining an aristocratic love of exotic plants with an emerging interest in botanical science. For sheer size and decorative detail, the most remarkable was the *Hortus Eystettensis* by Basilius Besler, a Nuremberg apothecary who recorded the plants in the Bavarian garden of his patron, the Prince-Bishop of Eichstätt. Published in 1613, the *Hortus Eystettensis* was described by a near-contemporary as the 'massiest' of herbals, its two enormous volumes requiring a wheelbarrow to cart them about.

Besler's engraved sunflower – he called it *Flos Solis major & Helianthemum* – is one of the most striking images in the entire work, and fully bears out the scope of his grandiose ambitions. Included with the plants of summer – an arrangement that reflected the weekly despatch of flowers from Eichstätt to Nuremberg during their flowering seasons – the sunflower's massive head occupies most of one page, its outer ray of cross-hatched petals curling at the tips like a fringed collar. The individual florets of the head swirl round from the centre in various stages of opening. The artist and his engravers must have driven themselves mad in their efforts to capture the intricacy of the florets' arrangement, which they actually achieve more accurately in the drawing of a smaller sunflower, called by Besler *Flos Solis proliferi*.

Other painted or drawn sunflowers seem necessarily more subdued. Despite their muscular stems, the two sunflower heads in the *Hortus Floridus* (1614–17) by Crispin de Passe the Younger look almost dainty in comparison, squeezed into an oblong quarto volume that fits neatly into the hand. But in the *Hortus Floridus*'s frontispiece to the flowers of autumn, another more menacing sunflower lurks in the shadows behind the dreamy-eyed goddess Flora, who clutches a cornucopia of tulips, roses, lilies and other more traditional garden flowers. The sunflower and pet greyhound painted mid-century by the English amateur Alexander Marshal is a strange confection of curling leaves and outer petals surrounding a relatively small, black-seeded head, while the large sunflower head and leaf painted early in the eighteenth century for Mary, the first Duchess of Beaufort, looks completely artificial, like a child's toy flower made out of felt.

GIVEN THE FLOWER's striking physical presence, it was only natural that the moralists would soon subvert the sunflower to their own ends. Most emblematic uses of the sunflower hinge on its supposed heliotropism, which, to European minds, supplanted that of the more modest heliotrope (*Heliotropium*), a member of the borage family. While many of the species in this genus are native to the Americas, the European heliotrope (*Heliotropium europaeum*) has small white flowers with five petals, much like those of perennial geraniums.

In Europe, the observation that plants turn towards the sun goes back to the ancient Greeks and the writings of Theophrastus, further amplified in the first century by the Greek-born Dioscorides and the Roman historian Pliny the Elder. Identifying the actual plants is problematic, however, as 'heliotrope' was not the name of one particular species; rather, it designated a solar plant that reacted mechanically to the sun's movement, either by turning its leaves or flowers or by opening and closing its flowers with the sun.

Of all the ancient writers on plants with heliotropic tendencies, Ovid exerted the most enduring influence in his retelling of the disastrous and unrequited love of the sad nymph Clytie for the sun god, Apollo. Upon discovering that Apollo loved her sister Leucothoe, Clytie betrayed her sister to their father after the girl had succumbed to Apollo in a blaze of glory. The sisters shared an oddly similar fate. Buried alive by her father – the traditional punishment meted out to an unchaste vestal virgin – Leucothoe was anointed with Apollo's fragrant nectar and turned into a frankincense tree, while Clytie languished unto death,

> and where her face had been
> A flower like a violet was seen.
> Though rooted fast, towards the sun she turns;
> Her shape is changed, but still her passion burns.

Once the sunflower had taken root in European consciousness, it ousted rivals for Clytie's heliotropic flower, even if Ovid had never set eyes on it. Still others would turn Clytie into the equally brash marigold, whose strident yellow made a mockery of Ovid's intended draining of life and vitality from the lovelorn nymph.

In matters of the heart, too, the sunflower was quickly amassing a variety of meanings: of ardent love – in the *Amorum Emblemata* of Rubens' teacher, Otto van Veen, for instance; and of marital fidelity – in Bartholomeus van der Helst's *Young Woman with a Sunflower*, or Ferdinand Bol's portrait of an unknown couple, painted in 1654. A girl depicted on her own with a sunflower was either thinking faithfully of her absent lover, or advertising her potential as a faithful wife.

The sunflower as an emblem of secular love was soon absorbed into Christian – and specifically Marian – iconography. Forget the sunflower's idolatrous past; here was a flower whose devotion to the sun was equal to that of the Virgin Mary towards her son, that 'loftie Cedar of flowers, wherin the Sun, could he nestle himself, would choose of al the rest to build his neast'. The sunflower's devotional character shines through in illustrations to the Jesuit Henry Hawkins's Marian meditations, *Partheneia Sacra.* In the chapter devoted to this 'miracle of flowers', the sunflower appears garlanded with other flowers sacred to the Virgin – stylized roses, violets, lilies, carnations, passion flowers and the like; in another, the flower lifts its head gaily to the sun, and droops under the moon. Hawkins turned even the flower's lack of smell to a moral advantage, suggesting that any fragrance, if added to its beauty and admirable singularities, would have made men 'stark mad indeed, with doting upon it'.

Devotion was also the theme of Anthony Van Dyck's multi-layered *Self-Portrait with Sunflower* painted in the same year, 1633, in which the artist, looking over his right shoulder, engages the viewer in a quizzical gaze. One hand plays with a gold chain given to him by his patron, King Charles I of England, while the other points to a giant sunflower set against billowing clouds. We see the sunflower not full face as the florilegia typically portray, but angled towards the artist. As a state-

1 Perennial dwarf Sun flower.
2 Ultramarine & Prussian blew Iris Major.
3 Blew Nigella, or Fennel flower.
4 Moon Trefoile.
5 Upright Sweet William.
6 Saxifrage.
7 Cinque foile.
8 Pansis, or Hearts-ease.
9 Maidens blush Rose.
10 Yellow Jasmine.
11 Blew Corn Flower.
12 Blush Belgick Rose.
13 The Francford Rose.
14 Double Martagon.
15 Orchis or Bee Flower.
16 Scarlet Colutea.
17 Fraxinella.
18 Moss province Rose.
19 Double Virginian Silk grass.
20 White Rose.
21 Dutch Hundred Lear'd Rose.
22 White Batchelors Button.
23 Rosa Mundi.
24 Mountain Lychnis.
25 Dwarf Iris Strip'd.
26 White Jasmine.
27 Scarlet Geranium.
28 Yellow Martagon.
29 Red Martagon.
30 Teucrium or Germander.
31 Mountain dwarf Pink.
32 Yellow Corn Marygold.
33 Purple sweet Pea.
34 Greek Valerian.

JUNE

From the Collection of Rob.t Furber, Gardiner at Kensington. 1730.

Design'd by P.t Casteels.   Engrav'd by H. Fletcher.

June's flowers in Robert Furber's *Twelve Months of Flowers* (1730) include a sunflower, Martagon lilies, a Bee orchid and roses galore.

Lotuses on a Summer Evening (1684) by the
Chinese artist, Yun Shou-p'ing.

Nymphæa Cærulea.

P. J. Redouté. — 70.

Pierre-Joseph Redouté's blue Nile 'lotus' (*Nymphaea caerulea*) from
Choix des Plus Belles Fleurs (Paris, 1827–33).

A playful incarnation of Vishnu, the Hindu god Krishna removes the clothes of the love-smitten cowgirls who are bathing in a lotus pool, *c.*1820–30.

The white Madonna lily brandished by the Angel Gabriel in Sandro Botticelli's *The Annunciation* (*c*.1490) signifies Mary's purity and virgin state.

Auguis &c.   Lilium &c.

Hog-nose snake with Martagon lily by the English naturalist Mark Catesby for
The Natural History of Carolina, Florida and the Bahama Islands (London, 1731–43).

Flos Solis maior.

Hand-coloured engraved sunflower from Basilius Besler's *Hortus Eystettensis* of 1613, recording the plants in the garden of his patron, the Prince-Bishop of Eichstätt.

Vincent van Gogh, *Sunflowers* (1887).

ment about art and patronage it is wonderfully complex, for Van Dyck's 'devotion' was of several kinds: of the artist for his patron and for his religion, most obviously, and for the rising power of nature as a suitable subject for art. Van Dyck would later paint his friend and kindred spirit, the virtuoso and natural philosopher Sir Kenelm Digby, with just such a sunflower.

But as the seventeenth century progressed, moralizing emblem books fell victim to their own popularity and slipped into sentimental cliché. Sunflowers naturally abounded, generally as signifiers of fidelity and yearning of a moral or secular kind. Daniel de la Feuille's *Devises et Emblemes*, published in Amsterdam in 1691, retained some sharpness in its sunflower images, helpfully translating its mottos into Latin, French, Spanish, Italian, English, Flemish and German. Yet the same images and thoughts were liberally 'borrowed' again and again over decades, cropping up, for instance, in *Emblems for the Entertainment and Improvement of Youth* of 1750 and its many subsequent editions, but having lost much of their definition.

One original artist who took a fresh look at the sunflower and subsumed it into his personal iconography was the English visionary poet, painter and printmaker William Blake. For Blake, the sunflower's supposed heliotropism hinted at woman's repressed and repressive sexuality, which to his mind operated largely by denying bodily pleasures to both sexes. Blake's fleeting two-stanza poem 'Ah! Sun-flower' appears in *Songs of Experience* sandwiched between 'My Pretty Rose Tree' and 'The Lilly'. These are clearly not the romantic outpourings of an uncritical flower lover. While the white lily does at least 'in Love delight', the sunflower poem drags its metric feet as if to emphasize the dangers of frustrated desire, and the subjects' inability to live in and for the moment.

> Ah! Sun-flower! weary of time,
> Who countest the steps of the Sun,
> Seeking after that sweet golden clime
> Where the traveller's journey is done:

Where the Youth pined away with desire,
And the pale Virgin shrouded in snow,
Arise from their graves and aspire
Where my Sun-flower wishes to go.

Some thirty years later, Blake returned to the sunflower image in his illustrations to Dante's *Divine Comedy*, commissioned by the patron of his last years, the English landscape painter John Linnell. As always, Blake reinterpreted Dante's ideas, most spectacularly substituting a giant sunflower for Dante's pure white rose of Paradise, vast in size and fragrant through all eternity. In Blake's revisioning, by contrast, the Virgin Mary sits enthroned in a sunflower as Queen of the Fallen World, naked except for a gauzy cloak and holding a lily sceptre and a looking glass, both sexual symbols for Blake but also attributes of rampant materialism. Once again, Blake uses the sunflower to warn against the female, who by her will exerts dominion over her mate in the only way she can – by denying him sex, yet forbidding him to seek satisfaction elsewhere. Henry Hawkins would have been sorely distressed to see one of his favourite devotional flowers fallen so low.

ALTHOUGH IT IS unlikely that Blake's radically recast sunflowers had much impact on public perceptions, reactions to garden sunflowers followed a similar trajectory to the flower's symbolic currency, progressing from the initial wonder expressed by early botanical writers of the sixteenth and seventeenth centuries, through the increasing familiarity of the Georgians with all the new sunflower varieties, to eventual disdain.

Philip Miller, gardener to the Society of Apothecaries at Chelsea, expressed surprise in the first edition of his monumentally successful Georgian guide to horticulture, *The Gardeners Dictionary*, that the sunflower had been a stranger to European gardens before the discovery of America. He listed seven different sorts of annual sunflowers, distinguished by type (whether single or double), flower colour (including various shades of brimstone) and seed colour (black, white and one with ash-coloured stripes). Although perennial varieties rarely set seed in England, Miller particularly recommended the 'Common Perennial or Everlasting Sun-Flower', which in his view produced 'the largest and most valuable Flower, and is a very proper Furniture for large Borders in great Gardens, as also for Bosquets of large growing Plants, or to intermix in small Quarters with Shrubs, or in Walks under Trees where few other Plants will thrive'. Along with Thomas Fairchild, the Hoxton nurseryman and author of *The City Gardener*, Miller recommended the perennial sunflower for city gardens, commenting that it 'doth grow in Defiance of the Smoak better than most other Plants'. Like another contemporary nurseryman, Robert Furber, he commended its use as a cut flower 'for Basons, &c. to adorn Halls and Chimnies in a Season when we are at a Loss for other Flowers. It begins flowering in *June*,' he added, 'and continues until *October*.'

But tastes change in garden plants as in everything else, and as more exotics reached the gardens of Europe and elsewhere – and as gardens shrank in size – the over-large, overblown sunflower began to fall out of favour. John Claudius Loudon included the briefest of entries in the index to his mammoth *An Encyclopaedia of Gardening* (1,469 pages in the first edition of 1822), remarking that it was 'of easy culture' and perhaps therefore not worth discussing in the text itself. Its simple habits appealed to Loudon's wife Jane, who pointed out in her classic *Gardening for Ladies* that the annual plant was suitable only where there was 'abundance of room, on account of the large size of its stalks and leaves'. Perennial kinds were much smaller, however, and very ornamental.

By the end of the nineteenth century, the sunflower needed apologists of the stature of the great Irish gardener, William Robinson, to defend its continued inclusion in better-class gardens. While admitting that all the perennial varieties were vigorous growers and that 'not a few' of the genus were 'coarse and weedy, unfitted for the flower-garden', Robinson believed that a fair number, including some not yet in general cultivation, could make their mark in even 'the best-kept flower-garden'. Although often dismissed as a cottager's flower, the annual sunflower was 'one of the noblest plants we have, and one of the most effective for various positions', he declared. As an advocate of wilder styles of gardening, Robinson advised planting it among tall shrubs in a sheltered part of the garden; here it would assume 'a dense branching tree-like habit' without the need for staking, and produce giant flowers over a foot in diameter.

A s t h e s u n f l o w e r ' s fortunes began to wane in the garden, so it played only an incidental role in the elaborate 'language of flowers' first codified in Napoleonic France, which sparked similar vogues in Britain and America. Aimed largely at women in polite society, this 'language' assigned meanings to flowers and devised a whole grammar to decipher how bouquets should be interpreted in the conduct of a love affair. Part game, part primer aimed at moral improvement, it was never intended to be taken too literally. Indeed, as authors from different cultures ascribed contradictory meanings to the same few flowers, any resultant dialogue would soon have given rise to serious misunderstandings.

The various meanings attached to the sunflower reflect how far it had fallen in public esteem. Although the author of one of the earliest and most literal French flower books, B. Delachénaye's *Abécédaire de Flore, ou Langage des Fleurs*, included a fine heliotropic sunflower in his bouquet, translated in the accompanying text to mean 'My eyes see only you', most authors referred to the flower's blatant showiness. 'Pride', 'haughtiness' and 'false riches' are not the sort of compliments a woman would welcome in a nosegay from a lover or potential suitor. The English novelist William Makepeace Thackeray judged the common sunflower to be similarly vulgar, commenting thus on the modest appeal of the simple, good-natured Amelia Sedley in *Vanity Fair*:

there are sweet modest little souls on which you light, fragrant and blooming tenderly in quiet shady places; and there are garden-ornaments, as big as brass warming-pans, that are fit to stare the sun itself out of countenance. Miss Sedley was not of the sunflower sort; and I say it is out of the rules of all proportion to draw a violet the size of a double dahlia.

By the time Thackeray published his satire on nineteenth-century Britain, the language of flowers was itself falling prey to the satirists. In France, where the fashion had first arisen, the caricaturist J. J. Grandville joined forces with the republican writer and editor Taxile Delord to produce a savage parody, *Les Fleurs Animées*, in which the flowers talked back. Grandville's sunflower is a distinctly unpleasant caricature of a kneeling flower with a blacked-up native face, dressed in a petal skirt and wing-like cloak of leaves. Delord takes the sunflower back to its supposed Mexican roots and mythological – if fanciful – sun worship. Set in Mexico City in the middle of the previous century, the story concerns the trumped-up condemnation by the Inquisition of a local headman and direct descendant of Moctezuma, Tumilco, who is accused of sun worship and sacrificing Christians. (In reality, it was the Inquisition that craved a good sacrificial burning.) After his life is spared on the intervention of a young dancer, Tumilco becomes a token Christian, living modestly until his final illness when he unexpectedly rejects the priest sent by his charitable neighbours and asks instead for the window to be opened. 'There is my God,' he cries, 'and the God of my fathers. Oh Sun, receive your child in your breast.' Tumilco dies and the story's satirical moral is made absolutely clear: you can sooner stop a sunflower tracking the sun than prevent heretics from returning to the cult of their ancestors.

DESPITE ITS INCREASINGLY tarnished reputation in Europe, and its gradual banishment from the garden, the sunflower made a miraculous recovery in painting and the decorative arts, although precisely why it became so fashionable many have found hard to explain. Oscar Wilde, as we have seen, paraded both the lily and the sunflower on his highly successful lecture tour of America in 1882, praising the latter's 'gaudy leonine beauty' and claiming the two flowers as the 'most perfect models of design, the most naturally adapted for decorative art'. The audience at his Boston lecture included sixty Harvard students sporting lilies in their buttonholes and sunflowers in their hands. But credit for launching the sunflower craze must surely go to the earlier generation of artist-craftsmen, among them William Morris, who incorporated sunflowers into his wallpapers and declared the single sunflower to be 'both interesting and beautiful, with its sharply chiselled yellow florets relieved by the quaintly patterned sad-coloured centre clogged with honey and beset with bees and butter-flies'. (For Morris's generation the term 'sad' was not necessarily a complaint, rather the opposite: the rage was for dull greens and amber yellows, although William Morris railed against a 'dingy bilious yellow-green' he was supposed to have brought into vogue.)

As far back as 1856 – when Oscar Wilde was less than two years old – Morris had featured sunflowers in his earliest published description of a garden, 'The Story of the Unknown Church', in which a long-dead medieval stonemason evokes the church he had built more than six hundred years previously, its cloister enclosing a lawn with a marble fountain carved with flowers and strange beasts, 'and at the edge of the lawn, near the round edges, were a great many sun-flowers that were all in blossom that autumn day; and up many of the pillars of the cloister crept passion-flowers and roses'.

In its dreamy medievalism, its nostalgia for a golden past that never was, its wild and garden flowers, its monks and castle, and its beauti-ful young woman with dark brown hair and eyes that were deep, calm and violet, Morris's story could stand as a blueprint for the fads and fantasies of the Pre-Raphaelite Brotherhood – and fantasies they certainly were in this case, since sunflowers, and passion flowers, too, were unknown in thirteenth-century Europe. Morris would recog-nize this himself when he praised the sunflower as a 'late comer to our gardens' to an audience of guild workers and Birmingham artists. But other sunflower aficionados had an equally shaky grasp of historical plant introductions, among them Morris's friend the English painter Edward Burne-Jones. In *Childe Roland to the Dark Tower Came* (1861), inspired by Robert Browning's poem of the same name, Burne-Jones implanted a riot of sunflowers in Browning's terrifyingly barren land-scape, thereby providing one of the earliest examples of the sunflower motif that would enthuse later decades.

After Morris and Burne-Jones, sunflowers proliferated across the art of Europe and America: sunflowers in a godly context (James Tissot, *Jesus Looking Through a Lattice with Sunflowers*, c.1886–94); in cool, Danish-style interiors (Michael Ancher, *Girl with Sunflowers*, 1889); in dazzling impressionistic sunlight (Claude Monet, *The Artist's Garden at Vétheuil*, 1881); in the hands of a ragged black Afro-American schoolchild (Winslow Homer, *Taking Sunflower to Teacher*, 1875); and in opulent drawing rooms furnished with oriental flair (Kate Hayllar, *Sunflowers and Hollyhocks*, 1889).

But it was in the decorative arts that the ubiquitous sunflower reigned supreme as one of the principal motifs of the Aesthetic Movement that began in the late 1860s, flourished through the 1870s and 1880s, then sank into a welter of parody and scorn shortly afterwards. You wore your sunflower on your sleeve or at least, if you were a fashionable woman, embroidered onto your velvet skirts. And you displayed it on every conceivable domestic object and surface: fabrics, wallpaper, tiles, gilded pots, song sheets, jewellery, smoking caps, calling cards, sculptural busts (as in the writhing *Clytie* by George Frederic Watts), ornamental plates, carved furniture, teapots, fire tongs, clocks – anything that might proclaim your aesthetic sensitivities. Such a 'sunflower affectation' filled Burne-Jones with disgust, according to his widow, and he vehemently denounced the 'feeble folly' of those 'sunflower-worshippers' to whom he had once stood as an unwitting godfather.

Some of these household subjects were intended to poke fun at the worst excesses of the craze. An enduring classic is a hermaphrodite teapot of 1882 from the Worcester Royal Porcelain Works. The male side displays a foppish young man wearing a 'greenery-yallery' jacket complete with sunflower buttonhole, while the figure on the reverse has metamorphosed into a lovelorn maiden dressed in a summer smock pinned with a calla lily, their mutual arms and limp wrists providing the teapot's spout and handle. An inscription on the base drives home the teapot's solemn warning of the 'Fearful consequences through the laws of Natural Selection and evolution of living up to

one's teapot' – a sly dig at both Darwinism and the influential Gros-
venor Gallery's display of a single teapot with the exhortation to 'live
up to it'. The ebonized wood and porcelain sunflower clocks designed
by Lewis F. Day for the London firm of Howell, James & Co. were, by
contrast, produced without any hint of irony.

The aesthetic sunflower spilled over into architecture, added as
a stock feature to the fashionable red-brick houses erected around
Chelsea and Kensington, in London's 'little colony' of Bedford Park,
and to the mansion flats built in mock Queen Anne style. Lower down
the social scale, even Board Schools and drab tenements were sometimes brightened with a solitary sunflower, added almost as an after-
thought, 'a modest conciliatory gesture to Art and Queen Anne'.

After such a surfeit of sunflowers, a counter-reaction was inevitable;
much of the scorn was directed at poor Oscar Wilde, whose ceaseless
proselytizing had pushed his favourite flowers to the fore. 'When he
wore a daisy in his buttonhole, thousands of young men did likewise,'
wrote the actress and royal mistress Lillie Langtry in her memoirs.
'When he proclaimed the sunflower "adorable", it was to be found adorning every drawing room.' The image would return to haunt him. A
Punch cartoon of 1881 has Wilde's head stuck inside the sunflower's
leonine mane that he would soon praise to his American lecture audience. The artist was Edward Linley Sambourne, and an editorial note
explained that this particular 'Fancy Portrait' was of 'O.W.':

> Aesthete of Aesthetes!
> What's in a name?
> The poet is WILDE,
> But his poetry's tame.

That same year Gilbert and Sullivan's comic opera *Patience* opened
in London and New York, lampooning Wilde's aestheticism and the
pretensions of artistic celebrities such as Dante Gabriel Rossetti and
Algernon Charles Swinburne. Sunflowers adorned the opera's programme cover for London's Savoy Theatre, as they doubtless adorned

"O. W."

"O, I feel just as happy as a bright Sunflower!"
Lays of Christy Minstrelsy.

Æsthete of Æsthetes!
What's in a name?
The poet is WILDE,
But his poetry's tame.

Cartoon by Edward Linley Sambourne for *Punch*, 25 June 1881, depicting the
Irish writer and aesthete Oscar Wilde as a sunflower.

many of the skirts and bodices of its female audience. Still playing after 500 performances, the opera struck a chord with the architectural press, wearied by aestheticism's 'inflated nothings'. The sunflower craze was symptomatic of a deeper malaise, declared the theatre critic of *The British Architect*: 'If there were nothing else to illustrate the fact, the sickening repetition of the sunflower in all sorts of decorative work (as though it were the sum total of beauty) would be enough to show how little good the general public have yet derived from the increased study of art.'

WHILE THE AESTHETIC Movement was fast losing momentum, sunflowers in art experienced their apotheosis in the glorious sun-drenched canvases painted by Vincent van Gogh in Arles as he waited feverishly for Paul Gauguin to join him in his 'Studio of the South', an idea that had fired his artistic vision but which lasted as a physical reality for less than a year.

Van Gogh had painted sunflowers before he travelled south: a fairly standard *Bowl with Sunflowers, Roses and Other Flowers* (1886) and a quartet of still lifes with great flower heads gone to seed (1887), which owed their inspiration to the sunflowers he had seen growing in the cottage gardens around Montmartre. These last paintings explored the effects of different brushstrokes and background colours, from the blue-and-yellow and darker reds of his *Two Cut Sunflowers*, to the highly textured surface of *Four Cut Sunflowers, One Upside Down*, in which the fringed petals flicker like flames, and the whole canvas flares with life in defiance of the chopped-off stems.

More sunflowers greeted his arrival in Arles; the splashes of colour in these Provençal gardens took on for him an amazing brilliance, 'and in the limpid air there's something happier and more suggestive of love than in the north'. Soon the sunflower with its vibrant yellows and solar symbolism came to represent all his hopes for a new beginning in both his creative and his everyday life; he told his ever-generous brother Theo that he was painting some big sunflowers 'with the gusto of a Marseillais eating bouillabaisse'.

Van Gogh's letters to Theo, and to his painter friend Émile Bernard, reveal how sunflowers came to dominate his artistic vision and his psychic health. After telling Bernard about his attempts to paint dusty thistles swarming with butterflies, he wrote of the half-dozen sunflower pictures with which he hoped to decorate his studio, 'a decoration in which harsh or broken yellows will burst against various BLUE backgrounds – from the palest Veronese to royal blue, framed with thin laths painted in orange lead' – an effect he likened to the stained-glass windows of a Gothic church. Bernard was then staying with Gauguin in the artists' colony of Pont-Aven in Brittany and although van Gogh wished to be with them, he drew comfort from re-imagining his sunflowers.

Van Gogh continued to work like a demon as he waited fretfully for Gauguin to join him. The plan was that Theo would fund Gauguin's stay, receiving paintings in return. But Gauguin still had to find money for the journey, which he constantly delayed. Vincent, meanwhile, was painting three sunflower canvases simultaneously, one with three huge flowers in a green vase; another with three flowers – one just a bud, another gone to seed – against a royal-blue background; and a third of twelve flowers and buds in a yellow vase, light on light, which he hoped would be the best. (None of these paintings turned out quite as he described.) 'In the hope of living in a studio of our own with Gauguin,' he wrote excitedly to Theo, 'I'd like to do a decoration for the studio. *Nothing but large Sunflowers*. Next door to your shop, in the restaurant [the inexpensive Bouillon Duval on the Boulevard Montmartre], as you know, there's such a beautiful decoration of flowers there; I always remember the big sunflower in the window.'

In van Gogh's fevered mind, the sunflower sequence had expanded to a dozen or so panels, 'a symphony in blue and yellow', on which he worked from sunrise to sunset, 'because the flowers wilt quickly, and it's a matter of doing the whole thing in one go'. By the time of his next letter to Theo, he had started on his fourth sunflower canvas – fourteen flowers, he said (in fact, fifteen), against a greenish-yellow background – and he continued to push his technique towards greater simplicity. Inspired by a Manet painting of huge pink peonies against a light background, he aimed to banish the fussy stippling of the pointillists, devising distinctive brushstrokes for each element in his painting. But the paintings were about more than art and style; they gave physical form to the new life he was about to begin. The room he promised Theo in a year's time ('or Gauguin, if he comes') would have white walls with a decoration of great yellow sunflowers, '12 or 14 to the bunch, crammed into this tiny boudoir with its pretty bed and everything else dainty. It will not be commonplace.'

Paul Gauguin arrived in Arles in late October 1888 and stayed for just nine weeks. During this time, the men lived and worked together, dissecting art and life in their conversations and in their pictures. For both artists their time at Arles was pivotal: for van Gogh, it represented a culmination of all his hopes, but for Gauguin it was a 'point of departure, instrumental in helping him chart his future course'. Gauguin was particularly impressed by van Gogh's sunflowers, declaring that he liked them better than the ones Monet had painted in a large Japanese vase; and he painted van Gogh painting his sunflowers in a portrait he called *The Painter of Sunflowers*. Against a background of Provençal blues, yellows and greens, the tormented Dutchman stares intently at a vase of imaginary sunflower heads, the time for their flowering having long since passed, as he labours to transfer his vision on to canvas.

By 23 December 1888, the dream of artistic collaboration was over. Gauguin left Arles after van Gogh had reportedly threatened him with a knife, then turned it on himself, severing part of his ear in a local brothel where he had taken refuge. He never saw Gauguin again, and after a short spell in hospital he returned to the Yellow House in Arles, painting three more vases of sunflowers copied from his efforts of the previous August, ostensibly to meet Gauguin's request for one of the Arles sunflower paintings to add to the two Parisian sunflowers van Gogh had already given him. Van Gogh categorically refused his request for an original but was happy to attempt a copy. Was he also trying to replicate – in midwinter – the joyful frenzy of their creation the previous summer? Sunflowers held such a special meaning for him, and these were the last ones he painted. Some three months before he died, he wrote to his youngest sister Willemien, seeking forgiveness that his paintings were 'almost a cry of anguish while symbolizing gratitude in the rustic sunflower'.

The sunflower stayed with Gauguin, too, recurring almost as a sign of bad conscience over the way he had treated his friend. Gauguin's *Caribbean Woman*, or *Female Nude with Sunflowers* conflated van Gogh's flowers with a *négresse* figure of his own. Yet other paintings of his were more one-sided borrowings, including a number of still lifes undertaken in 1899, apparently at the request of the Parisian art dealer Ambroise Vollard, and again in 1901, with *Sunflowers on an Armchair*, *Sunflowers and Mangoes*, and *Sunflowers with Puvis de Chavannes' 'Hope'*. Hope and sunflowers went together for Gauguin, as they had for his former friend, but hope in the end disappointed them both.

Flowers were a different matter, however. Writing to his mother from the asylum at Saint-Rémy-de-Provence in October 1889, van Gogh compared the art market to 'a sort of tulip mania from which the living painters get more disadvantage than advantage. And it will also pass like tulip mania.' Although the fever abates, the flower growers remain: 'And so I regard painting in the same way, that what remains is a sort of flower growing. And as to that I reckon myself fortunate to be in it.'

V AN GOGH WAS, of course, entirely correct in his castigation of the art market. Unsold in his lifetime, as were all but one of his paintings, aside from those 'bought' by brother Theo, his vase of fifteen sunflowers sold at auction to a Japanese buyer in 1987 for nearly $40 million, making it then the most expensive artwork in the world. (The record was broken a few months later by another van Gogh painting, of irises.) From New-World wonder to art-market phenomenon, the sunflower had travelled a long way, without losing its propensity to shock and delight in equal measure.

Its twentieth-century history is nonetheless a steadier affair, substituting economic for artistic importance as the cultivated sunflower transformed itself yet again into one of the world's four most important edible oil crops, especially important in the Soviet bloc states of central and eastern Europe. The story echoes the sunflower's beginnings in prehistoric America, when chance as much as design influenced its evolution. Reputedly introduced to Russia by Peter the Great, sunflowers are said to owe their popularity there to a decree from the Russian Orthodox Church prohibiting the consumption of certain oil-rich foods in the fasting days of Lent. Sunflower seeds, which contain a high proportion of oil, were then so little known in Russia that they were not listed and so could be eaten with a good conscience.

Cultivation increased rapidly, spreading to the Ukraine, where the acres of golden sunflowers explain how the flower became the nation's unofficial symbol; by the beginning of the twentieth century the sunflower was one of Russia's major crops. The Russian sunflower travelled back to North America with Mennonite and Jewish immigrants, and a variety known as 'Mammoth Russian' appeared in American seed catalogues from the 1880s. Breeding began in earnest, for pest and disease resistance, early ripening and higher oil content, lifting the latter from below 30 to above 50 per cent, and making sunflower seed the third largest source of vegetable oil worldwide, after soybean and palm. Even now, Russia and the Ukraine lead the global field in sunflower production.

Back in America, the humble sunflower demonstrated its continued ability to create its own mythology when Kansas adopted the plant as its state flower and floral emblem in 1903, in a statute that spun a mythic past of frontier life, celebrating the sunflower as the glory of the past, the pride of the present and richly emblematic of a golden future. The Kansas state legislature declared this native wild flower to be

common throughout her borders, hardy and conspicuous, of definite, unvarying and striking shape, easily sketched, moulded, and carved, having armorial capacities, ideally adapted for artistic reproduction, with its strong, distinct disk and its golden circle of clear glowing rays – a flower that a child can draw on a slate, a woman can work in silk, or a man can carve on stone or fashion in clay.

Many years later, the nearby state of Iowa tried to outlaw the sunflower as a noxious weed because of the havoc it wreaked on the soybean crop. In retaliation, Kansas picked a quarrel with Iowa's state bird, the eastern goldfinch, which feeds on sunflower seeds, threatening to declare it a public nuisance. Neither resolution was ever formally adopted and the row eventually subsided. The sunflower remains firmly fixed in the Kansan psyche, celebrated for its love of open spaces, neither hiding in the dark nor seeking solace in the shade. In the words of one nostalgic Kansan, 'It stood by the dusty roadside and out on the high prairie – and you always knew what it meant . . . It turned its gold petals and black center always toward the sun. No matter how fiercely the heat beat down, it faced the music and never blinked.' And as any Kansan will tell you, if you travel through the state in late August and early September, you will encounter a landscape dominated by sunflowers, looking bright and vigorous 'when everything else, including the residents, are brown and wilted'.

A native of New Jersey rather than the Kansas prairies, the beat poet Allen Ginsberg drew on the 'perfect beauty of a sunflower' to castigate the desolation of urban America, as he sat with Jack Kerouac on the 'tincan banana dock', hung-over like two old bums, beneath the huge shadow cast by a Southern Pacific locomotive. Unusually for Ginsberg, who wrote his 'Sunflower Sutra' in 1955 in Berkeley, California, the sunflower brings a glimmer of hope that America might rediscover its progressive roots and become beautiful again – a different sort of hope to van Gogh's sunflower dreams, but hope nonetheless.

TODAY, THE SUNFLOWER has reincarnated itself more widely as the emblem of good causes. Adopted as the trademark of the British Vegan Society and recognized around the world – except perhaps in the Asia–Pacific region, where the mark has metamorphosed into the lotus – it stands for the values of caring and compassion:

for animals and people, and for the earth as a whole. You are just as likely to find its cheerful, sunlit presence endorsing a hospice, a brand of margarine, or an estate agent's flyer wishing to breathe new life into an ailing market. And the sunflower lives on in art, most recently in the millions of hand-painted porcelain sunflower seeds with which the Chinese artist Ai Weiwei filled the great entrance hall of London's Tate Modern. '"*Sunflower Seeds*" invites us to look more closely at the "Made in China" phenomenon and the geo-politics of cultural and economic exchange today,' promised the gallery. Or you could simply stand and stare.

— 4 —

Opium Poppy

Not poppy nor mandragora
Nor all the drowsy syrups of the world
Shall ever medicine thee to that sweet sleep
Which thou owedst yesterday.

WILLIAM SHAKESPEARE, *Othello*

Black Poppy   White Poppy   Red Poppy

EVEN ON A rain-swept Sunday in early June, the opium poppies at London's Chelsea Physic Garden stopped me in my tracks, their translucent petals crumpled like silk in shades of pink, red and a gamut of ghostly purples. 'The poppy is painted glass,' wrote the Victorian art critic John Ruskin in *Proserpina*, his rambling study of wayside flowers; 'it never glows so brightly as when the sun shines through it. Wherever it is seen – against the light or with the light – always, it is a flame, and warms the wind like blown ruby.' Sodden and unilluminated, these poppies were glowing nonetheless as the limp young buds unfurled into proudly erect flower heads, their four petals splotched with basal purple enfolding a petticoat frill of pollen-bearing anthers around a radiating star – the stigmatic disc – at the flower's heart.

The opium poppy's power does not reside in its beauty, however. 'Joan Silver Pin', they called it in Elizabethan times, 'of great beautie, although of evill smell'. The royal apothecary John Parkinson was even plainer in his verdict, calling it 'faire without and fowle within'; for the power of this most beautiful of flowers lies in the opium it contains, a drug hailed as the most important remedy in the pharmacologist's entire *materia medica*, yet one judged capable of creating more misery by its abuse 'than any other drug employed by mankind'.

When I delved into its long history, the opium poppy's European origins – as a plant and as a drug – took me by surprise. Misled by its current notoriety, I had long viewed it as a more easterly plant, born in the badlands of countries such as Afghanistan, which today cultivates more poppies for their illegal drugs yield than any other nation.

But the opium poppy is in fact a plant of the western Mediterranean, which gathered strength as it moved eastwards and would later return to haunt those who had first recognized its potency.

The opium poppy's history is full of such paradoxes; constant undertones of fear and dislike are counterbalanced by periodic outbursts of reverence for its brilliance as a drug and as a garden plant. People were right to fear it, as its power was — and still is — very real. This power was particularly evident in the nineteenth century when the legal consumption of opium products was at its height, and Britain went to war to defend the 'right' of her merchants to bring illicit opium to China in defiance of the Chinese government's wishes. Yet by the end of the century, America would introduce desperate measures aimed at blocking the advance of opium smoking into her territory, and the world woke up to the dangers of the illegal drugs trade. Such are the ironies of this most perverse of flowers.

LIKE THE SUNFLOWER'S, the story of the opium poppy, *Papaver somniferum*, begins with men's stomachs, for it is as an oil plant that it leaves its first trace in human history, domesticated in the western Mediterranean some six thousand years ago. Remains of charred poppy seeds and occasional capsules have been uncovered from Neolithic and early Bronze Age settlements in northern France, Switzerland, Germany, Poland, northern Italy and southern Spain. The crop is closely related to the wild and 'weedy' poppies, previously known as *P. setigerum* and now usually classed as a subspecies of *P. somniferum*, that grow around the fringes of the Mediterranean basin to the west of Sicily and the toe of Italy, and along the North African littoral. From south-western Europe, the opium poppy then moved eastwards into central Europe and on to the eastern Mediterranean. Although most of these early finds tell us that poppies were cultivated for their food value as seeds or oil, the discovery of several beautifully preserved poppy capsules from a burial site in southern Spain suggests a connection with death rituals dating back to at least 2500 BCE.

The poppy's narcotic powers were also essentially discovered by Europeans and not, as you will sometimes read, by the ancient Mesopotamian civilizations of the Sumerians, Babylonians and Assyrians. The confusion was essentially linguistic. Among the many thousands of clay tablets excavated at Nippur on the Euphrates, a short distance south of modern Baghdad, was a detailed list of the animal, mineral and plant material used in medical prescriptions – in effect the world's oldest recorded list of *materia medica*, written in cuneiform script *c.* 2100 BCE by a Sumerian physician. Throughout much of the twentieth century, the ideogram transliterated as 'HUL-GIL' was identified with opium or the 'joy plant'. As the same ideogram appeared in later Assyrian plant lists and medicinal tablets, it was assumed that both opium and the opium poppy were known to the Assyrians. As a result scholars constructed a whole set of intriguing linguistic relationships linking narcotics in general and opium in particular to the root words 'to curse' and 'to rejoice' – the twin poles expressing the extreme effects of this most potent drug. Yet far from indicating the opium poppy, the symbol 'HUL-GIL' in fact refers to a kind of cucumber, quite possibly the stink cucumber, and the expert view today is that no word in Sumerian, Akkadian or Assyrian positively identifies poppy, opium poppy, or opium. Nor is the evidence of Assyrian bas-reliefs from Nineveh any more convincing, as scholars continue to argue over the identity of plants held by priestly physicians at a ritual scene.

Quite when the opium poppy arrived in Egypt is also disputed. The poppies depicted on the casket lid of Tutankhamun's tomb, and the dried poppy flowers found in his ornamental bouquet, are generally classed as common corn poppies, *Papaver rhoeas*, while an ancient Egyptian plant known as '*spn*' is identified only 'very dubiously' as the opium poppy. Its soporific effects were, however, much the same. Among the seven hundred or so medical remedies and magical formulae contained in the Ebers papyrus of *c.*1500 BCE, is this remedy to calm a crying child: '*spn*-seeds; fly dung from the wall; is made to a paste, [mixed with water?], strained and drunk for four days. The crying will cease instantly.'

More intriguing – and convincing – are reports by the Danish Egyptologist Lise Manniche that opium in some form may have been buried with the dead during Egypt's eighteenth dynasty (c.1400 BCE), although its ancient function and purpose remain obscure. According to Manniche, fatty material recovered from the tomb at Deir el-Medina of Kha, a high-ranking official involved with the royal tombs at Thebes, was subjected to laboratory analysis and introduced into a frog. After half an hour the frog began to leap about, reacting instantly to stimuli, but it later calmed down and its reactions slowed. A larger quantity injected into another frog caused paralysis and death, after initial excitement; and when dissolved in water and injected into a frog and a mouse, the drug induced deep sleep, after which the two creatures returned to normal. The chemical contained in the ancient substance was identified as morphine, one of opium's main alkaloids, isolated only in the nineteenth century.

Whatever ritual or medicinal use the ancient Egyptians made of opium, it seems unlikely that they were the first to revere its potency. As with the lily, that honour belongs to the Minoans of Crete who, possibly influenced by the Mycenaeans from mainland Greece, created the oldest surviving large-scale icon linking the opium poppy to the gods. This is the terracotta Minoan goddess with eyes closed, hands uplifted and lips clamped in a beatific smile suggesting either torpor or ecstasy, who wears in her hair three removable pins now recognized as poppy capsules, notched to release their precious sap. Known as the 'poppy goddess, patroness of healing' and dated to the second millennium BCE, she was discovered in 1936 in a sanctuary at Gazi near Heraklion in Crete, amid paraphernalia that may have been used to produce opium vapours, giving the drug a role in her worship.

Many smaller artefacts from mainland Greece confirm the link between poppies and a fertility goddess, among them a celebrated gold seal-ring from Mycenae, which shows a goddess under a sacred tree receiving gifts of poppy capsules, lilies and unidentified flowers. Living up to its later Elizabethan nickname of 'Joan Silver Pin', the opium poppy appears to have been a favourite ornament of ancient

Greek pinheads, such as the silver pin excavated at the sanctuary of Hera at Argos, inscribed with a dedication to the goddess.

WRITTEN EVIDENCE CONFIRMS the part played by ancient Greece and the lands of the Aegean in spreading the cult and culture of the poppy into the eastern Mediterranean. It had reached Corinth by the eighth century BCE at least, when the poet Hesiod wrote of a nearby town named Mekone, or Poppy Town, so named because of its extensive poppy fields. Others held that it was here the goddess Demeter first discovered the fruit of the poppy, which legend suggests consoled her as she searched for her daughter Persephone, snatched by Hades and taken to the underworld.

At much the same time, Homer used the poppy's limpness to describe in the *Iliad* the drooping head of the Trojan Gorgythion, killed by an arrow intended for his half-brother Hector. More controversial is the identification of *nepenthes*, the narcotic drug in *The Odyssey*, which Helen slipped into the drinks of her husband's guests returning from Troy.

> No one who drank it deeply, mulled in wine,
> could let a tear roll down his cheeks that day,
> not even if his mother should die, his father die,
> not even if right before his eyes some enemy brought down
> a brother or darling son with a sharp bronze blade.

Although widely assumed to be an opiate because of its ability to dispel anger and pain, *nepenthes* has never been conclusively identified. Homer tells us that Helen acquired the drug from Polydamna, wife of Thon, 'a woman of Egypt, land where the teeming soil / bears the richest yield of herbs in all the world'. Everyone in Egypt was a healer, claimed the poet, drawing on Egypt's contemporary reputation as the primary source of medical wizardry. But this proves neither the identity of the drug nor its supposed Egyptian origin. Indeed, writing some four centuries after Homer, Theophrastus – the great botanist of the classical age – hints that *nepenthes* might have been a figment of the poet's imagination, that 'famous drug which cures sorrow and passion, so that it causes forgetfulness and indifference to ills'. Others, too, have suggested that Helen stupefied her guests not with drugs but with her charms.

Far from clarifying the role of the opium poppy in Greek botany and pharmacology, Theophrastus omits it altogether from his three types of poppy: the horned poppy, the corn poppy, and a third kind (*Herakleia*) with a leaf like soapwort, used to bleach linen. Only the middle kind is a true poppy, much like today's corn poppy, *Papaver rhoeas*; he called it *rhoias*, 'which is like wild chicory, wherefore it is even eaten: it grows in cultivated fields and especially among barley. It has a red flower, and a head as large as a man's finger-nail. It is gathered before the barley-harvest, when it is still somewhat green. It purges downwards.'

The omission of the opium poppy is puzzling, especially as Theophrastus described how to harvest the poppy's juice for medicinal purposes: not from the stalks or roots but 'from the head, as in the case of the poppy; for this is the only plant which is so treated and this is its peculiarity'. The ancient Greek physician Hippocrates, who died about the time Theophrastus was born in 371 BCE, frequently mentioned opium and the opium poppy, especially in his gynaecological tracts, so perhaps midwives were more keenly aware of its painkilling properties than male physicians. Or perhaps Theophrastus kept silent because of the controversies that have always bedevilled its use as a drug.

Ancient knowledge about the different kinds of poppy and their effects on human physiology coalesced in *De Materia Medica* by the Greek-born Pedanius Dioscorides, who acquired his great knowledge of plants while travelling around the Roman Empire as an itinerant physician – perhaps in the wake of the Roman army – in the first century CE. Dioscorides distinguished between three kinds of poppy: one with white seeds, 'cultivated and set in gardens', whose seeds were made into bread and used with honey instead of sesame seeds; the wild corn poppy, *P. rhoeas*, whose heads could be boiled in wine to produce a sleeping draught or taken as a drink with honey and water to soften the

An opium poppy from the 'Vienna Dioscorides', an early
sixth-century Byzantine copy of Dioscorides' *De Materia Medica*
created for Princess Juliana Anicia.

bowels; and a third kind, 'more wild, more medicinal and longer than
these', which was the focus of his medicinal remedies.

From Dioscorides, we get a sense of opium's power as a drug but
also of the care and respect it demanded. While discounting from his
own experience the cautions of other authorities that it could turn men
blind and should be inhaled only, he declared that drunk too often 'it
hurts (making men lethargic) and it kills', nonetheless recommending
it for a range of conditions that called for a 'cooling' remedy. Boiled

in water and applied with hot cloths, the capsules and leaves induced sleep, as did a decoction taken internally. Pounded into small pieces and mixed into poultices with polenta, the heads could reduce inflammation and a streptococcal skin infection known as erysipelas. Boiled first in water and then with honey, the capsules produced a 'licking medicine' suitable for coughs and abdominal afflictions, while ground black poppy seeds drunk with wine were used to reduce diarrhoea and excessive discharges in women. Various parts of the plant could also be mixed with other ingredients and used for earaches, inflamed eyes, gout, wounds and as a general painkiller; while 'put up with the finger as a suppository it causes sleep'. The best poppy juice, according to Dioscorides, was 'thick, heavy, and sleepy in smell, bitter to the taste, easily pierced with water, smooth, white, not sharp, neither clotted nor growing thick in the straining'.

Dioscorides' very detailed descriptions set out the two main ways by which the Greeks harnessed the medicinal power of the poppy. The less potent method was to squeeze the pounded stems and leaves through a press, beat the resulting mash in a mortar, then turn it into lozenges; this was called *meconium*. Pure opium – a far stronger medicine – was harvested by slitting the fruit with a small knife, 'after the dew-drops have become well dried. The knife must be drawn round the crown without piercing the fruit within; then the capsules must be directly slit on the sides near the surface and opened lightly, the juice drop will come forth on to the finger sluggishly but will soon flow freely.' You were also advised to stand well back when preparing the latex, to avoid contaminating your clothes.

Pliny the Elder, a near contemporary of Dioscorides, added a few new facts: that poppy seeds offered a cure for elephantiasis, for instance, and that opium was a favourite recourse of suicides, giving the example of a man of Praetorian rank who killed himself with opium after an incurable illness had rendered his life intolerable. Condemned by earlier authorities as a deadly poison, the drug was then generally 'not disapproved of', although Pliny himself did not favour its medicinal use for sore eyes, upset stomachs or to reduce fevers.

Roman gardeners were more wholehearted in their approval. Opium poppy flowers grace the garden-room frescoes of Livia, wife of Emperor Augustus, at her villa at Prima Porta, and – most majestically – the garden paintings of Pompeii's House of the Gold Bracelet, where they are deemed worthy companions to resplendent Madonna lilies, camomile, morning glories and young date palms. At Pompeii, the flower heads are painted a milky lavender, shown in profile, full face and one with the seed-head clearly forming. The townsfolk may also have followed Cato the Elder in harvesting their poppy seeds to sprinkle on *globi*, fried cheesecakes spread with honey, and on *savillum*, a kind of sweet cheesecake.

Playing on the drug's power of consolation and oblivion, the poppy gathered more mythic associations that raised its status in the Graeco-Roman world. Although absent from the original *Homeric Hymn to Demeter*, which celebrated the ancient Greek goddess of marriage, good health, fertility and agriculture (known to the Romans as Ceres), the poppy soon attached itself to the goddess, fusing the opium poppy's power to assuage grief with the attributes of the corn poppy, traditionally found growing among the grain crops of barley and corn. Poppy capsules and sheaves of grain became the goddess's two principal symbols; and poppies may have played a part in the Eleusinian mysteries that celebrated both the winter descent of Demeter's daughter Persephone into the dark underworld of Hades, and her springtime return to her mother.

The opium poppy was also associated with the ancient Greek gods Nyx, the god of night; Hypnos, the god of sleep; and his son Morpheus, the god of dreams. In his *Metamorphoses*, the Roman poet Ovid situates the god of sleep's home deep in the hollow of a mountainside, beyond reach of the sun and human clamour, where

> Before the cavern's mouth lush poppies grow
> And countless herbs, from whose bland essences
> A drowsy infusion dewy night distils
> And sprinkles sleep across the darkening world.

Just such poppies would slip into the dark dreamworlds of German Romanticism, as in the 'sweet intoxication' of the poppies in Novalis's *Hymns to the Night* and their mirrored image in Philipp Otto Runge's painted *Moonrise*; these are poppies that mark the boundary between real space and the territory of dreams. Empowered perhaps by association with the more potent opium poppy, Demeter's corn poppies would much later metamorphose into the Flanders poppy of Remembrance Day, growing in ground disturbed not by tilling but by war.

AFTER ROME'S FALL in the fifth century CE, the use of opium declined for a time in the West but the poppy itself continued to thrive, planted sometimes in kitchen gardens – as in St Gall's idealized monastery plan – and sometimes among the medicinal plants of the infirmary garden, or bought specially for the sickroom. Emperor Charlemagne included it among the plants that were to be grown on his royal estates; and in the calm of the monastic garden at Reichenau Island in Lake Constance, the ninth-century abbot Walahfrid Strabo planted poppies in his small garden plot and pondered their significance in verse, calling them Ceres' poppies

> because, mourning the loss of her stolen daughter,
> She is said to have eaten poppy to drown her sorrow, deep
> Beyond measure – to forget, as she longed to forget, her grief of mind.

It was usual then to distinguish between two sorts of *Papaver somniferum*, the white and the black poppy, differentiated by the colour of their seeds rather than their petals. The white poppy was generally treated as a garden plant and the wilder black poppy as the 'medicinal', opium-yielding variety, although there is in fact no botanical difference between the two, and botanists now view the species as having developed from an ancient cultivated crop with semi-wild self-sown varieties, not found in a truly wild state.

The supposed distinction between black and white poppies

lingered into Elizabethan times. Of the black poppy, the herbalist and barber-surgeon John Gerard explained that it was the same as the white, 'saving that the flowers are more white and shining, spotted or str[e]aked with some lines of purple. The leaves are greater, more jagged, and sharper pointed. The seede is likewise blacker, which maketh the difference.' In his garden he grew single and double white poppies, a single purple poppy and possibly a double black poppy, but identifying pre-Linnaean varieties is always problematic. Like Pliny before him, Gerard seemed awed by opium's potency in the sickroom, declaring that it 'mitigateth all kindes of paines: but it leaveth behinde it oftentimes a mischiefe worse then the disease it selfe . . . Wherfore all those medicines and compoundes are to be shunned that are made of *Opium*, and are not to be used but in extreme necessitie.' Gerard's fear of the plant echoes that of the poet Edmund Spenser, who planted 'Dead sleeping *Poppy*' in *The Faerie Queene*'s *Gardin of Proserpina* [Persephone] along with 'mournfull *Cypresse*', 'trees of bitter *Gall*' and the 'blacke *Hellebore*'. No savoured flower of Elizabethan delight, Spenser's poppy was 'direfull deadly blacke both leafe and bloom, / Fit to adorne the dead, and decke the drery toombe'.

Revising Gerard's text in the 1630s, the London apothecary Thomas Johnson left the original entry for the poppy virtually unchanged, adding a showy new variety that demonstrated how poppies were developing into stars of the flower garden. This new sort had leaves that were 'much more sinuated, or crested, and the floure also is all jagged or finely cut about the edges, and of this sort there is also both blacke and white. The floures of the blacke are red, and the seed blacke; and the other hath both the floures and seed white.'

John Parkinson, royal herbalist to Charles I, added several more varieties in his book of garden flowers, selecting only those beauties deemed worth of respect: double white poppies, double red or blush poppies, and double purple or murrey poppies, their flowers 'eyther red or blush, or purplish red, more or lesse, or of a sad murrey or tawney, with browne, or blacke, or tawny bottomes: the seed is eyther of a grayish blew colour, or in others more blackish'. Unsure where his poppies originated, Parkinson tells us that many had been 'often and [a] long time in our gardens', sent from Italy and other places, and that the double wild kinds came from Constantinople, although 'whether it groweth neere unto it or further off, we cannot tell as yet'.

The poppy's great flowering in the gardens of Europe coincided with the age of the aristocratic florilegium, in which the sunflower also gained an appreciative following. Fine double poppies feature in the *Hortus Floridus* of Crispin de Passe the Younger (1614), and in Emanuel Sweert's *Florilegium* of 1612. But the finest of all appear in Basilius Besler's *Hortus Eystettensis*, already admired for its sunflowers. Here are the most evolved and decorative kinds of opium poppies, multicoloured and multi-fringed like pompom chrysanthemums from China and Japan, or dahlias from South America. Here, too, are lavender-eyed and two-tone varieties mixing red with white or purple-violet: monstrous blooms, it must be said, which have shed their dignity along with their beauty.

After Besler, the opium poppy's horticultural star could only gently wane in the flurry of more exotic plants crowding into the flower garden. A century or more later Philip Miller, gardener to the Society of Apothecaries at Chelsea, marshalled the many varieties of garden poppies in his *Gardeners Dictionary*, describing some as having very large double flowers, variously variegated, while others were finely spotted like carnations. 'During their short continuance in flower, there are few plants whose flowers appear so beautiful,' he admitted; 'but having an offensive scent, and being of short duration, they are not much regarded.'

The queen of 'paper mosaicks' in Georgian Britain, Mary Delany, nonetheless found a bright-red opium poppy attractive enough to turn into one of her most celebrated collages composed of minute strips of cut paper. Floating out of its black background, a leaf of her poppy wraps itself around the flower stalk as it might in three dimensions. Displaying skills of a more didactic kind, the physician Erasmus Darwin, Charles Darwin's grandfather, included the opium poppy in *The Loves of the Plants*, his ambitious if ponderous attempt to poeticize botany and teach his readers Linnaeus's system for classifying plants by their sexual parts:

> Sopha'd on silk, amid her charm-built towers,
> Her meads of asphodel, and amaranth bowers,
> Where Sleep and Silence guard the soft abodes,
> In sullen apathy PAPAVER nods . . .

So begins the poppy's entry in Canto II, and while frankly it never improves as a poem, it hints at opium's fantastic visions – 'the pleasure-dome, the airy music, the sorceress, the half-living statue, the embracing lovers in the icy wind' – reflecting Darwin's medical knowledge of opium's power to stimulate dreams, and the sensation of intense cold that accompanies withdrawal.

The poppy's beauty continued to flare periodically in the botanic and scientific canons of the age, as in Henry Phillips's *Flora Historica*, his companion to the *History of Cultivated Vegetables*. While his vegetable book had warned against opium used incautiously, and especially the dangers of dosing children with opiates, his *Flora* waxed lyrical over the poppy capsule, whose ingenuity in design he considered vastly superior to watches or miniature musical boxes, and a potent sign 'of the wisdom with which it has been formed by the Universal Creator'.

A more down-to-earth survey of the opium poppy's historical, geographical, nutritional, medicinal, botanical and horticultural virtues appeared in *The Ladies' Flower Garden of Ornamental Annuals* by Jane Loudon, author of *The Mummy! Or a Tale of the Twenty-Second Century*, published in 1827, whose inventiveness had caught the eye of the man who became her husband, the phenomenally prolific gardening writer John Claudius Loudon. As garden flowers, Mrs Loudon judged opium poppies 'very ornamental, and when judiciously intermixed, they produce a fine effect in a tolerably large garden; though they take up too much room to look well in a very small one'.

The Irish gardener William Robinson was similarly approving. An advocate of wild gardening with hardy naturalized plants, he praised the opium poppy as a beautiful and variously coloured hardy annual. 'The double scarlet, the double striped, and the double white are all varieties of this,' he wrote in the first edition of *The English Flower Garden*, 'and the flower-heads, being of great size, make a bold and striking effect when planted in masses.' He singled out for special praise the 'Paeony-flowered' variety of the species with its very double broad-petalled flowers in shades from pure white to dark crimson.

Gardeners today use opium poppies in much the same way: as bold emphasis plants, valued for their striking colour effects. The high priests of colour planting in the 1990s, Canadians Nori and Sandra Pope declared a fondness for single and double black forms, whose natural promiscuity they tamed by ruthlessly weeding out any misfits that dared to intrude on the colour design for their Somerset garden.

O F   C O U R S E, *Papaver somniferum* has earned its place among the most powerful flowers in history not for its garden effects but as a source of the narcotic and analgesic drug. While opium does not cure the ailments it is used to treat, it relieves their symptoms and, in the words of the Stuart apothecary John Parkinson, 'by procuring sleepe, easeth many paines for the present, which indeede it doth but palliate or cause to be quiet for a time'. As a stimulant, it induced initial euphoria, Parkinson said, but prolonged use 'bringeth very often more harme, and a more dangerous disease then it hath allayed, that is an insensiblenesse or stupefaction of a part or member, which commeth to be the dead palsie'.

Rooted in classical pharmacology, the drug's early history has already been told. By the time of Rome's fall, opium production had spread around the eastern Mediterranean, into Egypt and across to Asia Minor, which became a major centre of cultivation and production. In Byzantium, the poppy's ghostly flowers appear in the exquisitely illuminated, early sixth-century copy of Dioscorides' *De Materia Medica* made for a Byzantine princess, Juliana Anicia, daughter of the emperor Olybrius and a great patron of the arts. Arab medicine embraced the drug, passing it on to the Persians, then to other nations further east, aided by the spread of Islam, which proscribed the consumption of alcohol. When Persia's Shah 'Abbas II tried to enforce a ban on wine, opium use increased so sharply that he was forced to soften the prohibition and take measures against the opium trade. Carried by Arab merchants, the drug reached India and then China, reputedly through medieval India.

Just as western – essentially Greek – medicine travelled east and informed the great medical traditions that flowered in the Moslem world, so Arab, Islamic and Persian ideas returned to the West in translations, among them the *Tacuinum Sanitatis*, a medieval handbook on health and well-being based on an eleventh-century Arab medical treatise by Ibn Butlan of Baghdad. Opium appears indirectly, as one of the sixty-plus ingredients in theriac, recommended for cold temperaments and old people, especially if taken in winter in cold regions. The opium in such preparations was flavoured with nutmeg, cardamom, cinnamon and mace, or simply with saffron and ambergris. Highly prized in the late Middle Ages, it was often sent as a gift by the sultans of Egypt to the doges of Venice and the sovereigns of Cyprus.

From theriac developed a variable preparation known as laudanum, composed of opium – often known as 'opium thebaicum' – and other ingredients, available initially in solid form and later as a tincture. Credit for introducing laudanum to western medicine traditionally goes to the Swiss Renaissance physician Philip Theophrastus Bombast von Hohenheim (d. 1541), better known as Paracelsus, who rejected the medical orthodoxies of his day and travelled for years all over Europe and on to Russia, Lithuania, Egypt, Hungary, the Holy Land and Constantinople, practising as an itinerant physician and developing his own system of humanist medicine. Increasingly wild and embittered, he became in effect the Luther of medicine and was viewed by many of his contemporaries as a mysterious Doctor Faustus, able to perform miracles.

One such 'miracle' could surely be attributed to the opium he used in his treatments. Here, for instance, is Paracelsus' recipe for a sedative to be used in cases of the falling sickness (epilepsy):

Take *opii thebaici* 2 drachms, *cinamoni* ½ ounce, *musci ambre* ½ scruple of each, *corallorum* ½ ounce, *mandragore* ½ drachm, *succi hyosciami* 1 drahm, *masticis* 3 drachms. Mix these, crush them, prepare a lozenge and add stewed hop-juice. Put the compound into a quince. Close it again, then put it into a dough and let it bake in an oven as if it were bread. Take it out and crush it, one half-ounce to five ounces of *arcanus vitriolus*.

Following Paracelsus' example, poppy-based preparations proliferated in medical herbals throughout Europe. William Langham included nearly three pages of poppy remedies in *The Garden of Health* of 1597 – forty-six entries in all, some containing multiple prescriptions. Langham recommended poppies in cases of abscess, aches, backache, bellyache, broken bones, bruises, catarrh, consumption, colds, cough, gout, fever, women's flowers, fluxes, frenzy, headache, holy fire, hoarseness, inflammation, joint aches, kernels, hot liver, scrofula or the king's evil, 'sleepe to cause' (for which there were twenty-one remedies), hot swelling, thirst, throat kernels, ulcers and women's ailments. His remedies called for seeds or plants of the black, white and garden poppy, fashioned in various ways. Bruised with women's milk and egg white, ripe white poppy seeds could be applied hot to the temples and forehead to provoke sleep, for instance, as could a spoonful of syrup of poppy, or oil of poppy applied to the temples.

Far more cautious in his use of poppy preparations was William Turner, the great Tudor naturalist, physician and divine. In the second part of his herbal, he quoted the twelfth-century Moslem polymath from Spain, Averroes or Ibn Rushd, who classed the poppy as cold and moist according to the humours of Galenic medicine, the white poppy being cold to the third degree and the black to the fourth degree, declaring that 'the white bringeth a pleasant sleep, but ... the black is evil and maketh a dull or sluggish sleep'. Turner's fear of opium came from accidentally swallowing a little opium mixed with water while washing an aching tooth. Within the hour his wrists had swelled, his hands itched, 'and my breath was so stopped that if I had not taken a piece of the root of masterwurt, called of some pilletory of

Spain [*Peucedanum ostruthium*], with wine, I think that it would have killed me'. He gave advice on how to treat suspected opiate poisonings: induce vomiting by drinking pepper and the scrotum of a beaver in honeyed vinegar, wake the patient by thrusting stinking things up his nose, bathe him in warm water, then feed him fat meats and hot wine.

Gentler remedies found their way into the good housewife's medicine chest, using seeds harvested from white poppies sown in her kitchen garden at the new moon in February or March. In *The English Huswife* of 1615, Gervase Markham advised treating family members troubled with 'too much watchfulnesse' with a dram of dried and powdered saffron mixed with an equal amount of dried and powdered lettuce seed and twice as much pulverized poppy seed, moistened with women's milk and applied as a thick salve to the patient's temples. Powdered white poppy seeds and oil of violets applied to the back and kidneys could help reduce fevers; while fevers that started with a cold called for a concoction of dragon water, rosewater, brandy, vinegar and half a spoonful or less of mithridate – a compound similar to theriac, which usually contained opium. Poppy by-products also cropped up many times in the medical profession's early listing of drugs (in Latin), the *Pharmacopoeia Londinensis*, where they appear under herbs and simples, waters, syrups, lohochs (a thick linctus), conserves and sugars, chemical preparations (*nepenthes opiatum*), and – as laudanum – among the pills, in a recipe that also contained saffron, beaver, ambergris, musk and oil of nutmeg.

Doctors continued to prescribe laudanum pills for much of the seventeenth century, until Thomas Sydenham produced his famous recipe for liquid laudanum, which contained two ounces of strained opium, one ounce of saffron, a dram each of cinnamon and cloves, and a pint of Canary wine. A Puritan who fought on Cromwell's side in the Civil War, Sydenham is honoured as the 'English Hippocrates' and the 'prince of English physicians'. Prescribing liquid laudanum for dysentery and many other conditions, Sydenham declared his gratitude that 'Omnipotent GOD, the Giver of all good Things has not provided any other Remedy for the Relief of wretched Man, which is so able to quell more Disease, or more effectually to extirpate them, than Opiate Medicines taken from some Species of Poppies'. His tincture might not work any better than the pills sold in shops, but the drug was more convenient and easier to control, 'for it may be dropp'd into Wine, or into any distilled Water, or into any other Liquor'.

By the beginning of the eighteenth century, opiates were freely available in a variety of liquid and solid preparations, with different recommended doses for men and women of varying strengths. There were then no recommended doses for juveniles, although soothing opiate tinctures for children were common in Victorian times, with comforting names such as Godfrey's Cordial, McMunn's Elixir, Batley's Sedative Solution, and Mother Bailey's Quieting Syrup. Among the wonder drug's most enthusiastic supporters was the slightly mad Dr John Jones, who published *The Mysteries of Opium Reveal'd* in 1700. While perfectly aware of the dangers of over-indulgence, and of the distressing effects of trying to break the habit 'after long and lavish use', Jones waxed dangerously eloquent on the 'heavenly *Condition*' produced by a moderate dose of opium taken internally.

It causes a most agreeable, pleasant, and charming Sensation about the Region of the Stomach, which if one lies, or sits still, diffuses it self in a kind of indefinite manner, seizing one not unlike the gentle, sweet Deliquium that we find upon our entrance into a most agreeable Slumber, which, upon yielding to it, generally ends in Sleep.

If one kept active, by contrast, especially after a good night's rest, 'it seems . . . like a most delicious and extraordinary *Refreshment* of the Spirits upon very *good News*, or any other great cause of *Joy*, as the sight of a dearly beloved Person, &c. thought to have been lost at *Sea*'.

The pleasures and perils of opium consumption featured in travellers' tales throughout the eighteenth and nineteenth centuries. From his travels in Persia at the time of Shah 'Abbas II and his son Suleiman I, the Frenchman Jean Chardin reported that opium-taking was near universal in Persia as an acceptable alternative to wine, especially popular among eminent personages wishing to escape the burdens of state. Turkey was similarly afflicted, according to Baron de Tott, who travelled through the Turkish Empire and the Crimea during one of its periodic wars with Russia and relayed the strange antics of the opium eaters in Constantinople, where – as in Persia – opium was taken in the form of pills. In a nightly ritual at a row of little shops by the market square, customers would seat themselves on sofas shaded by trees, swallowing their pills with water, then waiting for them to take effect. After an hour at most these 'Automatons' would become animated, throwing themselves 'into a thousand different Postures, but always extravagant, and always merry. This is the moment when the Scene becomes most interesting; all the Actors are happy, and each returns home in a state of total Irrationality, but likewise in the entire and full enjoyment of Happiness not to be procured by Reason.'

However colourful their reports, travellers such as Chardin and Baron de Tott were mere spectators of the strange effects opium produced on others. In a growing corpus of drug literature, other authors offered insights into the experience itself, among them the strange impostor 'George Psalmanazar', who presented himself as the first native of Formosa (Taiwan) to visit Europe, although he was probably a French Catholic from Languedoc or Provence, describing in his posthumously published memoirs how he had successfully cut back his laudanum addiction to the lowest possible dose. But the classic story of opium addiction and withdrawal belongs to Thomas de Quincey, the English essayist and minor English Romantic figure, best known for his admiration of Samuel Taylor Coleridge and William Wordsworth, and for his *Confessions of an English Opium-Eater*, serialized in the *London Magazine* in 1821, which became an immediate best-seller when it appeared in book form the following year.

In common with many of his contemporaries, de Quincey began taking laudanum for a physical condition, in his case excruciating rheumatic pain experienced in 1804. Unlike Coleridge, whose gentler, laudanum-fuelled visions resulted in a tantalizing fragment of just fifty-four lines, depicting Kubla Khan's stately pleasure-dome in Xanadu, de Quincey succeeded in turning his opium habit into the central narrative of his life. Focusing on opium's 'fascinating power', he explains in his meandering *Confessions* how he fell prey to the drug and how he brought his habit under control, aiming 'to display the marvellous agency of opium, whether for pleasure or pain'.

For many readers now, the chief pleasures of de Quincey's *Confessions* lie in their opium-induced visions and dreams – at first confusingly architectural in their cities and palaces as if designed by Piranesi, crowded with dancing ladies, and later 'unimaginable' in their horror as the scenes shift to Egypt, India and China, where

I was stared at, hooted at, grinned at, chattered at, by monkeys, by paroquets [sic], by cockatoos. I ran into pagodas: and was fixed for centuries, at the summit, or in secret rooms; I was the idol; I was the priest; I was worshipped; I was sacrificed. I fled from the wrath of Brama through all the forests of Asia: Vishnu hated me: Seeva laid wait for me. I came suddenly upon Isis and Osiris: I had done a deed, they said, which the ibis and the crocodile trembled at. I was buried, for a thousand years, in stone coffins, with mummies and sphinxes, in narrow chambers at the heart of eternal pyramids. I was kissed, with cancerous kisses, by crocodiles; and laid, confounded with all unutterable slimy things, amongst reeds and Nilotic mud.

While laudanum gave Coleridge the desire to float like the Indian god Vishnu 'along an infinite ocean cradled in the flower of the Lotus', opium provoked in de Quincey a nightmare of sensations and dislocated experiences that struck a particular chord with the French. There are echoes of de Quincey in the prose poems written by the iconoclastic French poet, Arthur Rimbaud, who renounced poetry at the age of nineteen and became a gunrunner in Abyssinia. Two other French poets translated de Quincey's *Confessions*: Alfred de Musset in 1828 and, more memorably, Charles Baudelaire in *Les Paradis Artificiels* of 1860, three years after the first edition of his *Flowers of Evil* (*Les Fleurs du Mal*). Opium features among Baudelaire's poems, too, in the guise of a poison rather than a flower, while the dramatist Jean Cocteau would later write his own account of recovering from opium addiction. 'To lecture an opium addict,' he wrote, 'is like saying to Tristan: "Kill Isolde. You will feel much better afterwards."'

Of all French artists, de Quincey's most direct influence was on the Romantic composer Hector Berlioz, who composed his *Symphonie Fantastique* in a six-week frenzy of creativity in early spring, 1830. Like his English counterpart, Berlioz knew laudanum's dream-inducing euphoria at first hand, having experienced its alternating bouts of exhilaration and depression for a year or more. Then the deadlock broke and he found a way to formalize the delirium of his brain. After the unrequited love portrayed in the first three movements, Berlioz mirrors de Quincey in having his protagonist take opium, achieving not the death he had intended but a horrific vision in which he believes he has murdered his beloved and witnessed his own execution. In the final movement, his beloved returns as a vulgar courtesan to take part in her victim's funeral in a swirling witches' Sabbath that might have stepped out of Goethe's *Faust*. A *succès de scandale* after its first performance at the Paris Conservatoire, the symphony soon fed back into the world of literature, celebrated particularly by the Club des Haschischins whose members included French literati such as Gérard de Nerval, Théophile Gautier and Baudelaire, all dedicated to the study of drug-induced experiences.

By now the French were more taken with hashish than opium, but in Britain and North America, opium and especially laudanum remained the drug of choice to soothe society's sorrows and pains, and to inspire the visions of its artistic elite, as it had since the eighteenth century. Even if the reasons for taking it were medicinal in origin, patterns of addiction or near addiction were established that often continued through life. Those known to have taken opium or its derivatives included Clive of India (for a painful bowel condition); Lady Stafford, a contemporary of Horace Walpole (to fire her wit); the anti-slavery campaigner, William Wilberforce (initially for a serious gastro-intestinal illness); George III and George IV (the latter to curb the irritation provoked by his excessive drinking); Elizabeth Barrett Browning (her frail health is often attributed to the repeated use of opiates from an early age); Edgar Allan Poe (disputed); Florence Nightingale (on her return from the Crimea); Wilkie Collins (in almost constant pain from rheumatic fever, he built laudanum into the plot of *The Moonstone*); the Virginian planter and congressman, John Randolph; the actress Sarah Bernhardt (to counter the exhaustion of long performances); and Louisa May Alcott, the fêted author of *Little Women*. Most of the Romantic poets are on record as experimenting with opium except William Wordsworth, although his sister Dorothy took laudanum intermittently. 'W[illia]m and I walked up Loughrigg Fell by the waterside,' she wrote in her journal for Thursday 15 October 1801. 'I held my head under a spout. Very sick and ill when I got home – went to bed in the sitting room – took laudanum.'

Opium and its derivatives were not the exclusive preserve of social or cultural elites either, and in Britain they kept much of the population under sedation. Mrs Loudon tells us that opium was first successfully extracted from poppies cultivated in Britain by a Mr John Bull of Williton, who had obtained a reward from the Society of Arts in 1796 for harvesting opium that was 'in no respect inferior to the best Eastern opium'. Some years later a surgeon from Edinburgh had also succeeded in procuring opium of excellent quality and in considerable quantities. Cheaper than beer or gin, opium was in particular demand in the cotton-spinning districts of Lancashire, while in the fens of Cambridgeshire and Lincolnshire, cottage gardens were so awash with opium poppies 'that for several months of the year the Fenland people were largely drugged with opium, a fact to which their stunted physique was commonly attributed'.

A RTISTS, TOO, HAD recourse to opium's narcotic properties, and incorporated the flower symbolically into their art. Because of its sinister associations, the poppy seldom appeared in Christian art of the late Middle Ages or Renaissance, except in a devilish context. Blood-red poppies sprout by the devil's clawed feet in Bartolomé Bermejo's

St Michael Triumphant Over the Devil (c.1468), for instance, while the great Flemish illuminator Lieven van Lathem added the opium poppy's pale mauve flowers and languid seed-heads to the illuminated borders of *The Romance of Gillion de Trazegnies*. Framing a gruesome battle scene, these plants would have brought blessed relief to those with severed limbs.

Taddeo Zuccari, the Italian mannerist fresco painter, drew on the poppy's reputation to provoke erotic and demonic fantasies in his sixteenth-century drawing, *The Nightmare* or *Allegory of Dreams*. A dreaming young maiden lies on her back beneath a swirl of demonic apparitions and erotic images, clasping in her hand a magic staff and a spray of opium poppies, while a toad-devil lurks behind her pillow, inciting her to dream. Henry Fuseli must surely have known of it – or dreamed of it – for his own version of *The Nightmare*, painted in 1781.

A British artist closely linked to opium was Dante Gabriel Rossetti, whose work at times bore the trace of an opium trance. In *Beata Beatrix* he paid tribute to his dead muse and wife Lizzie Siddal, who had killed herself with an overdose of laudanum in 1862, just as William Hogarth's countess had committed suicide in the final engraving of *Marriage A-La-Mode* more than a century earlier. Although Rossetti had started work before Lizzie's suicide, the painting became a prophetic reconstruction of Lizzie as Beatrice, whose death held such mythic significance for Dante. (In later renderings, Rossetti would add a subtle overlay of Jane Morris, another of his great loves, to Lizzie's features.) Eyes closed in a beatific trance, she sits on the balcony of her father's palace overlooking the Arno, her hands lying open in her lap like those of a communicant about to receive the white poppy flower dropped by the red dove of the Annunciation. Behind her, the shadowy poet looks towards the figure of Love who holds a flaming heart.

WHILE ARTISTS WERE happy to draw poppies into their personal symbolism, polite society took a little longer to admit the poppy to its discourse. You will look in vain for poppies in the earliest guides to the language of flowers, the charming nineteenth-century conceit in which men and women exchanged gallantries in their floral bouquets, or at least read of the messages they might *want* to exchange. 'Charlotte de Latour', an early French exponent of the genre, omitted all trace of poppies from the first edition of her anonymous little floral 'dictionary' published in 1819. By the much enlarged edition of 1854, her bouquets still contained no poppies, but a white poppy appeared in her dictionary of plants and their emblems, signifying 'sleep of the heart' (*'sommeil du coeur'*), and a corn poppy in her dictionary of feelings, signifying 'consolation'.

And so the poppy took root as the floral sign for consolation, largely because – some said – it was created by Ceres to soothe her grief as she searched for her daughter. In America, too, the poppy played its part as the language of flowers became necessarily more nuanced. Now different poppies assumed very different meanings: the corn poppy, consolation; the variegated poppy, flirtation; while the opium poppy clearly signified death. It was left to the French to puncture the growing silliness of the genre in Taxile Delord's *Les Fleurs Animées*, illustrated by J. J. Grandville. In its short entry on the poppy, a flower-girl in doleful pinks, greens and greys shakes her capsules over a heap of comatose bugs, declaring perspicaciously that 'sleep is no longer enough for the man who wishes to forget his sorrows. Man does not want to sleep any more, he wants to dream. I was oblivion and am now become illusion.'

THE DATE OF Taxile Delord's gentle satire is significant: 1847, midway between the two Opium Wars of 1839–42 and the late 1850s promulgated primarily by Britain against China in support of the (illegal) trade in opium from British India into China. Drawing rooms might be wearying of floral conceits, but never had a flower wielded so much military power. It is a sorry irony that Britain should have gone to war to force Indian opium on the Chinese in the face of opposition from a Chinese government alarmed by the spread of opium addiction among all ranks of society. Even at the time, principled witnesses castigated Britain's opium policy as 'the greatest blot on the history and character of their country', but at stake for Britain were the twin gods of market dominance and profit.

India had long cultivated the opium poppy, reputedly introduced by Arab traders as Islam pushed outwards from its Arabian heartlands, and supported by India's Mughal rulers, who sold the monopoly for producing opium just as the British East India Company would later do. After Arab influence waned, the trade in Indian opium was taken over by the Venetians and then by the Portuguese, who established a permanent trading settlement at Macau on the mouth of the Pearl River, close to Canton (Guangzhou) in south-eastern China.

In Portuguese times, two sorts of opium were available on India's Malabar coast to the west: the most expensive, black and hard, came from Aden; slightly cheaper was the opium from Malwa in west-central India, described as soft and yellowish. India's other opium-producing area was Bengal in the east, centred around Patna and Ghazipur on the Ganges. As a Portuguese apothecary and diplomat informed his king early in the sixteenth century, opium in India was 'a great article of merchandize in these parts . . . kings and lords eat of it, and even the common people, though not so much because it costs dear'.

Although the poppy is not indigenous to China, small amounts had been grown in Yunnan province before the Arab trade, largely for medicinal purposes. Consumption began to increase as the Chinese took to smoking opium, a habit that reached China via the Dutch in the East Indies, where opium was smoked in combination with tobacco and local plants; by the mid-eighteenth century smoking was established as the Chinese way to consume opium. The Portuguese were then still dominant in the Chinese trade, importing Malwa opium from Portuguese Goa and attempting, unsuccessfully, to establish a monopoly on shipments to Macau.

Late entrants to the opium trade, the British began to expand their power base in India, initially through the East India Company, which came to rule large areas of the country until the British Crown assumed direct control halfway through the next century. By 1780, the Company had successfully ventured small shipments of opium to China and established a depot south of Macau for British-imported opium. But trading opium with China was problematic. Not only were the Chinese habitually distrustful of foreigners, restricting foreign traders to a small strip of land on Canton's Pearl River, but the opium trade was actually illegal, outlawed by a string of edicts from China's Manchu rulers, banning first the sale of opium (1729), then its consumption (1780), and finally its importation (1796).

Professing to keep its hands clean while pocketing the profits from its illegal sales, the East India Company established a triangular commerce with parallels to the slave trade between Europe, Africa and the Caribbean. As the monopoly buyer of all the opium produced by Bengal's farmers, the Company sold it at auction to licensed 'country traders' who shipped the opium to Chinese waters, where it was transferred to fast, flat-bottomed Chinese boats for smuggling into the country. Funds derived from the trade were paid to the Company treasury at Canton in return for bills of exchange on London, thereby helping to balance the trade gap between Britain and China – a gap heavily weighted in China's favour, as China wanted little in return for the shiploads of tea, silk and porcelain coveted by European markets.

For Britain's East India Company the trade worked well, almost too well. The price of a chest of opium rose almost six-fold between 1799 and 1814, attracting competition from Americans trading in Turkish opium, and from Malwa opium, shipped directly from Bombay, which came from areas under princely rather than Company control. Eventually even Malwa opium was forced to contribute to Company coffers through a transit tax; and the Company was able to manipulate opium prices to protect its interests, setting a trend for more opium at lower prices.

Corruption was rife and despite the Chinese government's best efforts to rid itself of the drug, imports to Canton on British accounts rose from 4,600 chests in 1819–20 to 23,570 chests in 1832–3. The situation then became confused, as smuggling along the Chinese coast opened up other entry points and the Company lost its opium monopoly. By the start of the first Opium War in 1839, however, the British were exporting 40,200 chests of opium from Bengal, and within China the number of opium smokers was also rising rapidly. One contemporary estimate for 1838 calculated as many as 4–5 million addicts among a population of some 400 million. Certain professions were particularly at risk, notably private secretaries and soldiers, and what began as an indulgence among the sons of the wealthy and privileged gradually spread to people of every description: 'mandarins, gentry, workers, merchants, servants, women, and even nuns, monks, and Taoist priests'. A contrary view argues that it is wrong to portray China as the passive victim of colonial interests; for many people in China, producing and consuming opium were normal – not deviant – activities, while Chinese opium policy was rooted in internal court politics that pitted Han scholars against the officials of the ruling Manchu dynasty. Britain was nonetheless engaged in an illegal trade, which hastened China's national decline.

Alarmed by the damage inflicted on China, the Emperor called on Commissioner Lin Zexu, a committed prohibitionist, to eradicate opium. Although he successfully forced British merchants to hand over some of their illegal stocks, the Chinese were powerless to stop the smuggling that continued along the coast. Within two years, the superior technology and agile tactics of a small British expeditionary force had defeated the demoralized Chinese army. The terms of the peace treaty were severe: China was forced to compensate merchants for their destroyed stocks; to cede the island of Hong Kong; and to open the ports of Amoy, Fuzhou, Shanghai and Ningbo to foreign trade.

The war had done nothing to legalize the opium trade, however. This required a second war, sparked in 1856 when the Chinese arrested a smuggling boat near Canton flying British colours, albeit with an expired licence. Hostilities were even more extensive and Britain joined forces with France in attacking Beijing. Peace forced further concessions from the Chinese: the opening of more treaty ports to trade with the West, and permission for foreigners, including missionaries, to enter the country. The now legalized opium trade was to be regulated by the Chinese authorities, Kowloon ceded to the British, and large indemnities paid to Britain and France. Viewed by many as both a cause and a symptom of China's social degeneration, the opium poppy could now also be credited with dismantling the country's isolationism. But moral responsibility for China's spiralling addiction to opium lay with Britain and those western powers that sought to profit from this trade.

IRONICALLY, WHILE THE West used force to maintain the supply of opium to China, the Chinese were exporting their opium-smoking habits back to the West. Attracted by the Californian Gold Rush, Chinese immigrants arrived in San Francisco, establishing ethnic communities to serve their needs as they spread throughout California and the American West. Opium dens appeared alongside restaurants, general stores, laundries and doctors' surgeries; and opium for smoking could be purchased legally in practically any US Chinatown, imported and distributed by Chinese secret societies. At first, only young Chinese men frequented them, as described in typically lurid detail by Mark Twain, who visited one Pacific-coast den at 10 p.m. when

the Chinaman may be seen in all his glory. In every little cooped-up, dingy cavern of a hut, faint with the odor of burning Josh-lights and with nothing to see the gloom by save the sickly, guttering tallow candle, were two or three yellow, long-tailed vagabonds, coiled up on a sort of truckle-bed, smoking opium, motionless and with their lustreless eyes turned inward from excess of satisfaction.

By the early 1870s opium had spread to the Anglo-American underworld and the habit penetrated further into society, threatening the values of the elite and middle classes. Xenophobia and moral panic ensued. As the *Reno Evening Gazette* declared in 1879, opium smoking was 'a foul blot on society – a hideous, loathsome moral leprosy, paralyzing the mind and wrecking the body. It is a foul cancer, eating the vitals of society and destroying all who are drawn within its horrible spell.'

The way to curb its power, it was felt, was not by making opium illegal (although that would eventually happen in 1909, when the US

Opium smoking in London: Gustave Doré's illustration
of the Lascar's room in Charles Dickens's *The Mystery of Edwin Drood*,
for *London: A Pilgrimage* (1872)

Congress approved a bill to prohibit the importation and use of opium for other than medicinal purposes), but rather to close the door to people seen as the primary dealers in opium. This prompted the introduction of a series of exclusion laws aimed at keeping out 'undesirables', identified initially as contract labourers from Asia, Asian women who might engage in prostitution, and foreign convicts; in time this was extended to all skilled and unskilled Chinese labourers. More legislation followed, making it illegal to grow opium poppies without a licence, and later to cultivate, grow or harvest the plant. ('Knowingly' or 'intentionally' growing opium poppies in the United States remains a felony, as the American food and garden writer Michael Pollan reported in *Harper's Magazine*, after a fellow journalist was arrested for just such an offence.)

The ban on Chinese immigration was rescinded only in the 1940s. Long before then, the still-innocent poppy fields in L. Frank Baum's children's story *The Wonderful Wizard of Oz* (1900) had given way to the sleazy images of opium addiction and crime peddled by pulp fiction and American movies. In Britain, too, the 'panacea' that had been used to pacify fretful babies was now vilified as an Asiatic peril, smoked in clichéd opium dens in vile back alleys of the sort visited by Dr Watson in Conan Doyle's short story, 'The Man with the Twisted Lip', where bodies with lacklustre eyes lay in 'strange fantastic poses' in long low rooms, 'thick and heavy with brown opium smoke, and terraced with wooden berths, like the forecastle of an immigrant ship'.

The final chapter in the opium poppy's story belongs to the laboratory, and the chemical advances that have bolstered its power for good and evil. Around 1804, the German pharmacist Friedrich Wilhelm Sertürner isolated a crystalline salt from opium, which he named morphium after Morpheus, the Greek god of dreams. He waited more than a decade before publishing his discovery; it was the first — and most significant — opium alkaloid to be identified, as well as the first active ingredient to be isolated from *any* medicinal plant or herb.

In all, the opium poppy contains more than forty alkaloids, which constitute around 25 per cent by weight of powdered opium and trigger its pharmacological effects. The poppy's essential contradictions — as a flower that is both beneficial and socially dangerous — are inherent in its chemical composition: some of these alkaloids depress while others excite the central nervous system. The most narcotic is morphine, while at the opposite extreme is thebaine, which produces strychnine-like convulsions. Other alkaloids derived from opium include papaverine, codeine and narcotine.

Although purified morphine allowed the prescription of exact doses, opium became more dangerous as its chemistry was better understood and manipulated. In 1874, the English chemist Alder Wright boiled together morphine and acetic anhydride to produce diacetylmorphine, a semi-synthetic opioid known as heroin in its illegal form. Wright's discovery languished, unused, until the substance was independently re-synthesized by the German pharmaceuticals company Bayer, who marketed it from 1898 as a non-addictive morphine substitute and cough medicine for children. Only later were its dangers recognized and its sale controlled from 1914.

Today, perhaps as little as 5 per cent of the world's annual opium harvest is used legally in medicine; the rest is consumed illicitly, much of it trafficked around the world to an estimated 12–21 million 'recreational' users, generating an estimated revenue of US $68 billion for the traffickers. Heroin is the most commonly used opiate, except among traditional opium-producing countries and their close neighbours, where opium is the norm. Globally, some 195,700 hectares are under cultivation to the opium poppy, nearly two-thirds of these in Afghanistan, although disease among Afghani poppies drastically reduced the amount of opium actually produced worldwide from 7,853 million tonnes in 2009 to 4,860 million tonnes in 2010.

Production reflects the realities of national and international politics. Mao Zedong's strict anti-opium policy virtually eradicated opium cultivation in China in the 1950s, but fluctuating production levels in Afghanistan present a less encouraging prognosis. While the Taliban seemed at first determined to cleanse Afghanistan of opium, pragmatism has prevailed since the movement was ousted from power, and its attitude towards the drug's production has become as ambiguous as that of both the government in Kabul and local warlords. Elsewhere, over the past decade, South-East Asia's 'Golden Triangle' has seen reductions in Vietnam and Thailand, although cultivation has increased in neighbouring Burma (Myanmar) and Laos. India no longer produces much opium, and the fields of opium poppies so vividly described by Amitav Ghosh in *Sea of Poppies*, the first of his Opium Wars trilogy, have mostly disappeared. No longer will their sweet, heady odour draw swarms of insects whose congealed bodies would add welcome weight to the harvest.

POPPIES, THOUGH, HAVE a habit of reappearing when least expected, as was discovered by one English gardener who moved in 2007 with her family to a small farmhouse in the Herefordshire countryside. After digging over her 'field' to prepare new flower borders, she was astonished the following spring by an explosion of red, mauve and lilac opium poppies, swaying gently in the breeze 'like a cavalcade of cardinals'. Here were Gerard Manley Hopkins' 'crush-silk poppies aflash' in his poem 'The Woodlark', echoing John Ruskin's bewitched description in *Proserpina*, and the resplendent scarlet double-flowered poppies of the sort praised by John Parkinson. An earlier house on the site had belonged to an apothecary; as poppy seeds last for a hundred years or more, perhaps some of his seeds had lain dormant ever since, waiting for someone to expose them to light, and so to life.

Rose

I see you, rose, half-open book
filled with so many pages
of that detailed happiness
we will never read.

RAINER MARIA RILKE, from 'Les Roses', trans. A. Poulin Jr

S OON AFTER THE publication of my book, *The Rose: A True History*, in 2010, I attended an auction at Sotheby's of some fifty water-colours of roses executed on vellum by the great Belgian artist Pierre-Joseph Redouté, flower painter to Napoleon Bonaparte's first wife, the Empress Josephine. All the watercolours went to a single, anonymous buyer. The most expensive, which sold for over £250,000 against an estimate of £50,000 to £70,000, was a dusky pink Autumn damask, renowned since the sixteenth century as the first western rose to flower more than once in a season. As flower and as art, this painted Damask is exquisite, its translucent petals darkening towards the centre, their softness in marked contrast to the spiny red prickles lining the pale green stem. Redouté's skill as a botanical artist even hints at its heav-enly fragrance: 'If sunshine had a smell this would be it,' remarked one retired perfumer of this particular rose.

The lotus may have lured me to explore the power of flowers, but the rose remains my undisputed favourite. For five long years I tracked its bewildering transformations – culturally and botanically – in a quest that took me from the White House Rose Garden to the cities and deserts of Iran and on to the world's largest rose garden at Sanger-hausen in the former East Germany. Looking at life through such a singular focus was both exhilarating and exasperating. As I said in the introduction to that earlier book, I travel to a city and look first for the rose gardens. I listen to music and hear only rose songs. I journey to a country and find roses everywhere.

The rose is a chameleon of a flower, and the range of its many incarnations is astonishing. Celebrated as a sacred symbol and as a token of womanhood, the rose unites Venus with the Virgin Mary, the blood of Christ with the sweat of Muhammad, the sacred and the profane, life and death, the white rose of chastity and the red rose of consummation. And the flower itself has evolved over the millennia, from a simple briar of the northern hemisphere to today's sumptuous garden queen, bred for beauty, strength, fragrance and 'charm' — qualities described to me by one rose grower as 'good doers' that will also capture the heart. But rose lovers beware: we get the roses we deserve, and the trend towards well-behaved, homogeneous blooms and bushes may destroy the very qualities that make the rose so precious.

IN THE WILD, rose flowers are pretty, usually modest in tone and often delicately scented, but they rarely catch your breath as might a pool of flowering lotus or a mountainside of wild tulips. Far more remarkable is the way the rose clings to life in the most inhospitable circumstances, its spiny prickles and pollinator-attracting scent aiding its survival strategies, and its natural promiscuity enabling it to hybridize in the wild, producing blooms with ever more petals and ever headier scent. A native of the northern hemisphere only, from the Tropic of Cancer up to the Arctic Circle, the rose has existed for millions of years, far longer than the so-called 'rose fossils' discovered in northern China and Alaska, both dating back some 35–40 million years.

The simple, five-petalled roses glimpsed in the 'Blue Bird fresco' that once graced a Minoan town house at Knossos on Crete, some 3,500 years ago, are clearly wild and similar to the wild Cretan roses of today, *Rosa pulverulenta*. Painted in a naturalistic setting of rocks and stony ground, they are celebrated as the world's oldest undisputed image of roses; but as wild flowers, they do not yet match the sophistication of the Cretan white lilies (see Chapter 2), which even then had found their way into town-house gardens and Minoan iconography.

Slowly, over the next thousand years, far more magnificent roses were mutating in the wild so that by the fifth century BCE, the ever-curious Greek historian Herodotus reported roses growing wild in the Gardens of Midas in western Macedonia, 'wonderful blooms, with sixty petals apiece, and sweeter smelling than any others in the world'. A century or so later, the Greek proto-botanist Theophrastus tells us that the citizens of eastern Macedonia were transplanting the best roses – some with as many as one hundred petals – from the slopes of Mount Pangaeus into their gardens, thus aiding the rose's steady transformation into the western world's favourite flower.

While the Greeks created meanings for the rose through their arts, the Romans brought it to the very heart of daily life, making it an essential accompaniment to cooking, gardening, perfuming, feasting, drinking and debauchery, as well as the rites of both living and dying. Roses even enjoyed their own festival, Rosalia, a movable and raucous feast timed to coincide with the rose harvest, which appears in calendars from the first century CE. Not to be outdone, the notoriously degenerate Syrian legions of Rome's imperial army adopted their own rose festival, the Rosaliae Signorum, when the legions' standards were decorated with roses, giving the soldiers an excuse for revelry on a grand scale.

For all his inaccuracies and garbled borrowings, the best guide to the roses actually grown in Roman times is Pliny the Elder in his encyclopedic *Natural History*, which described ten or so different sorts arranged according to place and scent. (Pliny believed that roses owed their qualities to the nature of the soil, and he mixed in a mallow and the rose campion, *Lychnis coronaria*, with his true roses.) The most esteemed roses, he said, came from the areas around Rome and Naples (ancient Praeneste and Campania), to which some people added the bright-red roses of Miletus on the western coast of Anatolia; the most scented came from North Africa, which together with Spain produced early roses throughout the winter. Roman Egypt also supplied early-flowering roses on a vast scale; at times it must have seemed as if the Empire was awash with roses.

For a glimpse of the roses so dear to Pliny's heart, take a look at the painted frescoes and mosaics of Pompeii and Herculaneum, which were sealed under a thick covering of lava and volcanic ash when Vesuvius erupted in CE 79, killing all who remained in the vicinity, including Pliny himself, but ironically preserving the cities' flamboyant culture of flowers. Roses were everywhere in these mercantile centres of the Campanian plain, planted with vegetables, herbs and other flowers in private gardens; grown for profit in commercial flower gardens; painted on house and garden walls to give an illusion of perpetual summer. Of all the garden scenes, some of the most exquisite are to be found in the House of the Gold Bracelet where, on the south wall of its garden room, a small brown songbird perches on a hollow reed to which is tied a prickly red-and-white rose displaying every stage of flower, from bud to full bloom.

But the Romans took their love of roses too far, as they did so many of their pleasures, and roses came to signify luxuriousness and decadence, which helps to explain the long-standing prohibition against wearing rose chaplets in times of war. Rulers were criticized, too, for wallowing in an excess of roses to mask the stink of real life, or to soften the impact of passing through piles of soldiers' corpses after a battle. Most notorious of all for his supposed addiction to roses was the Syrian boy emperor Elagabalus (Marcus Aurelius Antoninus, c.203–22), better known as Heliogabalus, who is credited with suffocating his dinner guests in a cloud of rose petals. Although his first biographer wrote not of roses but of 'violets and other flowers', the power of the rose is such that it hijacked the misdeed, taking the starring role in the monumental Victorian painting *The Roses of Heliogabalus* by Sir Lawrence Alma-Tadema, the Dutch-born Academician whose grand vision would later inspire the films of Hollywood. Roses might help to plot the gradual spread of empires, but they could equally contribute to their downfall.

After the slow decline of the western Roman Empire, culminating in its defeat by Germanic tribes in the fifth century CE, roses slipped out of the limelight, cleansed only gradually of their pagan associations by the Christian Church and restored to health and favour in the infirmary gardens of Europe's monasteries and religious orders.

By Charlemagne's time, three hundred years later, roses (in the plural) were listed among the seventy-three kitchen-garden plants and sixteen fruit and nut trees that were to be grown by royal decree on imperial estates, second only to the lily (in the singular), presumably the Madonna lily whose identification with the Virgin Mary gave it primacy.

Roses were also revered as the royal flowers of the Byzantines, and were nurtured by the great gardeners of the Moslem world, who borrowed from the conquered Persians their exquisite Paradise gardens, filling them with plants collected from foreign lands. A resident of Seville in Moorish Spain, the practical soil scientist Ibn al-'Awwam wrote about many kinds of roses in his celebrated treatise on agriculture of the early twelfth century: the mountain rose, the red rose, the white rose, the yellow rose, the Chinese rose (*ward al-sini*), the wild Dog rose (*nisrin*), the sky-blue rose, and another that was blue on the outside and yellow on the inside. The list is intriguing: by 'blue', did he really mean 'red', as the late garden historian John Harvey has suggested? And might this 'Chinese' rose represent the first recorded sighting on European soil of *Rosa chinensis*, or was it a different plant altogether? Some eighty years later, the learned Dominican friar Albertus Magnus compiled a shorter list of the garden roses known in Christianized Europe. These included the white rose, a red rose, a field rose – possibly the sweet-smelling *Rosa arvensis* – and a stinking rose, colour unspecified but conceivably the yellow *R. foetida* from the Caucasus and the Middle East, although this rose is absent from all other medieval works written in Latin.

Christendom's red and white roses climb the background trellis to two remarkable German paintings of the Madonna and child from the fifteenth century, Stefan Lochner's ethereal *Madonna in the Rose Bower*, c.1450, and *The Madonna of the Rose Bower* painted by Martin Schongauer in 1473 as an altarpiece for Colmar's church of St Martin. The latter is botanically the more interesting. It shows semi-double red roses with a clutch of golden stamens at their heart, almost certainly a garden variety of *Rosa gallica*, a native of central and southern

Europe, its habitat stretching eastwards into Iraq; and a very double pinkish-white rose, surely a forerunner of *R. alba*, the progeny of *R. gallica* and an unknown Dog rose. Also prominent in the foreground is a thornless blood-red peony; in Germany they are known as '*Pfing-strosen*', 'roses of Pentecost', commemorating the descent of the Holy Spirit on Christ's disciples after His ascension into heaven.

Almost certainly imported as precious rosewater before it came to Europe as a flower, the Damask rose was well established in European gardens by the sixteenth century, when it featured in early herbals. It may have originated in the caliphal gardens of the Muslim Empire or in Persia, which the French rosarian and scholar Charles Joret viewed as the cradle of the garden rose. Recent genetic investigation has found not two but three parents to the Damask, none of which

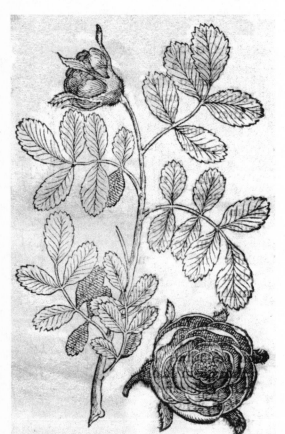

A double yellow rose from the Levant, described by the great Flemish botanist Carolus Clusius in his posthumous *Curae Posteriores* (Leiden, 1611).

coexists in the wild: *Rosa gallica* from Europe into south-western Asia; the scrambling, white-flowered *R. fedtschenkoana* from the foothills of the Celestial Mountains (Tien Shan) in Kyrgyzstan and eastwards into China; and the mysterious Musk rose, which inhabits a space somewhere in between. All three homelands are joined by the silk routes, the snaking, bifurcating routes that carried all manner of goods, people, ideas and religions to and from China's western borders to the southern shores of the Caspian Sea and onwards through Asia Minor into Europe. The carriers of the new roses westwards were the unsung heroes of plant diffusion – travelling scholars, monks, priests, immigrants, botanists scouting plants for the caliphs, merchants – rather than the warring crusaders who usually take credit in the West, without any supporting evidence.

The fourth rose to join the triumvirate of Gallicas, Albas and Damasks in European gardens were the Centifolias, born of Dutch horticultural wizardry in the late 1500s, possibly from Middle Eastern stock. Dutch and Flemish botanists were certainly the first to sing the praises of this magnificent new rose, round as a small cabbage, its spiced-pinks scent judged by the Edwardian doyenne of gardens Gertrude Jekyll as 'the sweetest of all its kind, as the type of the true Rose smell'. A splendid example of the garden rose's perfectly timed reinvention to meet the needs and desires of the age, it became the rose of choice for Dutch and Flemish master flower painters of the seventeenth century, showy enough to stand alongside the flared tulips and other exotic blooms entering Europe from Constantinople and beyond. And just when the rose was beginning to lose ground to these other imports, the influx of roses from China sparked a frenzy of rose breeding and *rosomanie*, which saw the rose in all its manifestations restored to favour on both sides of the Atlantic.

Home to over half the world's estimated 150 wild species of rose and to more endemic species than anywhere else, China almost certainly led the way in hybridizing the rose. Roses appeared in the imperial gardens near the ancient capital of Chang'an (modern Xi'an) in central China during the reign of the Han emperor, Wu Ti, more than two thousand years ago; and a millennium later, silk-screen paintings by the prominent Northern Song artist Cui Bai already displayed the high-centred buds of 'modern' rose cultivars. Yet despite such a profusion of roses, both wild and cultivated, the Chinese do not revere the rose to the same extent as western or Middle Eastern peoples, omitting it from the 'Four Gentlemen of Flowers' that represent the four seasons, for instance (see Chapter 7). And while early travellers to China reported fine roses for sale in Chinese nursery gardens, Chinese floriculture worshipped other stars, such as Moutan tree peonies, the sacred lotus, chrysanthemums, jasmine and camellias.

The China roses that took Europe by storm from the late eighteenth century onwards brought qualities that were startlingly new. These were the lightest of silks compared with the crumpled damasks of old Europe, in radiant colours that included clear reds, scarlets and yellows; their leaves, too, were a lustrous green and their buds elegantly pointed. While many lacked fragrance, a few carried the fresh and delicate hint of tea, or the 'faint sweet smell' of a harebell. Best of all, in contrast to most European roses, Chinese roses were repeat-flowering and bloomed long into autumn in an apparently everlasting display.

The advent of China roses resulted in a veritable mania of rose-breeding, led by the French among the coterie of amateur and professional rose-growers living in and around Paris during the First Empire, who projected their passions onto the Empress Josephine, considerably over-inflating her reputation as France's most iconic rose lover. Rose frenzy quickly spread to the British, Dutch, Germans and Americans, producing a bewildering medley of new cultivars and whole new classes of rose: Noisettes, Bourbons, Tea roses, Hybrid Chinas, Hybrid Perpetuals and – in 1867, with *Rosa* 'La France' bred by Guillot *fils* of Lyons – the ever-popular Hybrid Teas, which mark the division between 'old' and 'new' classes of rose. Rose parties became all the rage, in America and Britain, and by the 1880s the rose had replaced the camellia in privileged circles as queen of the cut flowers. At a midwinter party in New York, the Vanderbilts dazzled their 1,000 guests with 50,000 cut roses of the very best varieties, among them the velvety, long-stemmed *R*. 'Général Jacqueminot', which retailed at the exorbitant price of $1 a stem. But roses were popular among all classes of society, whether they lived in a cottage or a castle; and according to Dean Samuel Reynolds Hole, the proselytizing first President of Britain's National Rose Society, some of the best new roses were grown and exhibited by working men.

The trend among modern rose breeders of the twentieth and twenty-first centuries has favoured free-flowering roses that are resistant to disease, require minimal maintenance (America's KnockOut® Roses are even described as 'self-cleaning', like ovens) and, in certain breeding programmes, able to withstand climatic extremes – down-to-earth aims that nonetheless help to explain the rose's enduring popularity. Some growers explicitly include aesthetic factors in their breeding programmes. Britain's David Austin, for instance, looks for well-formed flowers, fine fragrance, attractive growth, good health and disease resistance, general sturdiness and that elusive quality – charm.

B EAUTY IS NOT the only source of the rose's appeal, however, or of its power. In pre-classical Greece the rose enjoyed an economic value as an ingredient in perfumes, and it has played a significant role in the *materia medica* of both West and East. Roses in perfumery have the longer pedigree, known to us from a storekeeper's clay tablet preserved by chance after a catastrophic fire destroyed the palace of Pylos in the south-western Peloponnese towards the end of the thirteenth century BCE. The tablet lists two sorts of scented oils – rose and sage – and an astringent herb, cyperus, added at an earlier stage to make the oil receptive to their fragrance. The oils were used in perfumed unguents to keep fabrics shiny and supple, and as grave goods for the dead. The Greeks, too, made a perfumed rose oil using fresh roses, spices, sesame oil, salt and red colouring from alkanet. Worn chiefly by men, it was also added to other perfumes to lighten their scent and was a special favourite of Theophrastus, who found its fragrance energizing. Pliny the Elder liked it too, omitting the rose from his condemnation of more extravagant perfumes.

Although Aristotle understood the principles of distillation, the ancient world made its perfumes by macerating flowers and spices with oils and fats, never by distilling them with water and steam. The art of distillation was perfected in the empire of the Arabs, its application to perfumery often attributed to the great eleventh-century Persian physician and polymath Ibn Sina (Avicenna), but it was already in use more than a century earlier, described by another Persian physician, the philosopher and alchemist al-Razi, known to the Latins as Rhazes. Long celebrated as the country of roses, Persia had developed a perfume industry from the beginning of the ninth century at least, much of it centred around the southern city of Shiraz. As the German traveller and physician Engelbert Kaempfer recorded after visiting the region in the 1680s, 'Even as the roses in Persia are produced in greater abundance and with finer perfume than those in any other country in the world, so also do those of this particular district in the vicinity of Shiraz, excel in profusion and in fragrance those of any other locality in Persia.'

The distillation of rosewater also produces a more concentrated oil that appears as droplets floating on the surface, which can be extracted by a process of double-distillation to produce 'attar' or 'otto' of roses. Legend credits its discovery to the marriage feast in 1612 of the Mughal emperor Jahangir to the ambitious and supremely beautiful Princess Nur Jahan, when the princess filled an entire canal with rosewater. As the pair rowed or walked by the water, they noticed an oily scum floating on its surface, which released the most delicate perfume known to the East. In fact, the technique for separating rose oil from rosewater was already understood, probably developed independently in Europe, the Arab world and India, and its description by the Italian Geronimo Rossi of Ravenna pre-dates the marriage feast by several decades. But the story illustrates the potency of this most romantic of perfumes. The much fêted rose otto came to Europe from Turkey and more particularly from around Kazanlik in modern Bulgaria, using Damask roses that still bear the town's name; Turkey and Bulgaria continue to vie for supremacy in the quantity and quality of their production.

The perfume industries of Morocco and France more commonly use Centifolia roses, from which they extract 'rose absolute' with solvents or carbon dioxide at high pressure.

While the scent of roses still infuses many modern perfumes, its popularity has waxed and waned as tastes swing between the floral and the feral, especially musk and civet with their undertones of excrement and sex. Despite her supposed love of roses, the Empress Josephine relished more obviously sensual scents; sixty years after her death, the smell of musk was said to linger still in her boudoir at Malmaison. After Josephine, lighter, fresher floral scents came back into fashion; in a mid-nineteenth-century work permeated with roses, the French perfumer Eugene Rimmel advised women to use 'simple extracts of flowers, which can never hurt you, in preference to compounds, which generally contain musk and other ingredients likely to affect the head'.

Roses were useful, too, in the simple business of keeping clean. Washing as an aid to cleanliness is a relatively recent invention; Europeans of the sixteenth century used friction and perfume to mask unpleasant odours. 'To cure the goat-like stench of armpits,' wrote the French author of a self-help guide of 1572, 'it is useful to press and rub the skin with a compound of roses.'

THE HEALING ROSE is just as potent as the perfumed rose, even if it lacks the medical history of the opium poppy. As with so much of western and Middle Eastern medicine, Pedanius Dioscorides provides the basic text in his great *De Materia Medica* of the first century, in which he distinguished between common Dog roses, not much used in Greek medicine, and cultivated roses, good for sore eyes, ears and gums; aches and pains of various descriptions; wounds and sundry inflammations; diarrhoea; spitting blood; and cosmetics. According to the Greek theory of humours, roses were hot and wet, and their effect generally cooling and astringent, 'but of an airish [humour] sweet and spicy', added the English divine and herbalist William Turner, quoting the Assyrian physician Mesuë, 'and fiery and fine, of which cometh the bitterness, the redness, the perfection, and the form or beauty'.

Each remedy required a different preparation, and Dioscorides also explained how to make rose oil, rose wine and deodorant rose pomanders, which women could wear like a necklace.

The rose most used in western and Arab medicine was the Apothecary's rose, *Rosa gallica* var. *officinialis*, claimed by the French apothecary Christophe Opoix of Provins to have been brought back from the Holy Land by the crusading Thibaut IV, king of Navarre and count of Champagne, although the parent species is a European native and Opoix's story is more likely a product of civic pride. Bushy but low-growing, the Apothecary's rose bears large semi-double flowers with characteristic golden stamens, known as 'threads' in Tudor times, and is highly scented. In England, it enjoyed its greatest popularity at the time of Queen Elizabeth I, when it was considered a 'cure-all' for more than fifty ailments in *The Garden of Health* by Turner's near-contemporary, William Langham, recommended for everything from general aches, backaches, belly griefs, bladder griefs, bloody flux, weak brains and sore breasts to vomiting, tongue ulcers, stopped urine, white discharges, windiness, worms and wounds. The pharmacologies of other nations naturally relied on their own native roses, such as the dried hips of *Rosa laevigata* used to cure premature ejaculation in Chinese medicine, and the astringent wild roses reported by early North American settlers as native remedies for burns and scalds.

Enamoured of his many varieties of garden rose, the herbalist and barber-surgeon John Gerard paints a delightful picture of the rose in Elizabethan sickrooms, its use proposed as a gentle remedy for purging stomachs of 'raw, flegmaticke, and now & then cholerick' excrements – Musk and Damask roses were especially suited – and, taken as distilled rosewater, to strengthen the heart, refresh the spirits, and for any ailment that required gentle cooling. As in Arab medicine, rosewater was particularly recommended for sore eyes, as it 'mitigateth the paine of the eies proceeding of a hot cause, bringeth sleepe, which also the fresh Roses themselves provoke through their sweete and pleasant smell'. With the rose, utility and beauty are closely linked, and Gerard's recovering patients would surely have delighted in his suggestions for adding rosewater to 'junketting dishes, cakes, sawces, and many other pleasant things', and for a morning feast of Musk rose petals eaten 'in maner of a sallade, with oile, vineger & pepper, or any other way according to the appetite & pleasure of them that shall eate it'. As well as providing pleasure, the aim was to purge the belly of 'waterish and cholericke humours', producing six to eight stools for every twelve to fourteen Musk flowers.

Red, white and Damask roses retained their role in English medicine throughout much of the seventeenth century, classed by London doctors among the five cordial flowers, along with violets, borage, rosemary and balm, and available medicinally in a number of different forms: as vinegars, decoctions, juleps, syrups, electuaries, lohochs, powders, pills, sugars, troches, oils and ointments, their recipes carefully laid down in the physicians' bible, the *Pharmacopoea Londinensis.* One of their most ardent supporters was the radicalized plantsman and medical rebel, Nicholas Culpeper, who took the Parliamentarians' side in the Civil War and died at the age of thirty-seven from a combination of wounds, consumption and furious smoking. An adherent of astrological gardening, Culpeper added French pox and leprosy itch to William Langham's list of ailments cured or calmed by the rose, maintaining that different roses operated under different planets: red roses under Jupiter, Damask roses under Venus, white roses under the moon and Province (Centifolia) roses under the king of France.

After the triumphal restoration of Charles II, the royalist sympathizer John Evelyn proposed a radical plan to banish all noxious industries from the capital, and to ring the city of London with sweet-smelling plantations of 'fragrant and odiferous *Flowers*', among them the Eglantine or Sweet Briar, 'the *Musk*, and all other *Roses*' – a plan that was part environmental tract, part allegory, intended to quell the 'presumptuous Smoake' of the Interregnum. And roses continued to play a role in the medicinal experiments of Robert Boyle, the Irish natural philosopher and scientist who had endured a sickly childhood and whose eyes gave him continual trouble. But as medicine became more professionalized, roses began to disappear from eighteenth- and nineteenth-century sickrooms; the cultivation of medicinal red roses in England shrank to a mere ten acres around Mitcham in Surrey, with further crops in Oxfordshire and Derbyshire.

By the beginning of the twentieth century, the rose was all but emasculated in mainstream pharmacology, valued only in folk remedies and among the wilder fringes of unorthodox medicine, and for its aesthetic properties. Rose-hips enjoyed a brief revival during the Second World War, when wartime children were fed spoonfuls of rose-hip syrup to replace unobtainable citrus fruits and other sources of vitamin C, until even this benefit was refuted by a German regulatory commission of 1990, which declared the use of rose-hips in treating or preventing vitamin C deficiency to be 'questionable'. So the announcement in September 2008 to a world congress on osteoarthritis that a patented rose-hip powder could bring relief to sufferers of this painful condition represented both a breakthrough and a vindication of one strand of ancient medicine, although aching joints as opposed to general aches and pains were absent from the conditions that rose preparations could reputedly cure. In the new study, however, researchers found that the powder was effective not simply in reducing inflammation, but also appeared able to protect cartilage cells from inflammatory assault and self-destruction.

T HE BEAUTY OF the rose, its many uses in everyday life (and death), and the sweet fragrance it imparted to lives conducted amid much squalor help to explain the flower's enduring acclaim. But the real power of the rose lies in the way people from different societies and different ages have used the flower to say something about themselves, in effect transforming the rose into a symbol of deeply held values – cultural, religious, political – or simply using the rose to tell their stories. No other flower comes close in western culture for the sheer variety of 'meanings' people give to the rose, although there is an intriguing difference between the western rose and the eastern lotus. In the West, the rose slowly accumulated meanings as it developed into a flower of great beauty, while in the East, the lotus played a part from the very beginning in the creation myths that sought to explain how the world began.

Of all its associations, the red rose as the flower of love has the longest history. Puzzling over why this should be, when the rose's fragrance contains none of the sultry erotic odours such as indol (a component of animal faeces whose purpose in flowers is to attract insects), the German chemist and perfume expert Paul Jellinek found his answer not in the rose's smell but in its colour and shape, which he judged suggestive of the female body and of kisses. In Jellinek's view, the ripening bud, with its subtle hints of 'the rounded abundance and fragrance of full maturity', and the ravishing scent as it opened to full maturity, 'are external manifestations of the flower's life processes which man sees and senses and which stimulate his erotic fantasy'.

The ancient Greeks saw it too and for me this is where the story of the rose truly begins: at the shrine of Aphrodite, goddess of love and human sexuality, where the poet Sappho planted roses in the second half of the seventh century BCE, invoking the goddess to appear in her 'graceful grove of apple trees' amid 'altars smoking with frankincense':

> And in it cold water makes a clear sound through
> apple branches and with roses the whole place
> is shadowed and down from radiant-shaking leaves
> sleep comes dropping.

The Romans ran with this notion as far and as fast as they could. To them, roses were the harbingers of spring, carried by nubile young women such as the bare-breasted maiden holding a basket of roses in the second-century floor mosaic of Neptune and the four seasons at La Chebba in Roman Tunisia. They were also – and very obviously – linked with Venus, the Roman incarnation of Greek Aphrodite who presided over all sexual dealings from the third century BCE, whether between mortals and gods or among mere mortals. In Ovid's *Fasti*, his calendar of Roman feast days, she takes April, the second month of the calendar after that of her husband, Mars; the poet exhorts Latin mothers, brides and those denied the garb of matrons – courtesans and prostitutes – to wash Venus's statue, dry her and restore her golden necklaces: 'now give her other flowers, now give her the fresh-blown rose'. In the first of the festivals dedicated to Venus and Jupiter, Ovid calls on prostitutes to celebrate Venus's divinity, and to 'give to the Queen her own myrtle and the mint she loves, and bands of rushes hid in clustered roses'.

From here, two strands developed that saw the rose linked with romantic love on the one hand and sex on the other. Both strands came together in the French medieval masterpiece, the *Roman de la Rose*, begun by Guillaume de Lorris in 1225 and finished some fifty years later by Jean de Meun, which became one of the most celebrated and controversial works of the time, lauded for its edifying humanism but bitterly condemned as scabrous and misogynistic in its graphic and, some said, gratuitous depiction of sex.

Constructed as a dream narrative, the poem describes the Dream Lover entering a walled garden, where he falls in love with a rose glimpsed in the 'perilous mirror' of the Fountain of Narcissus. Among the garden's many roses, the one he chooses brings Jellinek's verdict to mind. Glowing red and pure 'as the best that Nature can produce', the bud sits on a stem as straight as a sapling, neither bent nor inclined, filling the whole area with its 'sweet perfume . . . And when I smelled its exhalation, I had no power to withdraw.' But when he snatches a kiss, the rose bushes are whisked away behind the walls of a garrisoned castle, and the narrative, now continued by de Meun, enters a literal and verbal battlefield as allegorized figures debate their differences until the Lover launches his final assault on the rose, reached through a narrow aperture placed between two pillars. When he is certain he is 'absolutely the first' to enter by that route, he takes the bud at his pleasure in an act that to modern sensibilities seems indistinguishable from rape:

I seized the rosebud, fresher than any willow, by its branches, and when I could attach myself to it with both hands, I began very softly, without pricking myself, to shake the bud, since I had wanted it as undisturbed as possible

. . . Finally, I scattered a little seed on the bud when I shook it, when I touched it within in order to pore over the petals. For the rosebud seemed so fair to me that I wanted to examine everything right down to the bottom. As a result, I so mixed the seeds that they could hardly be separated; and thus I made the whole tender rosebush widen and lengthen.

One of the *Roman*'s fiercest critics was the lyric poet Christine de Pizan, who turned to poetry some time after the death in 1390 of her husband, a secretary to King Charles VI of France. Accusations and counter-accusations flew back and forth about the effrontery of seeking biblical support for sanctifying a woman's 'little rosebud'. Were the poem's defenders led astray by St Luke, thundered one of de Pizan's supporters, when he declared, 'Every male that opened the womb shall be called holy to the Lord'? Using poetry to advance her cause, de Pizan composed her riposte *Dit de la Rose* in 1402, in which she was asked, also in a dream, to found a chivalric order that would bestow its 'dear and lovely roses' only on those knights who upheld a woman's virtue and reputation, in obvious contrast to Jean de Meun, who viewed a woman's 'rose' as there for the taking. (Britain's Knights of the Garter follow in the tradition of decorating their collars with roses.)

De Pizan situated her narrative on St Valentine's Day, commemorated to this day as the occasion for lovers to exchange tokens of their affection – traditionally red roses – but then only recently 'invented' as a day for lovers, apparently by the English poet Geoffrey Chaucer and his circle. In his poem the *Parliament of Fowls*, Chaucer chose the feast day of the martyred St Valentine, 14 February, to mark the annual gathering of birds for the purpose of choosing their mates, although no one is quite sure why this particular saint should be linked to the first matings of spring, when the weather is hardly springlike.

In an irony worth savouring, it was Christine de Pizan, the arch-critic of the *Roman de la Rose*, who added roses to the celebration. She would have hated the ribaldry and innuendo with which many later writers treated the rose – most of all, Shakespeare, for whom the 'bud' of a girl's adolescence was ripe for the plucking but immediately lost its freshness as the flower opened and became (over)'blown'. Shakespeare was drawing on a rich seam of Elizabethan slang in which the rose took many meanings, pre-eminently sexual ones, as maiden-head, vulva, whore, courtesan, young girl, sexually used woman, syphilitic sore; to 'pluck a rose' might imply either taking a girl's virginity or pissing in the open air. Yet Shakespeare could equally use the rose to express the tragedy of time passing and a woman's fading beauty, as in Cleopatra's anguished cry:

> See, my women,
> Against the blown rose may they stop their nose
> That kneeled unto the buds.

The ripening rose also provided an arresting medical image for a woman's sexual parts in the anatomical textbook by Shakespeare's near contemporary Helkiah Crooke, a medical practitioner and later governor of Bethlem Hospital. Writing about female anatomy, Crooke described the hymen as being composed of 'little peeces of flesh and membranes', which together took the form 'of the cup of a little rose half blowne when the bearded leaves are taken away'. Taking a wider view, Crooke adjusted his metaphor to the 'Great Clove Gilly-flower when it is moderately blowne'.

And so it continues to this day, the rose blossoming into a metaphor for sexual love and for a woman's sexual parts in the work of poets, painters, dramatists, psychologists, psychoanalysts and medical pro-fessionals of all kinds. (Sigmund Freud is reputed to have compared the vulva to a rose, but the flower in question was the visually similar camellia.) In recent years, the British poet Jo Shapcott's medita-tions on the rose poems written in French by the Czech-born poet Rainer Maria Rilke led her to conclude that Rilke's roses were women, and 'more than that – petal – space – petal – these poems were ver-sions of female genitalia'. In the poems provoked by such a reading, Shapcott has her roses answer back, pointing out to Rilke where he is wrong, 'saying, in effect: "It's not like that, it's like this"'. Rilke's *Les*

Roses IX, for instance, with its 'troubling odour of naked saint', goes beyond temptation to become the ultimate lover, so far from Eve but still 'infinitely possessing the fall'. Shapcott's 'Rosa Sancta' will have none of it:

> Now you've made a
> a saint out of me,
> Saint Rose, open-handed,
> she who smells of God naked.
>
> But for myself, I've learned
> to love the whiff of mildew
> Because though not Eve, exactly,
> yes, I stink of the Fall.

For all their bickering, both poets point to the rose's extraordinary ability to express conflicting notions of the sacred and the profane, just as it had in the early centuries of the Christian era when the Church fathers did all they could to outlaw this flower so tainted by pagan associations. Springing, like Judaism itself, from the stony desert lands of Palestine and the eastern Mediterranean, the early Christians had no place for flowers; there are none in the Eden of Genesis and very few in either the Talmud or the Bible as a whole, at least in the original Hebrew.* Rose garlands and crowns were especially despised and the early fathers forbade their use, contrasting such wanton earthly diadems with Christ's crown of thorns and thistles. But gradually a remarkable transformation took place, which saw the rose cast off its pagan garb to emerge as one of the great symbols of Christian iconography, combining the white rose of Mary's purity with the red rose of Christ's martyrdom and in particular the Five Wounds of His

---

* The 'rose' of Sharon in the Song of Songs, and the blossoming desert 'rose' of Isaiah 35: 1, were supplied by later translators as neither botanists nor biblical scholars can agree on the flower intended by the original Hebrew, *'habasselet'*.

Passion, a cult that reached its peak in the late Middle Ages when the language used to express it became increasingly morbid and erotic.

The transition from sinner to saint was achieved over many centuries. In the early years, when the Church was subject to ferocious persecution, roses began to appear in the visions of Paradise experienced by Christian martyrs, and in the legends of saints such as St Cecilia, boiled in a bath and then beheaded because she refused to submit her God-promised virginity to her husband; and St Dorothy, whose martyrdom bore the same sweet smell of the roses of Paradise. (St Elizabeth of Hungary's 'miracle of the roses' is a later example, when the bread she was secretly carrying to the poor reputedly turned into roses, allowing her charity to remain undetected.) Then theologians and Church leaders began to draw roses into their thinking: St Ambrose, for instance, who declared that in Eden before the Fall, roses grew without thorns, indirectly incarnating Mary as the thornless rose, an idea later developed by St Bernard of Clairvaux in his sermons on the biblical Song of Songs.

Legend has it that St Benedict planted a little rose garden – *il roseto* – outside his hermit's cave at Subiaco, delighting his senses with the flowers and mortifying his flesh with its thorns. Even real roses were finding their way into the house of God, grown for their healing virtues in monastery infirmary gardens and eventually permitted in church decoration. The monks must have loved them, too. When Emperor Charlemagne's religious and educational adviser Alcuin of York bid farewell to his dearly loved cell, he celebrated its roses and lilies in verse: 'Thy cloisters smell of apple-trees in the gardens, and white lilies mingle with little red roses.' The rose naturally appears in the extraordinary gardening poems written in the mid-ninth century by another Benedictine monk, Walahfrid Strabo, when he was abbot of Reichenau. Reserving the rose until last, he celebrates it as 'the Flower of Flowers', revered for its beauty, its fragrance and the many healing virtues of its rose oil, 'a cure for mankind's ailments'. As we saw in Chapter 2, he ends his poem by musing on the spiritual meanings of the rose and the lily, two flowers, he says, 'so loved and widely honoured' that have stood throughout the ages as symbols of the Church's greatest treasures: the rose in token of the blood shed by the Blessed Martyrs and the lily as a shining badge of its faith.

After Walahfrid's time, despite the lily's continuing importance as the flower of Mary's innocence and purity, roses gradually inched ahead as the Church's supreme flower, celebrated by the Catholic Church as the Golden Rose, a sacred ornament of exquisite workmanship blessed by popes for centuries on Laetare Sunday and conferred on illustrious churches, sanctuaries, royalty, military figures and governments. Dante Alighieri brought his *Divine Comedy* to a close with just such a supreme flower: Paradise itself as a pure white rose, fragrant through all eternity, and vast enough to contain the two 'courts' of heaven, angels and human souls, with Mary Queen of Heaven sitting on the highest petal, closest to the sun. William Blake re-imagined this same rose as a giant sunflower (see Chapter 3), but for Dante, this Paradise-rose brought a mystic vision of eternal glory. The American academic Barbara Seward has called it one of the most complex symbols in literature – Dante's attempt to concentrate in a flower his answer to the riddle of the universe. Led through Hell and Purgatory to Heaven by his dead love, Beatrice Portinari, the poet conflated 'the rose of carnal and adulterous courtly love' with 'the mystic symbol of the soul's marriage to its God and with the flower of the saints, the Virgin, Paradise, and Christ . . . Love is the end as it was the beginning of Dante's journey and of all that is.'

As CHRISTIAN POETS have drawn on the rose for many of their most potent images, so have poets of the Moslem world, in old Persia especially, where the great poets of the thirteenth and fourteenth centuries, Sa'di (Musharrif al-Din Muslih) and Hafez (Shams al-Din Muhammad) – both from Shiraz, city of roses – sang frequently, even 'wearisomely', of roses. The snub comes from Vita Sackville-West, who nonetheless fell under the country's spell when she visited in 1926 to see her diplomat husband Harold Nicolson, then working at the Legation in Teheran; her short memoir *Passenger to Teheran* is packed with Persian roses.

Roses still permeate Iranian culture today, whether planted in gardens or laid on commemorative tombs; celebrated by poets, artists and mystics; transformed into rosewater and attar of roses; painted on decorative boxes or embedded in religious architecture; or paired with the traditional nightingale, *gul-o-bulbul*, lover and beloved in countless poems, paintings and tiles, like the one that sits on my desk in memory of a visit to Iran in 2009, which gave me more rose images than my rose book could possibly accommodate.

As in the Christianized West, the rose in Islam enjoys spiritual, even mystical connotations. Like the early Christian fathers, the Prophet Muhammad and his followers came out of the desert, so the flower itself is absent from the Qur'an, Islam's holy book containing the divine revelations received by the Prophet in the last twenty years of his life. Roses are absent, too, from the Paradise gardens promised by the Qur'an as a reward to believers and martyrs who can look forward to a place of green shade and gurgling fountains, plenteous fruit and cool pavilions – the delights of a desert oasis, in fact, where they can also expect to find themselves among the virginal *houris* of Paradise. But while the Qur'an anticipates no actual roses in Paradise, the Hadiths or collected sayings of the Prophet have given the rose a spiritual origin. According to these sources, as the Prophet made his miraculous night journey into the Divine Presence, some drops of his sweat fell to the ground, from which sprang the first fragrant rose. Later Hadiths elaborated further, suggesting that droplets of sweat falling from different parts of the Prophet's body created the different varieties of rose. When the Prophet saw a rose, they say he kissed it and placed it on his eyes. He also regarded the rose as the manifestation of God's glory; and mystics such as Jalal-al-Din Muhammad Balkhi (Rumi) from Afghanistan and Ruzbihan Baqli from Shiraz placed the rose at the heart of the mystic experience. 'The red rose is part of the splendour of God,' wrote Baqli; 'everyone who wants to look into God's splendour should look at the red rose.'

*

Earthly powers have also laid claim to the rose, much as they did the heraldic lily; today, the rose is the national flower of Bulgaria, Ecuador, England, Finland (a white rose), Iraq, Romania (the Dog rose) and the United States. Eleanor of Provence, the wife of Henry III, is said to have introduced the rose into English royal heraldry; and a crowned red rose – in heraldry, the colour is 'gules' – was one of the many badges used by Henry IV and subsequent sovereigns. Among his emblems, Edward IV used the rose *en soleil*, and the white ('argent') rose inherited from his Mortimer rather than his York ancestors, while the Stuart sovereigns combined the English rose with the Scottish thistle.

The rose's most famous political incarnation is the Tudor rose, created as an inspired act of spin-doctoring by the Lancastrian Henry Tudor, the future Henry VII, at the end of the so-called Wars of the Roses, after his defeat of the Yorkist king Richard III and his own marriage to Richard's niece, Elizabeth of York. To signify this union, Henry created his new emblem by setting the white rose of York inside the red rose of Lancaster, using the potent imagery of the rose to legitimize his tenuous claim to the throne. But the Wars of the Roses were no such thing – or, rather, the label was applied retrospectively by later historians who condensed a complex struggle enacted over more than thirty years into a simple conflict between two dynastic bloodlines that flowed only weakly through Henry Tudor's veins. In any event neither side fought their battles under roses: Henry's emblem was a red dragon and Richard's a white boar. While the Lancastrians did indeed have a red rose as one of their emblems, dating back to Edmund Crouchback, the younger son of Henry III and Eleanor of Provence, the white rose is only indirectly a Yorkist emblem.

Aided by Tudor propaganda, Henry's invented rose became firmly associated with dynastic succession and the Tudors' right to rule, replacing for a time the roses of courtly and Christian love. The particoloured Damask rose often known as the 'York and Lancaster' rose, *Rosa × damascena* 'Versicolor', appeared about this time; it may be John Gerard's 'blush rose', which he classed among the Musks and described as being 'of a white colour, dasht over with a light wash of carnation', and it is certainly John Parkinson's 'Rosa versicolor, the party coloured Rose, of some Yorke and Lancaster'. The candy-striped Gallica Rosa Mundi emerged later, some time before 1640, when Nicolas Robert painted it for Gaston d'Orléans.

Queen Elizabeth I displayed the Tudor rose in many of the portraits through which she adroitly manipulated her public image, among them the famous Pelican portrait of *c.*1574 by the court miniaturist Nicholas Hilliard, in which a crowned Tudor rose and a crowned fleur-de-lis appear in the top corners, signifying her dynastic claims to England and France. The queen took another rose as her personal emblem, the Eglantine or Sweet briar, a rose of the hedgerows that also found its way into gardens. Gerard described the wild sort as having leaves that are 'glittering, and of a beautifull greene colour, of smell most pleasant', and whitish flowers 'seldom tending to purple, of little or no smell at all'. The leaves of the garden sort were larger 'and much sweeter: the floures likewise are greater, and somewhat doubled, exceeding sweet of smell'.

Eglantine roses are traditionally associated with a charming miniature by Nicholas Hillard, *Young Man among Roses*, in which a gangly lovelorn youth leans against a tree, hand on heart, embowered in a thicket of scrambling white roses. The oval portrait is said to represent Elizabeth's favourite, Robert Devereux, second Earl of Essex, thirty-three years younger than his sovereign and eventually executed for treason after the failure of his Irish campaign. He wears the queen's colours, black for constancy, white for virginity; the dazzling whiteness of the flowers suggests that, rather than taking the Eglantine as his model, Hillier turned for inspiration to the musky Field rose, *Rosa arvensis*, the 'sweet musk-roses' of Titania's bower in Shakespeare's *A Midsummer Night's Dream*.

Political roses did not stop with English monarchs. Today the red rose is the emblem of the French Parti Socialiste, a very masculine clenched fist holding a red rose adopted in late 1969, and of British New Labour, devised in the party's rebranding begun by Neil Kinnock as leader and Peter Mandelson as director of communications. Nowhere is the political rose more prominent than in the United States, where the White House Rose Garden surrounding the Oval Office is a potent symbol of presidential power. It was here, in October 1986, that President Ronald Reagan declared the rose the national floral emblem of the United States of America in an emotional speech that wove roses into America's prehistoric and revolutionary past, and its most cherished values. 'More than any other flower,' he declared, 'we hold the rose dear as the symbol of life and love and devotion, of beauty and eternity. For the love of man and woman, for the love of mankind and God, for the love of country.'

And if you want to discover a gardener's political allegiance, look no further than the roses. When I visited the White House Rose Garden in 2008 during the Bush administration's last summer, five of the Rose Garden's ten rose varieties commemorated Republican presidents or their wives: 'Pat Nixon', 'Barbara Bush', 'Ronald Reagan', 'Nancy Reagan' and 'Laura Bush', while all the roses honouring Democrats had been uprooted, among them 'Lady Bird Johnson', 'John F. Kennedy' and 'Rosalyn Carter'.

T<small>HE ROSES CELEBRATED</small> so far have been sources of private joy and of public celebration. But roses cast a darker shadow that links them to the deeper mysteries of life, and death. The expression 'sub rosa', under the rose, refers to conversations that are privileged and not to be divulged, and secret fraternities have periodically sought to harness the powers of the rose to their own ends.

The link between roses and death was already present in the rites of ancient Greece, evident in the protective rose oil – 'rose-sweet, ambrosial' – with which the goddess Aphrodite anointed the body of the heroic Hector, slain by Achilles and dragged through the dust in revenge for the death of his friend Patroclus. The story is told in Homer's *Iliad*, composed towards the end of the eighth century BCE. Wealthy Romans also took roses with them to the grave; in an extraordinary feat of preservation, desiccated wreaths of *Rosa × richardii* – the 'Rosa Sancta'

Frederick Stuart Church's enigmatic etching, *Silence*, c.1880.

of Jo Shapcott's poem – survived intact in Roman tombs at Hawara in Lower Egypt, excavated in the late 1880s by the British archaeologist Sir William Matthew Flinders Petrie. Some are now held by the Royal Botanic Gardens at Kew, their roses darkened after nearly two thousand years to the colour of mummy flesh.

By an unnerving coincidence, the American painter Frederick Stuart Church put roses and mummies together in an etching of a mummified human head sniffing or kissing a (yellow) rose, executed a few years *before* Flinders Petrie's discovery of the mummified roses and later reproduced as a watercolour and an oil painting. The French were particularly taken with the image, calling it 'extremely strange but very personal', and critics continue to speculate over its meaning. Drawn to ideas of reincarnation, and to the works of Edgar Allan Poe and Odilon Redon, Church may have wanted to show the mummy imbibing life from the rose. Such transformative roses play a role in alchemy, the forerunner of chemistry, which originally pursued a material purpose – the transformation of base metals into gold – and only gradually acquired a more spiritual overlay that sought to transform the spirit into the gold of the awakened soul. In the alchemical process, the rose stands primarily as a symbol of conjunction, the 'chymical wedding' or mystical marriage of opposites between the active masculine principle (the Red King) and the receptive female principle (the White Queen). Here is a disturbing echo of the real-life marriage between 'red' Henry Tudor and 'white' Elizabeth of York, especially as the alchemical king and queen are often portrayed as roses, red for the male and white for the female.

Increasingly drawn to spiritual and psychological interpretations of alchemy, the great twentieth-century psychoanalyst Carl Gustav Jung proposed the rose as one of his transcendent symbols expressing psychological wholeness, along with the wheel and the mandala (from the Sanskrit word for circle), which the Jungian analyst Philippa Campbell explains as 'a circle that contains all that is paradoxical and has at its centre the radiating rose. If we trace a mandala in our chaos we are offered a symbol that allows us to bring that which is unattended and forgotten into consciousness.'

Long before Jung, the roses of alchemy had sported one of the Reformation's strangest offshoots, which flourished in Germany in the late sixteenth and early seventeenth centuries: the elusive brotherhood of the Rosicrucians, a society so secret that its very existence remained in doubt. The movement was linked to the rise of the Elector Palatine Frederick V, whose marriage to Princess Elizabeth Stuart, daughter of King James I of England, promised a new Protestant dawn. It was a short-lived dream that foundered after the Protestant Frederick accepted the crown of Bohemia in defiance of the Catholic Habsburgs, taking Elizabeth to Prague where they reigned for just one winter, immortalized as the Winter King and Queen.

Even before the wedding, two anonymous Rosicrucian manifestos had begun to circulate in Germany, followed by an alchemical romance, *The Chymical Wedding of Christian Rosencreutz*. All three texts centred on Christian Rosencreutz, the founder of an apparently revived brotherhood offering its followers a return to the 'truth, light, life and glory' enjoyed by Adam in Paradise, and all three created a furore. Yet amid the uncertainty surrounding the 'brotherhood', the instigators of the Rosicrucian movement had struck metaphysical gold when they fused the two great symbols of Christianity, the cross and the rose, using the rose to soften the cross of Calvary. And while Frederick's forces were crushed by the Habsburgs at the Battle of White Mountain, forcing Frederick and Elizabeth into permanent exile in The Hague, the Rosicrucian rose spread its suckering roots underground, exciting controversy wherever it appeared – in the Netherlands and France initially, and much later in the turbulent, *fin-de-siècle* atmosphere of late nineteenth-century Europe, swirling with hermetic cults. Then the Irish poet and patriot William Butler Yeats fell under its spell, even joining a Rosicrucian group known as the Hermetic Students of the Golden Dawn. For Yeats, the rose was the western flower of life, equivalent in power to the eastern lotus; in her gilded cover design for Yeats's *The Secret Rose*, published in 1897, Althea Gyles placed a four-petalled rose at the heart of a cross, within the twisting, serpent-like branches of a stylized Tree of Life.

For other poets, this darker, secretive rose could equally contain the seeds of destruction. Into his 'sick rose' from *Songs of Innocence and Experience*, published a century before Yeats, William Blake crammed the ills of modern society: venereal disease, prostitution, exploitation, corruption, the tangled relations of humankind. And his 'Pretty ROSE TREE' in the same collection turned away from the poet in jealousy, her thorns his only delight. For decadent writers such as Joris-Karl Huysmans, the rose was one of those 'pretentious, conformist, stupid flowers . . . which belong exclusively in porcelain holders painted by young girls'. In the same vein, the surrealist Georges Bataille vented his spleen on the rose as an ideal of bourgeois feminine beauty, declaring that 'even the most beautiful flowers are spoiled in their [centres] by hairy sexual organs. Thus the interior of a rose does not at all correspond to its exterior beauty; if one tears off all the corolla's petals, all that remains is a rather sordid tuft.'

And here, surely, is the point of the rose – not in Bataille's description of a rose but in the fact that he could make of it what he willed. A 'rose is a rose is a rose', perhaps, as Gertrude Stein famously declared, but which rose is that? Umberto Eco alighted on the rose for the title of his medieval thriller, *The Name of the Rose (Il nome della rosa)*, because, he said, it was 'so rich in meanings that by now it hardly has any meaning left'. Yet his sweeping dismissal ignores the very multiplicity that makes the rose so special. For it is precisely because the rose has so many meanings and so many manifestations that we can use it to tell our own stories, whether individually or collectively. President Ronald Reagan did just that when he gathered together a pot-pourri of rose facts and fictions for his declaration of the rose as the national flower of the United States of America. He was right in claiming that the discovery of rose fossils in Alaska proved that 'the rose existed in America for age upon age', but the rose that the first president, George Washington, is supposed to have named 'Mary Washington' after his mother belongs to the Noisettes, a class created after his death.

One of the oddest rose 'histories' is that of the Cherokee rose (*Rosa laevigata*), adopted in 1916 as the state of Georgia's floral emblem. One of only four supposedly 'native' roses included in the first *Flora* of America by Frenchman André Michaux, this rose was mythically linked to the forcible removal from their homeland of more than sixteen thousand Cherokee Indian people and their repatriation to Oklahoma. According to legend, the Cherokee mothers were grieving so much that they were unable to help their children, so the tribal elders prayed for a sign that would lift their spirits. The next day, wherever their tears had fallen sprang a beautiful rose: white for the mothers' grief, gold-centred for the land that had been taken away from them, the seven leaflets on each stem representing the seven Cherokee tribes.

Don't believe a word of it. The stems of *R. laevigata* usually have three leaflets, not seven, and it is not even an American native. It comes from China, where it was illustrated by Chiu-Huang Pen Ts'ao in his *Famine Herbal* of the early fifteenth century; no one knows how it had reached America and naturalized across the southern states by the time of Michaux's visit in the 1780s and 1790s.

In the story of the rose, myths count almost as much as facts. 'Rose, *oh reiner Widerspruch*' ('Rose, oh pure contradiction'): so begins the short epitaph Rilke wrote for his gravestone in the small mountain cemetery of the Burgkirche at Raron in Switzerland. Not even poets can hope to capture the essence of this most extraordinary flower.

— 6 —

Tulip

Here is a story of human folly.

ZBIGNIEW HERBERT, 'The Bitter Smell of Tulips'

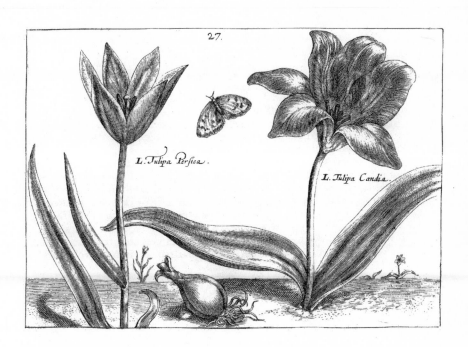

27.

L. Tulipa Persica.

L. Tulipa Candia.

SEVERAL YEARS AGO, my cousin sent me a packet of tulip bulbs from Amsterdam. They were gaudy Parrot tulips, their scarlet petals flamed with yellow and ruffled around the edges like primped silk. With some misgivings, I planted them by my front door and waited to be convinced. Their mid-spring flowers gladdened the heart and, despite my customary preference for plainer blacks and whites, I looked forward to their flowering the following year, having lifted and replanted them as the books say you should. But when they flowered a second time they reverted to plain reds on a yellow base, without the hint of a ruffle. Had I simply misremembered their flaring glory? Or had my prized tulips been spirited away by a covetous neighbour, like the black tulip in Alexandre Dumas's famous tale?

The story of the tulip is indeed one of hopes raised and dashed expectations. Surveying the landscaped wallpaper of Dutch tulip fields in early spring, or the massed ranks of tulips in Istanbul's parks at tulip festival time, I find it hard to imagine the fortunes paid for a single bulb of this most coldly formal of flowers, or the ruin wrought by too covetous a love for it. The American cultural critic Michael Pollan called today's tulips uniform and faithful, like paint chips. But my parrots were throwing something of their old selves into the ring: the ability to take us by surprise.

Unlike virtually all the other flowers in this book, the tulip has no utility whatsoever. Its symbolic role in the folklore, poetry and faith of Iran and Turkey finds no match in Europe, where it commonly signifies either the transitory nature of life or the extent of human folly.

Most tulips have little or no scent, and whatever power the tulip exerts comes from its beauty alone. Bulbs can be eaten, true, and sometimes were, usually when mistaken for onions, but the best that can be said of them is that they are not disgusting.

So what is it about the tulip that has turned so many heads, most famously in the Netherlands but just as dramatically in Ottoman Turkey where its story truly begins? The inevitable crash of Dutch tulip fever in the 1630s was mirrored by Turkey's resurgent tulip mania around a century later, when the country that first gave Europe its tulips went wild in its turn, and the passions it excited among the ruling caste cost the sultan his empire and the grand vizier his head. Yet the tulips favoured by Europeans and Ottoman Turks were utterly different creations, the flowers fat and flared in Europe versus thin and etiolated in Turkey. Beauty resides in the eye of the beholder, certainly, but beauty is a cultural construct as the tulip's story so clearly demonstrates.

D ESPITE HAVING INDIGENOUS species of its own, Europe was slow to recognize the tulip and then mistook it for another flower altogether. First to break the news of this beautiful 'red lily' growing in all the gardens of Constantinople was the French naturalist Pierre Belon, who travelled through Greece, Asia Minor, Egypt, Arabia and the Levant in the late 1540s, later publishing a full account of the many 'singularitez' he had observed. These Turkish 'lilies' clearly puzzled him, for while their flowers resembled white lilies, their leaves and roots were quite different.

Belon rightly remarked on the Turks' unequalled love of flowers, even scentless ones, which they delightedly tucked into the folds of their turbans, preferring single flowers to the mixed posies favoured by his compatriots. The Turks were skilled gardeners, too, and their markets did an excellent trade in foreign trees and plants shipped into Constantinople; as long as the flowers were beautiful, buyers did not grudge the cost.

These same foreign ships may have carried back to Europe the first Turkish tulips, for virtually all the early authorities credit Turkey and the extended Ottoman Empire as the source of the striking new tulips that arrived some ten years after Belon's initial sighting – as seed from Constantinople, as early-flowering tulips from the Crimean port city of Caffa (Feodosiya) on the Black Sea, and as later-flowering tulips from Cavala (Kavala) on the coast of eastern Macedonia. England's John Gerard spread the net a little wider, noting that tulips grew also in Thrace, Italy, Lebanese Tripoli and 'Alepo in Syria, from whence I have received plants for my garden'. The Frenchman Charles de la Chesnée Monstereul mistakenly located the tulip's birthplace in Ceylon (Sri Lanka), an error repeated by Alexandre Dumas in his nineteenth-century novel *The Black Tulip*, which named Sinhalese as the first language of 'that masterpiece of creation called the tulip'.

In fact the tulip's homelands stretch from southern Europe into western and central Asia, centred principally around the Tien Shan and Pamir Alai mountain ranges of central Asia, and also in the Caucasus Mountains, between the Black and the Caspian Seas. Some eighteen wild sorts of tulip grow in Anatolia – nearly a fifth of the world's hundred species or so – and more were brought from central Asia with the Turkic migrations, giving Turkey a primary role in the flower's onward transmission.

A S   T H E   T U L I P ' S   fame arose first in Turkey and the lands of the Middle East, it seems appropriate to begin its story here, with the Ottoman Turks under Mehmet II who conquered Constantinople in 1453. Under the Ottomans, Turkey witnessed a great flowering of its garden culture. Tulips, unknown in Byzantine art, took their place among the four classic flowers – '*quatre fleurs*' – of tulip, rose, hyacinth and carnation, appearing on many public buildings and fountains after this date, and in the celebrated Iznik ceramic ware produced from the end of the fifteenth century. While the Turks had loved the tulip long before the Ottomans conquered Byzantium, the Ottomans breathed a new naturalism into their art, allowing recognizable flowers to emerge from the stylized palmettes of earlier eras. Instead of looking to Greece and Rome, they borrowed their garden culture from the East, from

Persia and from a common Islamic tradition that the Mughals would take into Afghanistan and India, propelled by the gardening passions of emperors such as Babur and Jahangir.

Poetry was another medium in which the tulip took a starring role. As far back as the eleventh century, Persian poetry glowed with literal and metaphorical tulips, clothing the ground of plains and prairies, mountains and verdant hills, pleasure gardens and rocky deserts, their colour likened to rubies, cornaline, blood, the prince's standard, even a dash of ink at the bottom of a coral inkpot. The classic harbinger of spring, a role played in Rome by the rose, tulips reminded Persian and Turkish poets of lips and cheeks, the flower's wild origins setting it apart as 'a stranger from the distant steppes', barred from polite society and the conversation of roses.

In Turkey as in Persia, a love of flowers bore the mark of divine approval. According to a preacher of the Sümbüliye dervish order, all gardeners would go to heaven to carry on their work, as this was where flowers belonged. To Turkish mystics, the tulip was doubly blessed; as the late Islamic scholar Annemarie Schimmel explained, 'its very name, *lâle*, consists of the same letters as *hilâl* "crescent," the symbol of Islam, and, even more important, as *Allâh*.' But folk legend casts a darker shadow, attributing the tulip's origins to the Turkish folk hero Ferhad, who tunnelled through a mountain for ten weary years to gain the love of Sirin, then killed himself with an axe on learning that she had died during his labours. From his blood sprang bright red tulips, like the windflowers, or anemones, in the Greek legend of Venus and Adonis.

In court circles, the tulip and Ottoman floriculture generally gained ascendancy under Sultan Süleyman the Magnificent (r. 1520 to 1566), who had tulips embroidered on his gowns of satin brocade and embossed on his horse's armour. Turkish florists began raising tulip cultivars from wild forms, known collectively as *Lâle-i Rûmi* (Ottoman tulips), and their favoured shape changed from the pot-bellied flowers of early Iznik ceramics to almond-shaped blooms with petals stretched impossibly thin, like blown glass. The Ottomans were also planting tulips in vast numbers. In 1574, Sultan Selim II is said to have ordered 50,000 tulip bulbs from a Syrian sharif, although other reports talk not of tulips but of 500,000 hyacinth bulbs.

Confusion over the identity of the tulip filtered into the West, where it became known not as '*lâle*' but as '*tulipan*', an approximation of the Turkish word for turban, '*dülbend*'. The mix-up in translation is usually attributed to Ogier Ghiselin de Busbecq, the Habsburg ambassador to the court of Süleyman the Magnificent who spent some eight years at Constantinople and later recounted his experiences in a series of entertaining letters, supposedly written at the time but actually composed many years later when his memory was fading.

In a letter dated 1 September 1555, de Busbecq recalled his first journey to Constantinople in November 1554, almost certainly confusing it with a later journey he made in March 1558, when the tulips and other flowers he describes would have been in flower. After a day spent in Adrianople (modern Edirne, close to the Greek and Bulgarian borders), de Busbecq and his party set out for Constantinople, encountering 'quantities of flowers, narcissi, hyacinths, and *tulipans*, as the Turks call them. We were surprised to find them flowering in midwinter, scarcely a favourable season . . . The tulip has little or no scent, but it is admired for its beauty and the variety of its colours.'

Although tradition also credits de Busbecq with introducing the first Turkish tulips into European gardens, he was in fact responsible for neither event. Towards the beginning of April 1559, a red tulip had already burst into flower in the magnificent Bavarian garden at Augsburg of Councillor Johannes Heinrich Herwart, sprung from seed procured from either Byzantium or Cappadocia. As tulips need at least five years to flower from seed, Councillor Herwart's tulips were planted before de Busbecq even set out for Constantinople. Under the name 'Tulipa Turcarum', they were seen and described by the Swiss naturalist Conrad Gesner, then busy revising an annotated version of Dioscorides by Belon's old master, Valerius Cordus. Gesner appended his tulip notes when the work was published two years later, his appetite whetted by drawings he had received earlier of two tulips, a

Europe's first garden tulip, seen and described by the
Swiss botanist Conrad Gesner in 1559.

red and a yellow, possibly from contacts in Padua, Venice or Bologna.

Although Gesner described his tulip as having eight tepals (petals
and outer sepals), the accompanying illustration – the first European
woodcut of a tulip – shows a pot-bellied flower with six peeled-back
petal tips, its stem rising stiffly out of broad crinkled leaves that float
horizontally like seaweed. Its smell was pleasant, said Gesner, soothing and delicate but evanescent. The Swedish botanist Carl Linnaeus
would later name it *Tulipa gesneriana* in his honour, a name that
encompassed all Europe's first flush of cultivated tulips in the sixteenth and seventeenth centuries, which have since died out.

De Busbecq's description of Turkish *tulipans* nonetheless helps to explain the derivation of the word 'tulip' in most European languages. In both Persian and Ottoman Turkish, *'lâle'* was the generic term for wild flowers, in contrast to *'gül'*, which referred to cultivated flowers. In Ottoman Turkey, garden tulips were known as *'dülbend lalesi'* or 'turban *lâle'*, doubtless because these were the pretty blooms worn in their turbans by Turkish flower lovers, making the tulip's European derivation a partial rather than a full mistranslation. *'Lâle'* in Ottoman Turkish came to be used for wild flowers of a red colour; it entered mystical literature as the 'flower of blood' and the 'flower of suffering', while *'gül'* symbolized the soul in a state of *'haraka'* or grace. (In Iran to this day, the tulip remains the flower of martyrdom, seen in cemeteries honouring those killed in the Iraq–Iran War, and it appears in stylized form on the Iranian flag.) Over time, *'gül'* came to specify the rose just as *'lâle'* came to signify the tulip. And to European eyes, the first Turkish tulips really did resemble the fantastic turbans of the Grand Turk. 'After it hath beene some fewe daies flowred,' declared John Gerard, 'the points and brims of the flower turne backward, like a Dalmation or Turkes cap, called *Tulipa*, *Tolepan*, *Turban*, and *Tursan*, whereof it tooke his name.'

A FTER GESNER, TURKISH tulips proliferated in Europe's burgeoning botanical literature, just as they did in the best European gardens. The Flemish botanist Rembert Dodoens included them in the first edition of his book on ornamental and fragrant flowers of 1568, although they are absent from the herbal he published five years earlier. Pierre Pena and Matthias de L'Obel introduced a long-stemmed tulip from Venice in their collaborative herbal of 1570, *Stirpium Adversaria Nova*; and de L'Obel described several more in his herbal of 1581.

But the man who best records Europe's growing fascination with this flamboyant introduction from the East is the Flemish botanist Carolus Clusius, who first mentioned tulips in 1570 and wrote about them whenever he could thereafter, even when they had little relevance to his subject. A key figure in the story of European botany, Clusius had studied medicine in Montpellier under the great French physician and naturalist Guillaume Rondelet and gathered much of his information about tulips while supervising the imperial gardens at Vienna for the Habsburg emperor, Maximilian II.

The flower's earliest days in the Low Countries were hardly auspicious. From Vienna, Clusius tells the story of an Antwerp merchant who received a quantity of bulbs sent to him with exquisite cloths by a friend in Constantinople. Thinking they were onions, he ordered some to be roasted over glowing coals, then prepared with oil and vinegar; they cannot have been to his taste as he buried the remainder in his garden and quickly forgot about them. The few that survived were rescued by a merchant of Mechlin, one Joris Rye, a great plant lover, 'and I am bound to state [wrote Clusius] that it is due to his care and zeal that I could later see their flowers, which were a delight, and a joy for the eyes because of their charming diversity'.

By the time Clusius slipped tulips into his study of Spanish flora published in 1576, the varieties known in Europe included yellow, red, white, purple and variegated early-flowering tulips, and both red and yellow late-flowering varieties. Just seven years later, in his book on Austrian plants, he could identify thirty-four different kinds, among them a monstrosity of a three-flowered late tulip and four 'intermediate' tulips, which flowered midway between the others. A summation of all his tulip observations appeared in his collected masterwork, *Rariorum Plantarum Historia*, largely finished by 1593 when he moved to Leiden but not published until 1601.

Europe's rapidly expanding stock of tulips served to emphasize the flower's chief attraction: its astonishing colour palette, which Clusius had not seen in any other flower except the opium poppy. 'For the colour is either wholly yellow, or red, or white, or purple,' he reported, 'but sometimes one sees two or more of these colours mixed up in one and the same flower.' Contrary to others' claims, he had never encountered a blue tulip and he was scrupulous about describing only plants he had seen for himself, noting the smell of fresh wax or saffron in a certain yellow tulip and how its scent might weaken or disappear, and the way colours could change: attractive reds turning ungainly and dull, for instance, and dark purples fading to the colour of Damask or Provence roses.

Already the flowers were showing signs of the breaking colours that fanned the flames of tulip mania, when – in the words of English botanist John Rea – ordinary tulips changed 'into divers several glorious colours, variously mixed, edged, striped, feathered, garded, agotted, marbled, flaked, or specled, even to admiration'. Europeans were doubly bewitched because such changes were entirely unpredictable. Tulips grown from seed did not necessarily imitate their parents, and you could never predict when a plain tulip might 'break'. Gambling on its occurrence was the obvious response to such kaleidoscopic beauty.

Using observation alone, Clusius came close to discovering why tulips break into their constituent colours, having noticed from 1585 that tulips which had previously borne fine red flowers might suddenly produce a miscellany of reds and yellows, 'sometimes the yellow occupying the middle of the segment, sometimes the red, or both colours being arranged in rays, diverging along the edges'. The same happened with yellow tulips showing red and yellow, and purples showing white and purple. 'And this also I have also observed,' Clusius went on, 'that any tulip thus changing its original colour is usually ruined afterwards and wanted only to delight its master's eyes with this variety of colours before dying, as if to bid him a last farewell.'

As Clusius suspected, tulips that break are in fact sick plants, attacked by viruses transmitted by aphids; and the flaming and feathering admired as a sign of extreme beauty in reality heralded the plant's gradual demise. Without knowing the cause, breeders engaged in a veritable alchemy of the tulip as they sought to transmute plain colours into feathered gold. Unconvinced by the sickness argument, the French florist Charles de la Chesnée Monstereul refused to divulge the 'secret' of perfecting tulips, wishing to reserve it for 'Curious Sages'. John Rea singled out tulip colours likely to break ('*Orenge*, Brimston, Hair, Dove, Gredeline, *Isabella*, Shamway, or any other light or strange colour') and recommended planting the bulbs alternately in well-manured soil and that which is 'lean and hungry' to speed up the process.

Relying on the botanist and horticultural writer Richard Bradley as his authority, England's great eighteenth-century gardener Philip Miller quoted a Brussels grower whose land was virtually guaranteed to turn ordinary breeding tulips into fine variegated flowers, and a London gentleman whose tulip bed invariably produced fine striped tulips at each of its corners. Miller also passed on Bradley's advice to check the circulation of colours by binding some, but not all, of the vessels in a tulip's stem, but he discounted methods such as steeping the roots in coloured liquids, planting in coloured earths, inserting coloured powders into the roots, or drawing coloured silks through the roots. (All such sleights of hand vanished from his enormously successful *Gardeners Dictionary*, published seven years later, which simply recommended planting tulips in fresh soil each year.)

The apothecary John Parkinson warned the prudent against white tulips that suddenly turned red or yellow, suggesting that such an 'idle conceit' could result only from a gardener's trickery or one's own mistaking. As mystified as everyone else, the Dutch astrological gardener Henry van Oosten attributed the capricious breaking of some but not all tulips to the fact 'that one may be capacitated to receive the Influence, and the other not'.

All this lay ahead, however. In the tulip's early days in Europe, bulbs and seeds were eagerly passed from one plant enthusiast to another to mark their friendship and connection. The year after Clusius arrived in Vienna, the 'illustrious Ogier de Busbeque' — about to leave for Paris to look after the affairs of the Archduchess Isabella — gave him a quantity of tulip seed and bulbs, which he had received from Constantinople the previous year. Judging the seed too old to germinate, Clusius delayed planting for another year and must have been delighted with the prodigious number of tulips produced, especially when these flowered after five or six years in a great variety of colours. Some may have found their way to England, as the Welsh writer and geographer Richard Hakylut reported in 1582 that, within the past four years, 'there have bene brought into England from Vienna in Austria divers kinds of flowers called Tulipas, and those and other procured thither a little before from Constantinople by an excellent man called M. Carolus Clusius'.

Other rare tulips came to Clusius from various sources: from the 'generous Dame von Heyenstain', who gave him the offset of a single rare bulb from Byzantium with sulphur-coloured flowers (it was killed by the bitter winter of 1586, and Clusius had to abandon the seed he had sown in his small Viennese garden when he left imperial service); from the nobleman Jean Boisot in Brussels; and from Johan van Hogelande, secretary to the board of Leiden's Hortus Botanicus, who gave him a drawing and then his only bulb of a tulip with pointed petals that initially flowered green, turned light yellow at the edges, then flared into red. Clusius received another green tulip as a drawing from the naturalist and collector Jacques Plateau, observing that it looked like a small cauliflower but was 'not inelegant'.

Such genteel exchanges worked well when collectors shared a genuine interest in their rare plants. But the tulip was gaining a commercial value and Clusius's gardens in Vienna, Frankfurt and then Leiden were repeatedly robbed of their precious bulbs. In 1581, his servant disappeared and important plants – including chests of bulbs – were subsequently sold. The following year Clusius lost most of his variegated tulips, unique specimens that he later found growing in the garden of an aristocratic Viennese lady who denied having bought them from his servant. Other floral connoisseurs were equally at risk.

As the price of tulips continued to rise, market forces intruded rudely on a trade that had previously operated according to the rules of friendship. Now practically everybody was selling flowers, and the rich were buying them from artisans not from love but to flaunt them before their friends. Profoundly depressed, Clusius unburdened himself to a fellow humanist, Justus Lipsius:

To hell with those who started all this buying and selling! I have always kept a garden, sometimes for my own pleasure, sometimes so that I might serve my friends, who, I saw, took pleasure in that pursuit. But now, when I see all these worthless people, sometimes even those whose names I have never heard, so impudent in their requests, sometimes I feel like giving up my pastime altogether.

Whatever his private feelings, Clusius the plantsman-scholar continued to search for new tulip varieties and possible new uses for them. Remembering his failed attempt to test the aphrodisiac properties of tulip bulbs – the Viennese apothecary to whom he had entrusted his bulbs forgot to candy them like orchid roots before attempting his experiments – he was pleased to report that the apothecary Johan Müller had at last candied some tulip bulbs for a similar experiment, outcome unknown, although their taste was reported to be much more palatable than orchid roots. (John Parkinson tried the same experiment on himself but claimed not to have eaten enough to judge their 'Venereous quality'.)

Disenchanted by the tulip trade's increasing commercialization, Clusius turned his attention to wild tulips, which he included in his great masterwork of 1601: fragrant tulips from the Apennines (*Tulipa sylvestris*); from Narbonne in southern France (*T. sylvestris* subsp. *sylvestris*, collected by Matthias de L'Obel and sent to his friends in the Netherlands); from Spain (*T. sylvestris* subsp. *australis* from the mountains near Aranjuez, sent to the Netherlands by the king of Spain's gardener); and from Byzantium, assumed to be the little Cretan tulip, *T. saxatilis*, which came to him with the inscription 'Lalé di suoi fiori'. Clusius's final tulips appeared in 1611, two years after his death. Fittingly, they included the wild Persian tulip that bears his name, *Tulipa clusiana*, sent to him first in the form of a portrait and then as a bulblet by the Italian plant lover Matteo Caccini, who had a fine botanical garden in Florence. Imported originally from Persia, its flower was exceptionally delicate, slightly larger than the Narbonne or Spanish tulips, of a soft red on the outside but snowy white inside, its outer tepals long and pointed, the inner ones somewhat more rounded. A second – more expensive – Persian tulip bulb sent by Caccini produced a single leaf, which soon withered, and when Clusius lifted the bulb in May he found it quite flabby and empty.

Yet despite such setbacks, Clusius retained his trust in the extraordinary diversity of the plant world. 'Although it looks as if the pursuit of botany had reached its zenith,' he wrote when introducing his Persian tulip, 'yet almost every day we get knowledge of some new plant which nobody has described so far; so endless is this study.'

WHILE PROTO-BOTANISTS WERE celebrating the glories of the natural world, miniaturists such as Joris Hoefnagel were busy turning flowers into art. The son of a wealthy Antwerp diamond merchant, Hoefnagel moved to Frankfurt in 1591, joining the circle of Netherlandish artists and intellectuals who had gathered there around Clusius. Flowers developed into a major feature of Hoefnagel's work, as they did for many European artists. The tulip's rapid rise can be tracked through the increasingly fashionable florilegia designed to show off the botanic collections of their patrons – Basilius Besler's *Hortus Eystettensis* for the Prince Bishop of Eichstätt, for instance, and Pierre Vallet's book of flowers growing in the French king's garden – and to meet rich collectors' developing taste for exotic flora and fauna.

One of the most celebrated of the new florilegia was *Hortus Floridus* by Crispin de Passe the Younger, published originally in Latin in 1614 and soon afterwards in French, Dutch and English. Most plates show the plants growing in a flat Dutch landscape against a plain sky; the view point is so low the artist seems to be lying on his stomach. A handcoloured copy once owned by the great English botanist Sir Joseph Banks includes a fine yellow-and-red tulip named after John Gerard.

ALTHOUGH BRITAIN RECEIVED her tulips slightly later than continental Europe, their impact was no less dramatic. From the same John Gerard you catch a sense of wonder at the novelty and diversity of this 'strang and forraine flower', with which all the 'studious and painefull [painstaking] Herbarists'' wanted to become better acquainted. According to Gerard, one of the first to grow tulips in England was the apothecary James Garrett of London's Lime Street, home to a community of flower lovers, many of Flemish or Huguenot origin, which included the silk merchant James Cole and Matthias de L'Obel when he returned to live permanently in the capital. Clusius stayed here during his visits to London in the 1570s and 1580s, perhaps bringing some of the tulips that James Garrett planted in his garden near the city walls at Aldgate. Garrett's aim was to map the entire genus by sowing and planting tulips of his own propagation, together with those received from friends overseas, but after twenty years he gave up as new colours arose at each new planting; to describe them individually, said Gerard, would be like rolling Sisyphus' stone, or counting grains of sand.

Gerard nonetheless made a brave attempt to describe seven main sorts then flowering in Britain, including the Bologna tulip, the French tulip, the yellow tulip, various red-and-white tulips, one coloured like apple blossom, along with countless other sorts mentioned by Matthias de L'Obel. Thomas Johnson, the apothecary of Snow Hill in London, shied away from describing tulips altogether when he revised Gerard's herbal some thirty-five years later, directing his readers to the European florilegia of Johann Theodor de Bry, Emanuel Sweert, and the French king's gardener Jean Robin, and to the book of garden flowers by his fellow apothecary, John Parkinson. Tulips were garden flowers without medical significance, although Johnson noted that their bulbs could be preserved with sugar or otherwise dressed and were neither unpleasant nor offensive, 'but rather good and nourishing'.

Writing specifically for gentlewomen, whose 'love & liking' of flowers was born of their leisure, Parkinson's splendid book on garden flowers gave tulips a central role in his frontispiece of the Garden of Eden and in his text, where they appear between lilies and daffodils, sharing a little of both their natures. In all, he identified some 140 different sorts of tulip, 'found out in these later dayes by many of the searchers of natures varieties, ... our age being more delighted in the search, curiosity, and rarities of these pleasant delights, then any age I thinke before'. Many of the early-flowering varieties he identified by place of origin: Caffa, Bologna, Italy, France, Crete, Armenia, Constantinople and Clusius's rare Persian tulip, which he had seen only recently. He mentions, too, a white tulip shown to him by his friend John Tradescant, who would shortly take up his post as keeper of the royal gardens, vines and silkworms at Oatlands Palace for Charles I and his French wife, Queen Henrietta Maria.

From Tradescant, we gain a sense of how tulips were entering British gardens. While not especially renowned as a tulip fancier, the elder Tradescant bought 800 tulip bulbs in Haarlem and 500 more in Brussels when he travelled through the Low Countries and northern France buying vast quantities of plants and trees for his then master Robert Cecil, Lord Treasurer of England, who was busy creating a fine new garden at Hatfield House. The year was 1611, two decades before the onset of tulip mania, and the tulips cost him ten shillings a hundred, far less than the rare Martagon lilies and irises he also bought in Brussels, or the twenty-six shillings he spent on two pots of gillyflowers and one pot of seed. He later acquired more tulips for his own garden at South Lambeth, dutifully recording their names in his copy of Parkinson's book of garden flowers, now in Oxford's Bodleian Library, including a 'Tulipe Caffa' sent to him by Sir Peter Wyche, ambassador at Constantinople. Like Thomas Johnson, he passed over individual tulip names in his garden catalogue, merely listing 'a great variety of elegant tulips' and '50 sorts of tulips, variously flamed'.

Aided by Elias Ashmole, Tradescant's son John was at least able to name thirty different varieties among his many other 'gallant Tulips'; five of these were painted by his friend Alexander Marshal, a merchant and gentleman of independent fortune as well as a keen horticulturist, entomologist and amateur artist of rare talent. Marshal stayed with the younger Tradescant at South Lambeth in 1641, making daily visits to Oatlands Palace and doubtless already at work on his 'Booke of Mr. TRADESCANT's choicest Flowers and Plants, exquisitely limned [painted] in vellum'. That album is now lost but Marshal's own florilegium survives, with its five tulips also grown by Tradescant, the purple-and-white 'Zebulom' and four prized red-and-white varieties: 'Admiral de Man', 'Louis of Portugal', 'Agate Robin' and 'Pas Citadel'.

Another admirer of this last variety was the Welsh florist Sir Thomas Hanmer, who began the Civil War fighting for King Charles I but later obtained permission to take his family to France. After his wife died in Paris, Hanmer returned to England, married again and settled at Bettisfield in the Welsh Marches, where the local soil and air killed off most of his rare tulips. He lamented their fate to his good friend the diarist John Evelyn, eight years his junior, whom he advised on plant-ing the flower garden of his Deptford home, Sayes Court, and to whom he sent roots and bulbs, including tulips.

Despite his personal loss, Hanmer commended the tulip as 'the Queene of Bulbous plants, whose Flower is beautifull in its figure, and most rich and admirable in colours, and wonderfull in variety of markings'. To fill his days of enforced leisure under Commonwealth rule, he poured his love of plants and gardening into a Garden Book, finished in manuscript by 1659 but left unpublished for nearly three centuries. Supplemented with notes from his pocket book, it opens a window onto a beautifully preserved, mid-seventeenth-century garden, packed with all the latest flowers, and catching fashions on the point of change.

Like Parkinson, Hanmer selected only the brightest and best of his beloved tulips, describing their gradations of colour in words that are now all but lost to the language: amaranthe (purple), aurora (deep orange), bertino (blue-grey), furille-mort (dead-leaf colour), gilvus (very pale red), grideline (flax grey), isabella (greyish yellow), minimme (dun colour), murrey (mulberry), quoist or queest (dove grey), and watchet (sky blue). At first in England, he tells us, gardeners valued only pure white tulips striped with purples and reds, but French tastes had crept in and now 'we esteeme (as the French doe) any mix-tures of odde colours, though there bee no white with them, and such as are markt with any yellowes or Isabellas are much priz'd; all which new colour'd Tulipes wee call Modes, being the fashion, yet new flowers with good Purples or Violets and White are still very deare and valuable'.

As John Evelyn explained, it was not the amount of colour that brought fame to a tulip, but rather the quality, vivacity, mix and position of the varied shades, 'in the *botomes*, *strakes & forme*', which all had to follow certain rules known as *Transcendents*: that the colours should be evenly laid, splendid, perfect and distinct inside and out, placed so 'that one kill not & obscure the other but add luster rather to it like a good piece of painting'. It was important, too, that the streaks, known by the French word *'panache'*, should start at the bottom and extend up to the brim like a shell.

Hanmer clearly had the gift of friendship as well as gardening. In dedicating his *Flora* to Hanmer, John Rea called him the 'truly Noble, and perfect Lover of Ingenuity', explaining that Hanmer had first brought to England the gallant tulip named after him, 'Agate Hanmer', 'a beautiful Flower, of three good colours, pale gredeline, deep scarlet, and pure white, commonly well parted, striped, agoted, and excellently placed, abiding constant to the last, with the bottom and Tamis [anthers] blew'. Hanmer's friendships even crossed enemy lines, for in June 1655 he sent a 'very great mother-root of Agate Hanmer' to another renowned tulip fancier, Cromwell's Major-General John Lambert, who had bought Queen Henrietta Maria's fine Italianate villa and garden at Wimbledon. Hanmer entrusted the mission to 'Rose', presumably John Rose who gardened for King Charles II after the Restoration, and he repeated his gift of tulips the following year, sending the general fine varieties such as 'Belle Susanne' and 'Belle Isabelle'.

In his garden at Bettisfield, Hanmer grew his tulips in four little bordered beds in the midst of a bordered knot, planting them carefully in rows, together with jonquils, narcissi, fritillarias, anemones, gillyflowers, cyclamen, irises raised from seed by John Rea, spring crocuses, hyacinths, polyanthas and one double crown imperial. His instructions for growing tulips show equal care, covering the best kinds of earth (one part sand and two parts willow earth, or two parts rich mould from the fields and a little cow dung, rotted and sieved); planting beds (slightly mounded, no more than four feet across to

Lambert K.ᵗ ofʸᵉ Golden Tulip.

The Parliamentarian Major-General
John Lambert's love of the tulip
is here lampooned in a pack of playing
cards produced by Royalist exiles
in the Netherlands.

allow weeding and viewing); and weather protection (linen cloths supported on wooden frames). The cloths could be pulled aside to admit sunshine and proper viewing: 'And now the Florists fly about to see and examine and take the chiefe pleasure of gardens, admiring the new varietyes that Spring produces, and being impatient of delays open the very buttons scarce yet coloured, but with a little sticke or two for the purpose, lest they should prejudice them with the touch of their fingers.'

SIR THOMAS HANMER may have developed his love of tulips in France, which exhibited a peculiarly Gallic form of tulip fever well before the mania erupted in Holland, and which remained largely unscathed by its aftershocks. France produced one of the first treatises devoted exclusively to tulips, the *Traitté compendieux et abregé des tulippes et de leurs diverses sortes et espèces* (Paris, 1617), which claimed that nature had tried to outdo herself in creating each beautiful variety.

It is said that in the first two decades of the seventeenth century, single tulip bulbs changed hands for the price of thriving businesses (a brewery valued at 30,000 francs, for instance), and were welcomed as dowries by prospective sons-in-law. More tulip treatises followed throughout the century, repeatedly crowning the tulip *Reine des fleurs* or Queen of Flowers and making wild claims about its growing popularity. Most bombastic of all was Charles de la Chesnée Monstereul's *Le Floriste François* of 1654, which focused exclusively on tulips as if these were the only flowers worth growing. Having erroneously given the tulip a Sinhalese origin, the author attributed its lack of smell to its transportation from warm to colder climates; had it retained its scent, he declared, the tulip would have united all the perfections of the floral kingdom. And once the Portuguese had given it to the Flemish, the French – 'adoring these terrestrial divinities' – took it home with them and, being 'more curious spirits than any other nation', had found the means to perfect it.

Tulips undoubtedly made a fine show in French gardens as their numbers swelled, from the two dozen varieties singled out by the first tulip treatise of 1617, to La Chesnée Monstereul's total of 450 by mid-century. One of the best-stocked gardens belonged to Pierre Morin from the extended family of Parisian nurserymen who supplied plants to curious gardeners throughout Europe, including the Tradescants at South Lambeth. John Evelyn visited at least twice, finding much to admire: Morin's oval garden, which he copied for Sayes Court; his rare collections of shells, flowers and insects; and his plantings of tulips, anemones, ranunculuses and crocuses, all of which Evelyn judged to be 'of the most exquisite' and 'held for the rarest in the World', drawing crowds of like-minded admirers throughout the season. On a return visit in 1651, Morin told him 'there were 10000 sorts of *Tulips* onely', although whether he meant in his garden or in general is not clear. Morin listed a hundred named tulips in his plant catalogues, the rarest of his stock. Customers with shallower pockets were assured that he had many lesser varieties for sale at a fair price.

*

EUROPE'S TULIP MANIA belongs most surely to the Dutch,
however, who let their normally phlegmatic nature run away with
them, attracted on the one hand by the extraordinary – and extra-
ordinarily capricious – beauty of this Turkish wonder flower, and on
the other by the prospect of untold wealth, after rare tulips had caught
the imagination of connoisseurs and collectors, and their prices,
already high, began inexorably to rise.

The story has been well told by others, among them Anna Pavord's
The Tulip, Mike Dash's *Tulipomania*, Deborah Moggach's fictionalized
Tulip Fever and most recently Anne Goldgar's painstakingly researched
Tulipmania, which calls into question several cherished myths about
what exactly happened, and why. It is hard to ignore parallels between
the increasingly unhinged tulip market of seventeenth-century
Holland and the packaging of complex financial derivatives that
triggered the global economic crash of 2008. By the time tulip mania
peaked in 1637, bulbs were traded, sight unseen and frequently un-
owned, to buyers without the money to pay for them but who hoped
to sell them on at ever more astronomical prices. It was a market in
futures that had lost all connection with reality; a *'windhandel'*, they
called it at the time – a trade in wind.

But there is no doubting the extraordinary beauty of the tulips then
in vogue. For all their Calvinist leanings, the Dutch had long nurtured a love of flowers, and of paintings that celebrated the pleasures
of the physical world. Travellers such as keen-eyed Peter Mundy, an
employee of the East India Company, were delighted by their little
gardens and flowerpots stuffed with rare bulbs and flowers, and by the
paintings hanging in the shops of quite ordinary tradesmen. Tulips
brought these two loves together; and the tulip's rise coincided for-
tuitously with the perfection of the new genre of flower painting by
artists such as Jan Brueghel the Elder, Ambrosius Bosschaert and his
sons, Roelandt Savery and Daniel Seghers. Outlandish and strange,
their tulips appear bathed in a seductive sheen, often placed at the
all-important top right-hand corner of the composition and mixed
with flowers from different seasons. Although the models were real,

sketched in gardens because the artists could not afford to purchase the rarest blooms, these are exercises in horticultural fantasy like the tulip trade itself. And for householders who could no longer afford the flowers, a painting by all but the highest rung of flower painters was almost certainly more affordable.

'A fool and his money are soon parted,' declared Roemer Visscher in a popular emblem book of 1614, illustrated with two fat tulip blossoms whose prices must even then have raised eyebrows. As in any market, prices were driven by desire and scarcity, leading the botanist Joost van Ravelingen to conclude that the most valued tulips were not necessarily the nicest or most beautiful but merely the rarest, especially when owned by one master who could manipulate their value.

The prices charged for 'Semper Augustus', one of the most famous flamed tulips of all, bear out this view. An early admirer was the Dutch chronicler Nicolaes van Wassenaer, who named it the foremost beauty for 1623, having seen it growing among a variety of tulips planted around a mirrored cabinet in the Heemstede garden of Dr Adriaen Pauw, the pensionary (leading official) of Amsterdam. Wassenaer was clearly entranced: 'the colour is white, with Carmine on a blue base, and with an unbroken flame right to the top, never did a Florist see one more beautiful than this'.

The price for one 'Semper Augustus' bulb was then quoted at 1,000 guilders (f.1,000), more than a decade before tulip fever had reached its peak. The following spring, with only twelve bulbs of 'Semper Augustus' in existence, the price had risen to f.1,200 each, although the single owner – presumably Dr Pauw – held back from selling them for fear of driving prices down. The same happened in 1625, when the price had risen to f.3,000 but still the owner would not sell. By 1633, one bulb reputedly changed hands for f.5,550 and by 1637 – the year of the crash – the asking price was f.30,000 for three bulbs. At a time when average annual incomes were only f.150, a single 'Semper Augustus' bulb could buy you the most expensive house on an Amsterdam canal with a small garden and coach house.

Inevitably, the high prices achieved for the rarest tulips attracted a new clientele into the market, the sort of people so roundly condemned by Clusius. But in the main, buyers and sellers came from the 'middling' classes: connoisseurs, several important artists and ordinary citizens such as merchants, skilled craftsmen, manufacturers and professionals, often connected by ties of family, religion, trade or location. Their speculative ambitions drew the attention of moralizing pamphleteers, who portrayed the participants to the tulip drama in a fool's cap or a chariot of fools, while prices continued to rise. In 1636, the year before the crash, one anti-tulip pamphleteer calculated that the price paid for a single 'Viceroy' tulip bulb (f.2,500) might more usefully purchase twenty-seven tons of wheat, fifty tons of rye, four fat oxen, eight fat pigs, twelve fat sheep, two hogsheads of wine, four barrels of beer, two barrels of butter, three tons of cheese, a bed with linen, a suit of clothes and a silver beaker.

As the trade was in bulbs, sales took place outside the flowering season, generally between June and October. Some growers commissioned tulip portraits, usually of a single specimen, sometimes named and sometimes priced. Gathered together into tulip albums, these functioned partly as sales catalogues but also as objects of beauty in their own right when painted by notable artists such as Judith Leyster, Antony Claesz and the German Jacob Marrel. Most sales took place in taverns under the auspices of 'Colleges' of flower growers, established to govern transactions between buyers and sellers. Prices were agreed either by arbitration or by public auction, after which everyone – buyers, sellers and witnesses – got drunk at the buyer's expense. The trade was so flourishing that the States of Holland contemplated introducing a tax on tulips, without gaining the necessary agreement from all its constituent members.

Then the unthinkable happened, if the hearsay evidence of the pamphleteers is correct. On Tuesday 3 February 1637, a group of tulip buyers and sellers gathered at a Haarlem tavern to conduct their business. A member of the College began the day's trading by offering for sale a pound of tulip bulbs priced at f.1,250. No one bid. The auctioneer dropped the price to f.1,100 then f.1,000, but there were still no takers. Rumours had already begun to circulate about the fragility of the tulip trade and news of the failed auction brought it to a standstill. It seems the Jeremiahs were right in their prognosis that once the market was swollen with more sellers than buyers, confidence would evaporate and the market would collapse.

An auction did in fact take place two days later, at Alkmaar, when the average price paid per bulb was a little under f.800 (equivalent to nearly two years' pay for a master carpenter in Leiden) and a few prized bulbs achieved much wilder prices: a 'Viceroy' reportedly sold for f.4,203 and an 'Admirael van Enchuysen' with an offset for f.5,200. But it seems unlikely that the sellers, the orphans of Wouter Bartholomeusz Winckel, ever realized their profits. Threatened with ruin by the failed auction at Haarlem, growers hastily convened a conference in Amsterdam for 23 February at which they hoped to resolve the crisis by agreeing a cut-off date of November 1636 for tulip contracts. All contracts drawn up prior to this were deemed bona fide and therefore enforceable, while contracts agreed after November could be annulled on payment of 10 per cent of the agreed price. Holland's High Court subsequently overturned this decision, declaring *all* uncompleted transactions invalid since the beginning of 1636, and entrusting local magistrates with the task of untangling any resulting legal wrangles.

The demise of tulip fever inevitably claimed some casualties, although Anne Goldgar's careful sifting of the records suggests that reports of individual bankruptcies were much exaggerated, most vociferously by the anti-tulip pamphleteers whose tirades have coloured subsequent reports. Some individuals undoubtedly lost money, among them the landscape painter Jan van Goyen, who famously spent large sums on tulips in the last few weeks of the craze and died in penury twenty years after the crash. But van Goyen also speculated heavily in land, and documented bankruptcies attributable solely to tulip fever were few. The Dutch economy as a whole was not seriously undermined, despite the more lasting damage to the Dutch psyche.

As a mark of its resilience, the tulip lived on in the gardens and paintings of the Dutch Golden Age, undergoing no more than a modest retreat as painters counted the cost of their own, and their clients', failed investments. Despite an inevitable sharp drop after the giddy heights of 1637, fine varieties of tulips still commanded decent sums. 'Incredible prices For tulip rootes,' wrote Peter Mundy when he travelled around the Low Countries in 1640, three years after the crash. The year after the fever had abated, the Dutch artist Jacob Gerritsz. Cuyp painted a whole field of flamed and feathered tulips against a flat Dutch horizon, attended by a butterfly and a pair of admiring frogs. Had his tulips all been 'Semper Augustus', their combined value might at one time have bought him a whole street of Amsterdam's finest canalside houses. Elsewhere in Europe, prices for fine new varieties remained high, and the French writer Alexandre Dumas opened his novel *The Black Tulip* in The Hague in 1672 as if the crash had never happened.

E UROPE WAS CURED, perhaps, but less than a century later a second bout of tulip fever erupted, this time in Ottoman Turkey during the reign of Sultan Ahmed III (r. 1703–30) and especially the years from 1718 when the sultan's son-in-law Ibrahim Pasha of Nevshehir shared the reins of power as grand vizier. The country that had given Europe the tulip now suffered the consequences of its own obsession with this most fateful of flowers. Later historians called it '*Lâle Devri*' ('the Tulip Era') to reflect the floral preoccupations and cultural excesses of the sultan and his grand vizier, whose shared passion for the tulip coloured every aspect of Ottoman public life.

The two men were well suited to each other. Cultured, hedonistic and exceptionally greedy, the sultan left affairs of state to his grand vizier, devoting himself instead to pleasure and to a series of construction projects in a style that blended Ottoman baroque with French rococo. Mosques, mausoleums and fountains sprang up all over Istanbul, while new palaces (*yalis*) with their kiosks and fine gardens turned the waterfronts of the Bosphorus and the Golden Horn into an earthly paradise. Refined and cultured in his turn, Ibrahim Pasha looked to satisfy his sultan's prodigal whims, bringing an initial peace to the Ottoman Empire and making overtures to the West that caused resentment among more conservative elements of society, as did his tight grip on the machinery of state.

With the advent of Ibrahim Pasha, the tulip came to symbolize the continuous festivities and extravagances of Sultan Ahmed III's court. The flower had by now transformed itself into the elegant almond shape prescribed by Sultan Ahmed III's chief florist, Seyh Mehmed Lâlezarî, its tepals stretched into daggers with pointed tips. For a century or more it had been the task of the sultan's chief florist to oversee the raising of new tulips and narcissi, presiding over a council of expert florists who examined the new cultivars, selecting and naming only those judged to be faultless, and entering their details in the council's catalogue. Unlike Dutch cultivars, new varieties rarely received the name of their grower, but rather celebrated the tulip's grace or distinctive features, such as 'Slim One of the Rose Garden', 'Scarlet Swallow', 'Light of Paradise' and 'Bringer of Joy'.

In his manual of flowers (*Mizanü 'l-Ezhar*), Seyh Mehmed Lâlezarî set out twenty rules governing the perfect tulip. In essence, these required that its six petals should be long and equal in length, neither jagged nor double, the outer and inner segments closing neatly to conceal both filaments and blotches. Colours should be pure and clear, and only white was allowed for the background of variegated sorts (rarely shown in tulip albums, so perhaps less prized). Further rules covered pollen (which should not soil the flower); stems (long and strong); bulbs (neither too large nor too small); and leaves (long but not so long as to hide the flower).

In all, some 1,500 'Istanbul tulips' were recorded. Grown by only a handful of tulip enthusiasts, these have now completely disappeared. As in Europe, prices began to rise dramatically: a single bulb of the much coveted cultivar 'Mahbud' ('Beloved') might fetch between 500 and 1,000 Ottoman gold coins and, to prevent speculation, the state began officially to control prices by issuing fixed price lists. For the two years 1726 and 1727, when the number of varieties listed increased from 239 to 306, the most expensive bulb was 'Nize-i Rummânî',

'Pomegranate Lance', priced at a mere 7.5 Ottoman gold coins.

No such attempt was made to curb the flamboyance of the sultan's tulip festivities, however. At tulip time, Ahmed III would proceed majestically to his palaces built on the edge of the water, accompanied by mass promenades of the people. Barges sailed to the new Sa'dabad palace on the Golden Horn, built to French plans, and to other places of recreation. Most famous of these was the Ciraghan, the 'Palace of Candles' on the European side of the Bosphorus, begun by Sultan Murad IV for his daughter and magnificently reconstructed by Ibrahim Pasha for his wife, the sultan's daughter. The sultan came here often to enjoy the festivities, when small night lights illuminated the tulip gardens, and tortoises with candles on their backs meandered through the flowers. In the sultan's own tulip garden, guests were required to wear costumes that harmonized with the flowers; one night the women of the harem played at shopkeepers, serving the sultan as their only shopper. Out of season the festivities continued unabated, and the sultan's palace was adorned with tulips and pinks even at the height of winter.

Such unbridled and unpopular extravagance could not last, especially as the empire itself was beginning to crumble. Outright revolt was finally provoked in September 1730 after Persia had regained land occupied by the Turks, and Persian soldiers massacred a Turkish garrison stationed at Tabriz. The sultan and his grand vizier were both on holiday and Ibrahim Pasha's two sons-in-law were busy tending their gardens on the Bosphorus. The court did not return for another two days. Fearing for his own skin, the sultan eventually ordered the strangling of the grand vizier and his sons-in-law but it was too late; the sultan himself was forced to abdicate in favour of his nephew, Mahmud I, who had the ringleaders of the revolt executed in turn.

The tulip, so inextricably identified with the excesses of the sultan's regime, had played its course. The gardens and palaces of recreation were all destroyed, and although the tulip would return to Istanbul – and even now is celebrated in an annual festival, when Gülhane Park below the Topkapi Palace glows with masses of bowl-shaped and pointy tulips, and the Bosphorus at Emirgan echoes to the sound of concerts and folk dances that keep alive a memory of the sultan's fabulous festivities – a European visitor to Istanbul in the early 1930s reported that 'the cult of the Tulip has gone'. Ibrahim Pasha's famous garden was turned into a Ford car factory, and nothing was left of the Ciraghan or 'the quaint old wooden overhanging Yalis, with their dainty gardens which skirted the shores of the Bosphorus, from the Marmora to the Black Sea'.

T HESE TWO OUTBREAKS of tulip fever, one Dutch, one Turkish, reveal the flower's extraordinary power to attract devotees through beauty alone. While Ottoman culture had embraced the tulip as a symbol of Paradise, touched with divinity, in Europe it was generally stripped of religious associations; and when the apothecary Thomas Johnson equated tulips with the 'lilies of the field' of Christ's Sermon on the Mount, it was on account of their 'wondrous beautie' and 'infinite varietie of colour', greater than that possessed by any other sort of flower.

Yet dissenting voices were raised even then, perhaps because the much vaunted tulip is curiously hard to love. Resplendent and dazzling on the one hand, cultivated tulips can also appear stiff and unbending, a masculine sort of flower in contrast to the feminine softness of the rose. The tulip showed this other face in *Antheologia, or the Speech of Flowers*, a tiny anonymous work that appeared during the strait-laced Commonwealth years under Oliver Cromwell. Delicately subversive in tone and generally attributed to the lukewarm royalist Thomas Fuller, best known for his *Worthies of England*, it contains a light-hearted dialogue between the flowers of a garden in Thessalonia, then under Turkish occupation.

First to speak was the rose, lamenting that she had been displaced by the tulip, despite her own acknowledged precedence 'under the *Patent* of a double *Sence, Sight, smell*' and her even more sovereign virtues when dead, in curing a host of ailments with her cordials and conserves. What is this upstart tulip, asked the rose, but 'a wellcomplexion'd stink, an ill favour wrapt up in pleasant colours'? As for its use in medicine, no physician had honoured it with a mention, or a Greek or Latin name. And yet 'this is that which filleth all Gardens, hundreds of pounds being given for the root thereof, whilst I the *Rose*, am neglected and contemned, and conceived beneath the honour of noble hands, and fit only to grow in the gardens of Yeomen'.

The tulip's reply was suitably haughty, dismissing the rose's complaint as that of a mere vegetable, which should not presume to raise itself above the judgement of *'Rationable* creatures'. Surely men were the best judges of the 'valew of *Flowers'*, said the tulip, and while no healing virtues had yet been discovered, that did not mean it had none.

And this I am confident of, that *Nature* would never have hung out so gorgious a signe, if some guest of quality had not been lodged therein; surely my *leaves* [petals], had never been *feathered* with such variety of *colours*, (which hath proclaimed me the King of all Lillies) had not some strange vertue, whereof the world is yet ignorant, been treasured up therein.

In the debate that followed, the violet upheld the rose's complaint; the flowers had paid tribute to the rose as 'our Prime and principall' for as long as they could remember, while the tulip had been in gardens for sixty years at most. A native of open fields, of reputed Syrian extraction, it was little better than 'a gentler sort of weed'. By solemn vote, the flowers concluded that the tulip should be rooted out of the garden and cast on the dunghill as a foreign interloper.

B UT THE TULIP was not quite finished. Although the rose would eventually regain her crown, fantastically coloured tulips retained a British following as one of the original florists' flowers grown by dedicated flower fanciers, first under the aegis of florists' societies and later in the floriculture of the Victorian age, which flourished at all levels in society, from the gentry to the labouring classes, spawning societies dedicated to horticulture in general and to particular classes of flowers. It was to be the tulip's last great reincarnation.

In use since the 1620s at least, the term 'florist' then referred to

PAPÁVER SOMNÍFERUM. *WHITE POPPY.* ☉

G. Harell. Del. Pub.ᵈ by W Baxter Botanic Garden Oxford. C. Mathews. Sc.

An opium poppy (*Papaver somniferum*) from *British Phaenogamous Botany* on British flowering plants (1834–43) by Scotsman William Baxter, Curator of the Oxford Botanic Garden.

LEFT: In *Beata Beatrix* (c.1864–1870), Dante Gabriel Rossetti portrays his dead wife, Elizabeth Siddal, as Dante's Beatrice Portinari; its ghostly opium poppy hints at Siddal's death from a laudanum overdose.

BELOW: Detail showing red and white roses and a prominent red peony in Martin Schongauer's *Madonna of the Rose Bower* (1473), painted for the Church of St Martin in Colmar, Alsace.

A bouquet of roses (1805) painted by Dr Robert John Thornton and engraved by Richard Earlom, Thornton's only painting for his flamboyant *Temple of Flora, or Garden of Nature*.

A lady holds a bowl of rose flowers in a Mughal miniature,
c. 1700–40, from an album given to Lord Clive of India.

Five tulips showing the bowl-shaped flowers favoured by European tastes,
from Basilius Besler's *Hortus Eystettensis* of 1613.

An exquisitely elongated 'Istanbul tulip' from an Ottoman tulip
album of 1725, when Turkish tulip fever raged.

Pierre-Joseph Redouté's Lady's slipper orchid (*Cypripedium calceoleus*) with its characteristic pout, from his monumental *Les Liliacées* (1802–16).

Cattleya Orchid and Three Brazilian Hummingbirds (1871) by Martin Johnson Heade – the orchid worn by Odette de Crécy in Marcel Proust's *À la Recherche du Temps Perdu*.

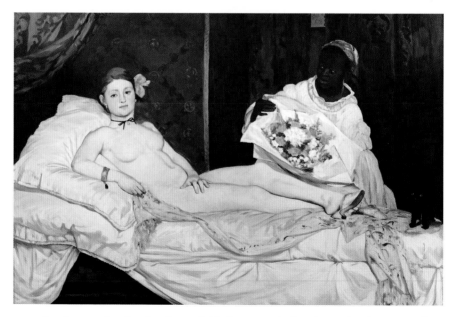

Announcing her profession by the orchid she wears in her hair, the *demi-mondaine* in Edouard Manet's *Olympia* caused a scandal when first exhibited at the 1865 Paris Salon.

enthusiasts who grew flowers for their beauty rather than their utility, much like the amateur flower lovers in Clusius's circle. They concentrated on certain flowers only, which they grew to defined standards, testing their skills in competition with their fellows. The original florists' flowers (tulips, carnations, anemones and ranunculuses) were later joined by auriculas, hyacinths, polyanthuses, pinks and, in the 1830s, by pansies and dahlias. All shared common characteristics: their flowers were circular in outline, bearing smooth-edged petals that were neither fringed nor jagged, neat if double and variegated whenever possible. All were capable of producing seed and of vegetative propagation, allowing their growers to develop and reproduce new kinds.

Britain's florists' societies were following the lead set by similar Dutch societies, convened to hold 'sweet Conversation and pleasant Consortship' under the protective eye of St Dorothea, patron saint of flower lovers. First recorded in the 1630s in Norwich, home to successive waves of Huguenot exiles from the Low Countries and France, British florists' feasts reached their peak in the 1770s and 1780s. Gatherings were held in taverns, like the Dutch tulip auctions, and the winning flowers passed around the dinner table. But by the end of the century, the feasts had descended into drinking parties, their decline further hastened by the economic gloom cast by the Napoleonic Wars.

Interest in florists' flowers remained high nonetheless, especially in tulips, which British growers had begun to cultivate from seed instead of relying on stock imported from Holland and France. Southern growers at first held sway, charging prices for new varieties that went beyond the pockets of working-class growers further north; by 1820 their tulips had practically beaten the Dutch tulip into second place, or so it was claimed. But from about 1840, growers in the north and the Midlands began producing seedlings of note, and by 1880, this 'gorgeous flower', once held in high esteem in Britain and throughout continental Europe, was 'now little grown south of the Trent or north of the Tweed'.

Florists' naturally competitive instincts provided the spur to such developments. Following the lead set by the Horticultural Society of London (today the Royal Horticultural Society), provincial horticultural societies sprang up around the country, organizing competitive shows for head gardeners, florists and cottagers, and presenting the winners with silver spoons accompanied by much patronizing comment. With competition came the codification of rules by which standards could be judged, much as the sultan's chief florist had dictated the rules for tulips at the time of Ahmed III, and much as earlier authorities such as Philip Miller had attempted informally.

First to define the standard for tulips and other florists' flowers, in 1832, was the vituperative George Glenny, founder of the *Horticultural Journal*, who claimed credit for declaring the perfect shape for a tulip flower to be a one-third portion of a hollow ball, complaining afterwards that 'having done so, I had at first half a dozen mongrels yelping at my heels, against my decision; and as soon as the public would have it so, they turned round, and described the same thing, with unimportant deviations, *as their own*'. Ignoring the self-coloured 'breeder' tulips, Glenny's rules dealt with the all-important matters of form, purity and markings for the three main kinds of show tulips: roses (crimson, pink or scarlet on a white ground); bybloemens (purple, lilac or black on a white ground); and bizarres (any coloured marking on a yellow ground). How the colours broke was crucial. Feathered flowers were to have a close, even feathering around the petal, forming an unbroken edge when expanded, while flowers with a central flame only were to have no colours breaking through to the petal's edge. The ground in all flowers, whether white or yellow, was to be clear and distinct, and the least stain, even at the bottom of a petal, would render a tulip 'comparatively valueless'. This last rule placed Glenny firmly in the camp of southern growers, who hated the smudged bottoms allowed by judges from the north.

For all the judges' disagreements, the old-fashioned tulip was the perfect florists' flower. Naturally inclined towards variegated markings, florists adored the marbled effects seen to perfection in flower paintings from the Dutch Golden Age, and the wayward variegations of flaming and feathering that were still not properly understood. As seedlings take several years to flower, and as they do not come true from seed, producing a tulip with perfectly feathered markings demanded the skills and perseverance of an alchemist. It was a form of tulip fever all over again, a lottery in which everyone hoped to emerge the winner.

The old florists' tulips enjoyed their greatest success from the mid-1800s until about 1870 when their fortunes began to ebb, displaced in the public's affection by the new styles of wilder gardening championed by figures such as William Robinson. Author of *The English Flower Garden* and the hugely influential *The Wild Garden*, Robinson nonetheless found space in his garden for late-flowering tulips descended from *T. gesneriana*, which he called a 'very handsome plant in the wild state', and he drew attention to 'some really beautiful plants' among the wild tulips, including *T. clusiana*, which he described as 'delicate in tone, humble in stature, and modestly pretty in appearance'.

But the alchemical tricks used to encourage tulips to break were scorned, and florists' tulips 'fell into neglect and obloquy'. One who mourned their passing was Sir Sacheverell Sitwell, from the Derbyshire Sitwells of Renishaw Hall, who, despite his love of the beautiful wild species 'so deservedly popular' in the 1930s, wanted gardeners to plant a bed of old English tulips. The only problem was expense: at about a shilling a bulb, he calculated in 1939, this might cost some £8–10, or anything up to £1,760 in today's money. As ever with the tulip, money has the final word. Perhaps we should not be too surprised that the tulip has left little trace in western literature, beyond a rather flat poem by Théophile Gautier, and better ones by more recent poets, such as Sylvia Plath's upsetting tulips that watch her on her hospital bed, snagging the ambient air and eating her oxygen, and James Fenton's yellow tulips that remind him of love's ambush in a summery wood.

*

TODAY, THE TULIP trade is again big business. Worldwide, the flower bulb industry is estimated to have an annual turnover of more than $1 billion, with tulips and lilies the most popular bulbs. Since Turkish tulips first arrived on Dutch soil, the Netherlands has transformed itself into the world's leading bulb producer, topping the list of tulip-producing countries with its estimated 87 per cent share of global production by area. This translates annually into more than four million Dutch tulip bulbs, of which just over half are used for cut-flower production at home and abroad. Tulips are grown commercially in fourteen other countries, headed by Japan, France, the US and Poland. Turkey does not appear in global production lists, although it is named as one of three countries with emerging programmes for flower bulbs, alongside Brazil and Chile.

Now that the breaking virus is understood, commercial growers have laboured to breed uncertainty out of their stock, hence the uniformity of tulip fields at flowering time when almost one-third of the Dutch acreage is taken up by just eighteen cultivars. You can still find heart-stoppingly beautiful wild varieties, but the elongated Istanbul tulips of *Lâle Devri* linger only in the memory. As for the flared and feathered tulips that possessed the burgers of Haarlem, Amsterdam and Alkmaar, to see them at their best you may need to seek out the modern-day equivalents to the old florists' societies, dedicated to the breeding and showing of the old varieties.

Britain has one such tulip society left: the Wakefield and North of England Tulip Society, founded in 1836. In May 2012 I attended its annual show, held in an anonymous community hall on the outskirts of Wakefield, bright with patriotic bunting. Here, for an afternoon, I could imagine myself among the curious tulip fanciers of old, peering myopically at exquisite single blooms thrust into beer bottles and marshalled into long neat rows on a trestle table running the length of the room: plain-coloured breeders, and flamed and feathered old English tulips, judged according to their esoteric categories of bizarres, bybloemens and roses, in a buzz of restrained rivalry and understated congratulation. Lovers of old-fashioned tulips flock to this event from all over Britain and from as far afield as Holland and Sweden, to show and to admire. Their tulips are as beautiful and as strange as anything the Dutch masters could produce and, had this been an auction, I know I would have parted with my money – doubtless more than was wise.

— 7 —

Orchid

The air was thick, wet, steamy and larded with the cloying smell of tropical
orchids in bloom . . . The plants filled the place, a forest of them, with
nasty meaty leaves and stalks like the newly washed fingers of dead men.
They smelled as overpowering as boiling alcohol under a blanket.

RAYMOND CHANDLER, *The Big Sleep*

I KNEW TROPICAL ORCHIDS before I had properly encountered our native British ones. When I was eight, my family moved to Malaya as it then was, to a satellite new town outside the capital, Kuala Lumpur, where we grew orchids in the garden, almost certainly varieties of the Scorpion orchid from the Arachnis family. They looked suspiciously like giant spiders so I gave them a wide berth, preferring the intoxicating fragrance of frangipani, the flame-red flowers of hibiscus and the graceful casuarina trees that hid the bulldozed wasteland beyond the fence.

My feelings towards orchids remain ambivalent. On my first visit to a London orchid show I found their infinite variety bewildering. They were just so impossibly different, sourced from all corners of the globe, many sporting bizarre appendages uniquely evolved to secure the plant's continued survival. (Orchids were, unsurprisingly, Charles Darwin's favourite flowers.) My companions had arrived early at the show, keen to purchase a Peruvian Slipper orchid that had been smuggled into Florida, costing its 'discoverer' two years' probation and a $1,000 fine, but which was now legally on sale. The plastic bag they showed me contained a few strappy leaves and roots like pasty earthworms, for which they had paid £100. I felt mystified, increasingly bemused by the obsessiveness I witnessed in those around me: one man collected only *Bulbophyllum*, a diverse but relatively unprepossessing genus, of which he owned more than 450 species and forms. Here was tulip mania's mad singularity of purpose transferred to a protean flower that encompasses the exquisitely delicate and the downright

ugly, among them varieties sprouting monstrous lips and unidentifi-
able dangly bits ('What can they all be for?' asked John Lindley of the
spirals dangling from a bizarre Mexican import, *Cycnoches maculatum*),
and I felt vaguely defeated by a passion I did not share.

I persevered, however, taught myself the most popular orchid
families and by my second orchid show was at least able to recog-
nize some of them as acquaintances if not friends. Others disturb
me still with their rude contrivances while the cloned supermarket
orchids leave me cold. You want to prod them to check they are real,
and knowing that some can flower for weeks is not necessarily in
their favour.

But the more I studied the orchid, the more intrigued I became by
its evident duality. You can see this most clearly in the wildly different perceptions of orchids in eastern and western cultures. Since the
time of Confucius at least, the orchid in China has been a plant of great
refinement and virtue, revered for growing modestly in inaccessible
places where its beauty is largely unseen. The West, by contrast, has
a much earthier view of the orchid, equating it primarily with sex,
and not especially wholesome sex either. Even their names betray
this duality: '*lan*', the Chinese word for orchid, referred originally to
fragrant flowers used to ward off evil spirits, while the West settled on
'*orchis*', the Greek word for testicles, which the tubers of terrestrial
orchids are said to resemble.

Might the power of the orchid reside in the tension created by these
wildly conflicting views of the world's strangest flower?

TODAY, THE ORCHID family (Orchidaceae) is one of the largest
plant families on earth with the greatest diversity of flora. The
Royal Botanic Gardens at Kew estimate there are some 25,000 species in 850 genera, compared with the rose's paltry 150 species in a
single main genus, *Rosa*; hybrid orchids add at least 155,000 more recognized varieties, as of March 2012, increasing at the rate of 250–350
per month. While some species have disappeared due to over-col-
lecting or the destruction of their habitats, between 200–500 new

species are identified each year. In November 2011, for instance, the Dutch orchid specialist Ed de Vogel discovered the world's only truly night-flowering orchid, *Bulbophyllum nocturnum*, in a forest zone earmarked for logging on an island off Papua New Guinea. The photograph accompanying press reports shows three greenish-yellow sepals arranged around the flower's miniscule petals from which dangle long, greyish-green appendages that bear an uncanny resemblance to the fruiting bodies of certain slime moulds also found in the region. Botanists speculate that the orchid is pollinated by night-feeding midges tricked into thinking they are landing on food: ingenious, certainly, but hardly pretty.

Their current wide distribution suggests that orchids existed on earth before the continents began to split away from the original land mass of Pangaea, at least 100 million years ago. From their original home – almost certainly tropical – they drifted away with the tectonic plates: *Dendrobium* orchids (one of the largest genera) spreading throughout China, India, South-East Asia, Malaysia, Australia and New Zealand; *Vanilla* orchids (the family's main economically useful plant) ending up in tropical America, Africa and Malaysia; the Slipper orchids, *Cypripedium*, travelling to North America, Europe, Russia, China and Japan but not crossing south of the equator; the related *Paphiopedilum* extending through the tropical and subtropical regions of southern China, India, South-East Asia and down into Indonesia; and their *Phragmipedium* relatives crossing through Central America into Panama and the Andes into South America. Some – possibly younger – genera remain more localized, such as the ever-popular *Cattleya* orchids, found only in South and Central America; today, wild orchids inhabit all continents except Antarctica, from Alaska down to Tierra del Fuego.

In their growth habits, orchids are either terrestrial, producing underground tubers, or epiphytic, growing on the trunks and branches of trees and drawing water and nutrients from the air through aerial roots; they may also be lithophytic (growing on rocks), saprophytic (living off dead organic matter), or entirely subterranean, such as the rare and threatened *Rhizanthella* orchid, endemic to Western Australia, considered such a curiosity when it was first discovered in 1928 that wax models were exhibited at scientific meetings and museums throughout the state. In size, orchids range from a couple of milli- metres in diameter to a ton in mass; and they grow either vertically as a single stem (monopodial) or laterally with pseudobulbs and mul- tiple shoots along a horizontal rhizome (sympodial). Uniting all the multiplicity of orchid types and forms is the structure of their flowers: an outer whorl of three sepals, similar in substance and colour to the petals, and an inner whorl of two lateral petals plus a third, greatly modified petal, which forms the lip or labellum that gives many var- ieties their distinctive pout.

ORCHIDS HAVE THE longest history of cultivation in China, which boasts by some counts upwards of 1,000 species spread over more than 150 different genera. Classic Chinese varieties include the cool-growing *Cymbidium* orchids such as *C. ensifolium*, *C. goeringii* and *C. floribundum*, which grow throughout the Yangtze River Valley. The flowers of Chinese orchids are generally small and yellowish-green, often marked with purple streaks or spots, and delicately perfumed 'with the scent of kings'. In fact, the Chinese word for orchid, 'lan', which derives from the verb 'lan' meaning to check or ward off, re- ferred originally to several fragrant plants worn by Chinese youths to keep evil spirits at bay. Only when scholars became familiar with *Cymbidium* orchids (*chih-lan*) as houseplants did they codify the word in writing, linking it to a particular flower but missing the flower's lin- guistic associations.

Chinese reverence for the orchid dates back at least to the writings of the great scholar and philosopher Confucius (551–479 BCE), when political and military power had migrated southwards into what is now Zhejiang province and the adjacent areas, where *Cymbidium* and other orchids grew wild on the steep rocky slopes and among the bamboo woods. Confucius compared the superior man (*chün-tzu*) to the wild orchid; for just as the orchid spreads its fragrance when it blooms unseen and unappreciated in the deepest valley, so the superior man continues to strive for self-discipline and virtue even when living unrecognized in poverty or distress. Being with virtuous people, said Confucius, is like entering a hall of orchids, *chih-lan*. 'In the course of time one becomes accustomed to the superior ways of life and gets used to fragrance.'

Basking in Confucius's approval, the orchid found its way into poetry as a metaphor for virtue and loyalty, admired above all other flowers by Ch'ü Yüan (339–278 BCE), one of the authors of the *Songs of the South*. It stood in contrast to the aggressive and persistent weed, *hsiao-ai* (artemisia): 'Rather be repressed like an orchid and broken like jade, than be the flower of an artemisia' was a saying of China's first imperial dynasty. Blossoming in out-of-the-way places, the orchid came also to represent womanly elegance, joyous elation and restrained nobility; finding a lovely courtesan living in a secret place was like 'finding a delicate orchid in a secluded valley'. The orchid's modesty and restraint also appealed to Buddhist sensibilities, as in this poem written in the eleventh century by Su Shih, a major poet of the Song era:

> In the quiet valley I can see no orchids growing –
> By accident, a gentle breeze betrays their presence.
> It is a liberating fragrance, pure and unsullied –
> One sniff of it is enough to give enlightenment.

Huang T'ing-chien, another Song poet and the exact contemporary of Su Shih, considered the orchid's fragrance pre-eminent, worthy of the title 'national fragrance'. 'It thrives in the forest,' he declared, its perfume undiminished by the absence of an audience, 'and it survives the snow and frost without undergoing any change in its nature.'

Despite the high esteem accorded to the orchid, it appeared relatively late in Chinese art; only the lotus was seen with any frequency from the time of the First Emperor onwards. Paintings of the Tang dynasty (618–906) famously captured landscapes with glimpses of distant trees, shrubs, bamboos and leaves, but flowers were largely absent. A culture of gardens and flowers assumed importance only in the Song dynasty (960–1279), when flower-and-bird paintings were especially popular; but few Song paintings of orchids survive. An outstanding exception is Ma Lin's *Orchid* of the thirteenth century, meticulously rendered in subtle shades of lavender, white and malachite green, which transcends realism to hint at the flower's implicit qualities of movement and stillness, blossoming and dying, fragrance and emptiness. After the Song dynasty fell, orchids assumed a subversive role in monochrome paintings by the minor artist Cheng Ssu-hsiao, whose solitary orchids float above an empty background, refusing to root themselves in soil stolen by the Mongol invaders.

Ink-and-wash orchids were admirably adapted to express the Spirit or Breath of the Tao (*Ch'i*), and were favoured especially by the literati and women artists 'in whose work the *shên* (divine) quality seemed to float across the painting'. Helping to develop the painters' spiritual resources were much later manuals such as *The Mustard Seed Garden Manual of Painting*, whose first complete edition of 1701 included orchids among the 'Four Gentlemen of Flowers'; these relate to the Confucian virtues of the superior man and to the four seasons: Orchid (spring), Bamboo (summer), Chrysanthemum (autumn) and Plum (winter).

According to the manual's authors, the secret of painting orchids lies in the circulation of the spirit (*ch'i yün*). The painter's hand should move like lightning, drawing four leaves crossed by a fifth and placing flowers naturally in a variety of positions. 'Stems and leaves should have movement like the tail of a soaring phoenix; the calyx should be light as a dragonfly.' The flowers' fragrance, too, could be conveyed by a quick flick of the wrist. 'Through brush and ink it is possible to transmit their essence.'

Just as eastern gardeners appreciated an orchid's leaves as much as its flowers, so Chinese painters learned first to draw orchid leaves, which should be 'painted in a few strokes, and they should have a floating grace in rhythm with the wind, (moving like a goddess) in

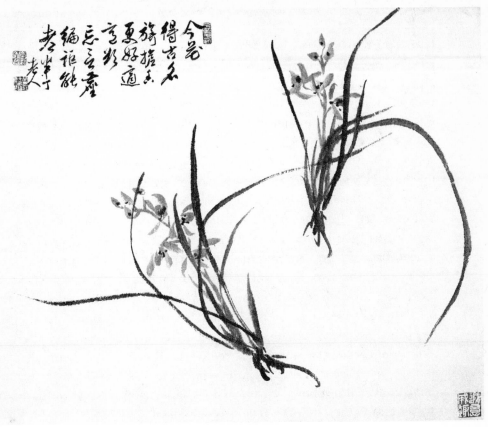

Orchid in the traditional style by the noted Chinese
flower painter, Chen Banding (d. 1970).

rainbow-hued skirt with a moon-shaped jade ornament swinging from
her belt. No breath of ordinary air touches them.' Having mastered the
leaves, the novice progressed to the flowers. Here, the critical skill was
learning how to dot the stamen at the orchid's heart, likened to 'drawing in the eyes of a beautiful woman. As the rippling fields of orchids of
the River Hsiang give life to the whole countryside, so dotting the heart
of the flower adds the finishing touch. The whole essence of the flower
is contained in that small touch.'

Chinese gardeners applied the same sensibility and dedication to
growing their favourite orchids. The oldest extant treatise on orchids –
by Chao Shih-kêng in 1233 – described twenty-two orchids in two basic

types: purple-flowered and white-flowered. As well as *Cymbidium* species, these are thought to include *Aerides*, *Calanthe*, *Habenaria* and *Phajus* varieties. In less than fifteen years another treatise appeared, by Wang Kuei-hsüeh, with thirty-seven varieties. Cultivating orchids was then very popular among the leisured classes, and largely followed the beliefs and practices of the Taoist religion. A manuscript from about this time – repeatedly copied by Chinese orchid enthusiasts for the next seven hundred years – evolved a monthly programme of orchid care, developed from the Taoist practice of casting horoscopes and expressed in diagrams that reflected seasonal weather changes, the straight lines representing the Yang principle (male: sunlight and warmth) and the broken lines the Yin (female: shade and coolness).

The Chinese taste for orchids arrived in Japan a thousand years or more ago, introduced by returning Japanese monks and by Chinese monks who had settled in Japan. Although orchids never quite reached the same level of popularity as in China, particular varieties appealed to different sectors of Japan's markedly feudal society – to the intelligentsia and those touched by Chinese culture; to rich merchants who craved unusual or showy leaves; and to the shogun class of military overlords and their territorial barons or *daimyos*.

In the mid-nineteenth century, for instance, the nobility favoured varieties of *Neofinetia falcata* with speckled or striped leaves, following the lead of the shogun Tokugawa Ienari, who ordered his *daimyos* to collect exceptional varieties and held gatherings to admire their markings. Pots were covered with gold and silver nets, and admirers held paper masks over their lips to avoid breathing over the orchids. On their biennial journeys to the capital, *daimyos* were reputed to take orchids with them in their palanquins, to savour their exquisite fragrance. Some two hundred *Neofinetia* varieties were then in cultivation, perhaps twice as many as now.

Today, the Japanese differentiate between western orchids (*Yo-Ran*, principally varieties improved from flowering tropical orchids) and oriental orchids (*Toyo-Ran*, principally derived from *Cymbidium* species native to the temperate regions of eastern Asia, and also the genera *Dendrobium*, *Goodyera* and *Neofinetia*). Two epiphytic *Dendrobium* orchids are native to Japan, among them *D. moniliforme*, known to the German naturalist and physician Engelbert Kaempfer, who visited the Japanese island of Deshima towards the end of the seventeenth century, when Japan was largely closed to foreigners (see Chapter 2). And orchids continue to play a supporting role in Japanese flower arranging, viewed as suitably elegant although not among the traditional stars of plum, peach, cherry, azalea, peony, wisteria, iris, morning glory, lotus, chrysanthemum and maple.

AFTER THE GRACE and reverence with which orchids are greeted in China and Japan, the western view of the orchid comes as a rude surprise. Ever since the ancient Greeks, westerners have looked at the orchid and thought of sex, a connection traditionally ascribed to Theophrastus, who included an 'orchis' in the final book of his seminal *Enquiry into Plants*, which examined the medicinal properties of herbs. This book's authorship is now disputed; while it may contain an original core by the man whom westerners revere as the father of botany, it lacks the detailed plant descriptions and classification for which Theophrastus is justly famous. Whoever wrote it, the author was interested not in the orchid as a plant but in how it affects sexual intercourse – an idea considered so shocking early in the twentieth century that the standard translation by Sir Arthur Hort, a former fellow of Trinity College, Cambridge, omits the offending passage altogether.

What the missing text says, in effect, is that some plants have the power to increase both fertility and infertility. In the case of the orchid, the larger tuberous root was said to make a person more effective in intercourse when given in the milk of a mountain-reared goat, while the smaller root would hinder and prevent intercourse. It is an idea that recurs endlessly in herbals of the ancient world right through to the seventeenth century, usually drawing on minor variations found in the *De Materia Medica* of Dioscorides, which appeared in the first century: that if the orchid's greater root is eaten by men, they will beget men children, and if the lesser root is eaten by women, they will conceive girls. 'It is further storied,' wrote John Goodyer in his 1655 translation of Dioscorides, 'that ye women in Thessalia do give to drink with goates milk ye tenderer roote to provoke Venerie, & the dry root for ye suppressing, dissolving of Venerie', thus putting Thessalian women firmly in control of sexual relations.

Theophrastus and Dioscorides both called the plant an '*orchis*' after the Greek word for testicles, which the tubers of terrestrial orchids were said to resemble. Fool's Stones, Fox Stones, Dogstones, Goat's Stones, Sweet Cullions and Hares-bollocks were among the common names for wild orchids in sixteenth-century England – 'stones', 'cullions' and 'bollocks' meaning much the same thing. Sex featured in later Latin names, too. Linnaeus named the Slipper orchids *Cypripedium*, after Cyprus – an island sacred to the goddess of love – and '*pedilon*', the Greek word for slipper. More than a century later, the German bot-anist Ernst Hugo Heinrich Pfitzer retained the Venus/Aphrodite con-nection when he named the related genus *Paphiopedilum* after Paphos, Aphrodite's mythical birthplace on the island.

Dioscorides identified four varieties of orchid, including one he called *Saturion* or *Satyrium*, which bore leaves in threes similar to docks or lilies, but smaller and reddish:

It has a naked stalk, a foot long, a white flower similar to a lily, a bulbous root as big as an apple – red, but white within, similar to an egg, sweet to the taste and pleasant in the mouth. One ought to drink it in black hard wine for fever spasms, and use it if he wishes to lay with a woman. For they say that this also is an aphrodisiac.

In categorizing orchid tubers as aphrodisiacs, Dioscorides is mindful of the ancient Doctrine of Signatures, which attributed the power of plants to their physical form, but he did not restrict his orchid 'cures' to sexual ailments. Of an orchid similar to the Bee orchid, for instance, he noted that its roots could dissipate dropsy, clean ulcers and repress herpes, and that if smeared on the skin it would soothe

inflamed parts and repair fistulas. Sprinkled on dry it could stop a
tissue-eating disease, while drunk in wine it could heal the intestines.

China's very different perception of the orchid naturally produced a different reading. Of *Dendrobium* species found growing on
rocks, for instance, the sages reasoned that the plant must possess
unusual strength to draw nourishment from such hard material,
and that a medicine derived from such a plant would strengthen the
weak. In China's earliest pharmacopoeia, the *Shên Nung Pên Ts'ao
Ching* or *Divine Husbandman's Materia Medica*, roughly contemporary
with Dioscorides although drawing on an earlier oral tradition, the
Dendrobium orchid was credited with the power to heal internal injur-
ies and induce the power of Yin. It was also said that imbibing the drug
persistently in small quantities would stimulate the appetite and lead
to a long life.

But sex continued to dominate western perceptions of the orchid,
in botanical and medical descriptions and in its iconographic meanings. The wild orchid nestling against the unicorn's belly in the magnificent 'Unicorn Tapestries' of the southern Netherlands is clearly
intended as a symbol of fertility and procreation. Created in the high
Middle Ages, the tapestries show the hunt and capture of the unicorn, an allegory of Christ's death and resurrection, which by 1500
had become secularized as the lover's capture by his lady. The orchid
appears in the final tapestry, the 'Unicorn in Captivity', which shows
the unicorn-lover chained and fenced but happy in his confinement
against a backdrop teeming with symbols of fertility and wedded bliss:
bursting pomegranates, orchids, English bluebells, bistort, carnations, stock-gillyflowers, columbines, St Mary's thistle, even a little
frog, renowned for its noisy mating.

Slowly, however, as the science of botany developed, interest shifted
from the orchid's claimed influence over human sexuality to how
the flower reproduced itself – a mystery for most plants until late in
the seventeenth century, but particularly baffling for orchids, whose
seeds are microscopic, and most orchids, notably the terrestrials,
need specific fungi to survive beyond germination. The German

proto-botanist and Lutheran minister Hieronymus Bock (a surname Latinized as Tragus) speculated that orchids produced not seed but a fine dust, believing that they arose naturally in fields and meadows where the semen of birds and beasts had fallen to the ground. The German Jesuit Athanasius Kircher concurred that orchids appeared where livestock had been brought together for mating, much as Virgil's bees and wasps had sprung forth from the carcasses of bulls and horses.

All the while, the number of known orchids was growing at a bewildering rate. The royal apothecary John Parkinson listed seventy-seven native or European varieties in his herbal of 1640, *Theatrum Botanicum*, which he tried to bring into 'some methodicall order' by grouping them into separate ranks, but placing the Lady's slipper orchid elsewhere. A century later, the gardener Philip Miller identified twenty orchids that deserved a place in every good garden for the 'extreme Oddness and Beauty of their Flowers', despite difficulties in transplanting them from the wild. Each bore a colourful common name, such as the 'Lizard Flower, or Great Goat-stones', the 'Common Humble Bee *Satyrion*, or Bee-flower', and the 'Handed *Orchis*, with a greenish Flower by *some call'd* The Frog *Orchis*'. These last names came from the flower's astonishingly varied third petal or lip, 'sometimes representing a naked Man, sometimes a Butter-fly, a Drone, a Pigeon, an Ape, a Lizard, a Parrot, a Fly, and other Things'.

As the eighteenth century progressed, the mechanics of sexual reproduction in plants became better understood; the great Swedish botanist Carl Linnaeus even tried to introduce a classification system for plants based entirely on sexual characteristics (it proved inadequate, unlike his enduring system of binomial plant names). Having already written a monograph on orchids, Linnaeus condensed their number to sixty-two species in eight separate genera, which he assigned to the Gynandria class in which a flower's male sex organs are attached to and standing on the female. Orchids were still considered a dangerous subject for polite society, however. When Charles Darwin's grandfather Erasmus attempted to introduce Linnaean botany to an audience of young ladies in his heavy-footed poem *The Loves of the*

Plants, he included the sullen opium poppy (see Chapter 4) but stayed silent on the more obviously sexualized orchid.

It was Charles Darwin himself who cracked the sexual puzzle of the orchid, using his study of the plant to prove his theory that plants favour fertilization by the pollen of another flower, rather than self-fertilization, and that the 'contrivances' by which orchids achieve this are 'as varied and almost as perfect as any of the most beautiful adaptations in the animal kingdom'. For twenty years he had watched native orchids growing in abundance around his Kentish home, commandeering family and friends to help in his observations and amassing vast amounts of data about the insects attracted to orchids, their role in transferring pollen from one flower to another, and those ingenious 'contrivances' developed by temperate and tropical orchids to achieve their goal of cross-pollination. One such example was the 'shooting mechanism' of *Catasetum* orchids, by which pollen is flung at the pollinator; another, the mimicry by which some orchids attract their pollinators. In a letter of October 1861 to Sir Joseph Hooker, then assistant director at Kew and himself an orchid aficionado, Darwin declared, 'I never was more interested in any subject in my life than this of Orchids.'

For Darwin, the orchid provided ample proof that living things were not created as an 'ideal type', fixed for all eternity according to the Omnipotent Creator's original plan, but rather that the 'now wonderfully changed structure of the flower is due to a long course of slow modification'. The whole purpose of the flower, in Darwin's view, was to produce seed, which orchids accomplished in 'vast profusion' – so many, in fact, that seeds from the great-grandchildren of just one plant of the Spotted orchid would 'clothe with one uniform green carpet the entire surface of the land throughout the globe'.

If Darwin celebrated the orchid's ingenuity in ensuring its own survival, another giant of nineteenth-century England was positively appalled by the flower: the art critic and social thinker John Ruskin, who exchanged visits with Darwin in the 1860s. No scientist himself, Ruskin judged Darwin 'delightful' but rejected his theory of natural selection and maintained that a seed's purpose was to produce the flower, not the other way round. For Ruskin, a flower's beauty, like everything in nature, was designed expressly for man's instruction. Far from sharing Darwin's fascination with orchids, he judged certain species 'definitely degraded, and, in aspect, malicious'.

One can only assume that the orchid's blatant sexuality lay at the root of Ruskin's dislike (his marriage to Effie Gray was, after all, annulled on the grounds that it was never consummated). In his one work devoted exclusively to flowers – the increasingly deranged *Proserpina, Studies of Wayside Flowers* – he banished all reference to orchids and Orchidaceae, renaming the family 'Ophrydae' from the Greek word '*ophrys*' or eyebrow. In place of testicles Ruskin saw 'the brow of an animal frowning' and 'the overshadowing casque of a helmet'; and in defiance of the rules of botany, he sought to reclassify his *Ophryds* into just three divisions: a group he called 'Contorta', found in English meadows and alpine pastures; a second group, 'Satyrium', for blooms of 'Satyric ugliness' that habitually dressed 'in livid and unpleasant colours', twisting their stalks and their prominent lower petal round and round, 'as a foul jester would put out his tongue'; and a third group of epiphytes he called 'Aeria' or airplants. In Ruskin's botany, plants with feminine names ending in 'a' could be either pretty or good (or both), but the neuter 'um' ending of plants such as Satyrium would 'always indicate some power either of active or suggestive evil . . . or a relation, more or less definite, to death'.

Poor Ruskin; rejecting the sexuality of flowers, he chose instead to see them as expressions of divine beauty – a beauty that he allowed to illuminate the deathly poppy but not these devilish orchids, which had no place in his world. As he wrote in 1875 to Kew's librarian and keeper of the herbarium, 'My feeling about the orchids is complicated with many moral and spiritual questions wholly overwhelming to me . . . I have notions which I dare not print for fear of the world's thinking me mad.'

Expunging the word 'orchid' from the botanical dictionary could not, however, mask orchids' extraordinary success at exciting desire in the pollinators they want to attract, and Ruskin's views were simply wrong. A good third of orchid species are thought to deceive their pollinators with false offers of sex or food. The garden writer Michael Pollan went to Sardinia in search of a certain type of Bee orchid, which mimics the appearance, scent and even the 'feel' of a female bee, but then ensures pollination by frustrating the bee's desires. 'The flower, in other words, traffics in something very much like metaphor. *This stands for that.* Not bad for a vegetable.'

D ARWIN AND RUSKIN were writing about orchids in the second half of the nineteenth century, when 'orchidelirium' had been raging fiercely in Britain and the West for several decades. Like tulip mania, the passion for orchids was fanned by scarcity and the desire to possess a plant of rare beauty. Added to this, orchids were notoriously difficult to grow; indeed, until their individual requirements were properly understood, exotic orchids were little more than curiosities, admired, perhaps, but beyond the capabilities of ordinary gardeners.

The first American orchid to arrive in Europe, as cured pods rather than growing plants, was vanilla (*Vanilla planifolia*), which the Spanish found in Mexico, where it was used to flavour chocolate, the Aztec ruler Moctezuma's favourite drink. According to an Aztec herbal of 1552, the dried flowers were also ground with other ingredients, placed inside a Mexican magnolia and hung about the neck as a charm to safeguard travellers. Even before the Spanish conquest, vanilla pods reportedly reached Europe as a perfuming agent, although it would be 300 years before vanilla was successfully transplanted to its current centres of production in Indonesia, Madagascar, China, Mexico, the Comoros and elsewhere. Clusius included the dried pods in a late work on exotic fruits and trees, having received a specimen from Hugh Morgan, apothecary to Queen Elizabeth I, but he provided little information about where it came from or what its uses were.

As the world gradually opened up to European inspection, doctors, naturalists, diplomats and priests travelling to the tropics sent back reports and sometimes dried herbarium specimens of more native

orchids: Hans Sloane from his travels in Jamaica (although he mistook the epiphytic orchids he saw for other plants); the Dutch colonial
administrator Hendrik van Rheede tot Drakenstein from the Malabar
coast of southern India; Engelbert Kaempfer from Japan and Java;
the Jesuit missionary Georg Joseph Kamel from the Philippines; and
the German botanist Georg Eberhard Rumphius from the Dutch East
Indies. The Dutch can also take credit for cultivating the first tropical orchid in Europe: a Caribbean orchid listed as an *Epidendrum* (the
name then given to all epiphytic orchids), introduced from Curaçao to
the Dutch garden of grand pensionary Casper Fagel, and handsomely
illustrated in Paul Hermann's *Paradisus Batavus* of 1698 – the first
woodcut of a tropical orchid to appear in Europe.

It would be more than thirty years before England succeeded in
flowering its first tropical orchid: a species now known as *Bletia
purpurea*, despatched from New Providence Island in the Bahamas
(sender not recorded) to the Quaker cloth merchant Peter Collinson.
Although the plant arrived in a desiccated condition, Collinson took
the tubers to Admiral Sir Charles Wager, who owned a fine garden of
exotics at Parsons Green in London. Wager had them mulched in a bed
of bark for the winter, and by the following summer they had produced
purple flowers. Philip Miller gives a confusing account of this particular orchid's provenance, suggesting that his own roots of the plant
had come from the Bahamas, Jamaica ('where the late Doctor *Houstoun*
found it growing plentifully on the Mountains') and from Collinson's
American plant hunter John Bartram in Pennsylvania, where it surely
would not have survived a winter outdoors.

But tropical orchids were nonetheless slow to enter cultivation
in Europe. Although Linnaeus had included orchids from Asia, the
Caribbean and South America in *Species Plantarum* (1753), those he
examined personally would almost all have been dried herbarium specimens. Records for the royal gardens at Kew show, by contrast, the
rate at which living orchids were gradually entering the collections
of wealthy patrons. In 1768 Princess Augusta, the Dowager Princess
of Wales, was growing just twenty-four sorts of orchid at Kew, mostly

European natives and much the same ones that Philip Miller had included in his *Gardeners Dictionary* of the same year. Twenty-one years later, George III's gardener William Aiton recorded a more impressive collection, with native orchids from Europe, North America, the Cape (despatched by Kew's first plant collector, Francis Masson), Canada, Newfoundland and the West Indies (*Bletia purpurea*, for example, which Aiton credits to Dr William Houston). Also included was *Phaius tankervilleae*, which came from China and was introduced in about 1778 by the Quaker plantsman Dr John Fothergill.

The great expansion in Kew's tropical orchids began during the tenure of Aiton's son William Townsend Aiton, whose updated *Hortus Kewensis* of 1810–13 contained thirty-two pages of native and foreign orchids, including forty-six tropical species from the West and East Indies, South America and Asia, and some twelve more from Australia and South Africa. Nearly all the tropical orchids were lowland or terrestrial species, as epiphytes could not survive the growing methods then employed.

Credit for introducing many of Kew's early tropical orchids goes to some of the great names in plant exploration and botanical imperialism: Sir Joseph Banks, who had travelled to Australia with Captain Cook and advised King George III on all matters scientific and horticultural; Vice Admiral William Bligh, whose concern for his precious cargo of breadfruit sparked mutiny on the *Bounty*; William Kerr, Kew's first resident plant collector in China; William Roxburgh, superintendent of Calcutta's Botanic Garden; and Gilbert Slater and Thomas Evans, both with East India Company connections and fine gardens of exotics on the outskirts of London.

With strange new orchids arriving from afar, orchid fever was slowly spreading among the upper stratum of society, fanned by a remarkable coincidence of factors at once technical, social, cultural and political. Technology and methods of cultivation were advancing, and gardeners began to realize that '"Rule of Thumb" succeeds not in growing orchids but in killing them', just as the strange, unearthly beauty of tropical orchids caught the fancy of rich collectors able to finance collecting expeditions around the globe and to grow their precious booty back home. Commerce played a part, too, as a small band of specialist nurseries financed collecting expeditions of their own: first Loddiges in Hackney; then James Veitch of Killerton, Exeter and later Chelsea; and from the 1870s, Frederick Sander at St Albans in Hertfordshire.

As with any craze, rumour and counter-rumour played their part. One of the earliest imported orchids to set the pulse racing was *Cattleya labiata*, reputedly collected by William Swainson in the Organ Mountains of Brazil in 1818 and sent as packing material around a consignment of other tropical plants to a renowned collector of exotics, Mr William Cattley of Barnet near London. Cattley was curious enough to plant his packing material, so the story goes, producing the first of the species to flower; when later collectors failed to find any trace of this finely coloured orchid – a pale lavender with a prominent crimson lip – it joined the list of supposedly 'lost orchids' that drove people wild.

In fact Swainson found his *Cattleya* a thousand miles north of Rio in Pernambuco, sending it on to William Jackson Hooker, who would shortly take up the chair of botany at Glasgow University before assuming the directorship of Kew. Hooker judged his *Cattleya* 'the most splendid, perhaps, of all Orchidaceous plants, which blossomed for the first time in Britain in the stove of my garden in Suffolk, during 1818, the plant having been sent to me by Mr W. Swainson during his visit to Brazil'. Either Swainson or Hooker sent it on to Cattley, as a fine drawing of one flowering in Barnet in November 1820 appeared in a part-work of rare and curious exotic plants growing in British gardens. The author was John Lindley, soon to become Assistant Secretary to the Horticultural Society of London and the world's leading orchidologist. Like Hooker, Lindley considered it 'the handsomest species of the order we have ever seen alive', and took the opportunity to name the genus after his friend and patron Cattley, 'whose ardour in the collection, and whose unrivalled success in the cultivation of the difficult tribe of plants to which it belongs, have long since given the strongest claims to such a distinction'.

In addition to fine plants, the craze for collecting orchids depended on example – patrons with the wealth and passion to make each new find desirable and therefore valuable. Leading the field among the British upper classes was William George Spencer Cavendish, sixth Duke of Devonshire, aided by his talented young gardener Joseph Paxton, whose prestige would earn him a knighthood and a seat in Parliament. Both gardener and duke became avid orchid enthusiasts, their acquaintance dating back to 1823, when Paxton went to work at the Horticultural Society's experimental garden in Chiswick, on land leased to the society by the duke. Three years later Paxton joined the duke at Chatsworth in Derbyshire, where he assisted in the gardens' extraordinary transformation. Wealthy enough to send a dedicated plant collector, John Gibson, to the mountains of Assam, the duke built up within ten years the largest private collection of tropical orchids in Britain – upwards of 240 varieties by 1834, or nearly a quarter of all types then known, when just a few years earlier the Jardin du Roi in Paris could muster only nineteen orchids in total. (By 1840, Lindley was able to catalogue 1,980 species known to him.) Profoundly deaf, the duke never married and flowers became a 'necessity of his existence'. In later years, when succumbing to bouts of melancholy, his pleasure was to be wheeled before some object of beauty, on which he would gaze to cheer his spirits, such is the curative power of flowers.

Recognizing that Britain was becoming in effect the graveyard of tropical orchids – a remark attributed to Joseph Dalton Hooker – Paxton insisted on separate houses for orchids from different climates, maintaining lower temperatures and more efficient ventilation than were then the norm, and keeping walkways well watered. For epiphytes, he followed Sir Joseph Banks in recommending a planting basket containing chopped moss and vegetable mould, spreading a little more moss over the roots and hanging the basket from the rafters. Once the orchid had been coaxed into flower, 'it may be taken down, and hung up in a warm room of a dwelling house, where, if treated with care, its flowers will continue for a long time'.

Chatsworth's success with orchids was warmly applauded by John Lindley, who dedicated his great work on orchids, *Sertum Orchidaceum*, to the duke, commending to him 'this history of some of the most beautiful of his favourite flowers'. Lindley could barely contain his excitement as he described the weird and wonderful introductions then entering cultivation, such as the Mexican orchid, *Stanhopea devoniensis* (now *S. hernandezii*), which first flowered at Chatsworth in 1837, opening its 'large rich leopard-spotted blossoms, in all the perfection of their singular form and deep soft colours' and releasing a heady scent of wintersweet, heliotrope and a perfume called Maréchal. Enjoying its first British flowering in the same year at Loddiges' Hackney nursery was a charming Chinese orchid, *Dendrobium nobile*, bought in the markets of Macao by John Reeves, an inspector of tea for the Honourable East India Company, and later supplied as a living plant to Loddiges nursery. From Burma came minute epiphytic orchids resembling insects and tiny animals (*Oberonia rufilabris*). 'If the Brahmins had been botanists,' mused Lindley, 'one might have fancied they took their doctrine of metempsychosis [the transmigration of the soul] from these productions.' Also from Mexico, and imported by a Mr Barker from Birmingham, came *Cycnoches maculatum*, which might once have kept botanists talking for a fortnight, but which now excited only a passing glance of admiration from devotees: 'Surely it is one of the most curious productions of nature in her wildest mood,' wrote Lindley. 'Did any one ever see such a flower before? Which is the top, which is the bottom? What are we to call that long club foot? which is cloven, too; and what the crooked fingers daggled with blood, which spread from the middle of one of the leaves, as if about to clutch at something?'

A name that crops up repeatedly in works by Lindley and other writers of the times is James Bateman, the creator of the splendidly eclectic, high-Victorian garden at Biddulph Grange in Staffordshire and a renowned orchid scholar himself. Bateman's particular favourites were South and Central American orchids, and he pioneered cool cultivation techniques suited to *Odontoglossum* species from the cloud forests of Central America. In a field noted for hyperbole, his monumental work, *The Orchidaceae of Mexico and Guatemala*, is one of the largest volumes ever produced, meriting a cartoon by his friend

The librarian's nightmare: woodcut from a drawing by George Cruikshank
in James Bateman's *The Orchidaceae of Mexico and Guatamala* (1837–43).

George Cruikshank in which this 'librarian's nightmare' had to be
raised by pulleys.

Like the Duke of Devonshire, Bateman used his wealth to finance
plant-hunting expeditions, and he established a special relationship
with George Ure Skinner, a Scottish trader resident in Guatemala
who came to orchids late (birds and insects were his first loves in
natural history) and then threw himself wholeheartedly into scouring
the forests, 'as if bewitched by the magic of the flower, seeking its
secret habitats'. Skinner's Guatemalan orchids helped Bateman to
build up an impressive collection at his family home of Knypersley
Hall; and Veitch's Chelsea nursery later set aside a whole glasshouse
to receive Skinner's introductions. In all, he takes credit for nearly
a hundred new species, among them *Barkeria skinneri*, which Bateman asked Lindley to name after its discoverer, and *Lycaste skinneri*;

the white variety of the latter, renamed *L. virginalis*, is Guatemala's national flower.

You can sense Skinner's delight on finding an epiphytic orchid, *Epidendrum stamfordianum*, while paddling his canoe beside the margins of a great lake near Isabel, Guatemala, where he had been detained by cholera. The orchid hung suspended over the water, emitting a perfume of violets. 'For twenty minutes I stood gazing at it before I could prevail upon myself to disturb it; but I found it in such abundance, and in such splendid flower withal, that I at length nearly filled my canoe before I could stay my hand, fancying each specimen finer than the one before it.'

In an intriguing echo of tulip fever, Skinner was responsible for arranging auctions of orchids at Mr Stevens's auction rooms in 38 King Street, Covent Garden, where collectors sold their new plants and orchid enthusiasts could dispose of their collections, among them James Bateman and Mrs Lawrence of Ealing Park, one of the few women of the time to collect orchids on any scale. The first auction devoted purely to orchids was held in 1842, and auctions continued through to the 1880s, selling plants from Skinner himself and some of the great collectors of the day: men like the Bohemian Benedict Roezl, described as 'perhaps the most intrepid orchid collector who ever lived'; Jean Linden, a native of Luxembourg, who helped to establish Belgium's orchid trade; the Pole Josef Ritter von Rawicz Warszewicz; nurserymen Loddiges and Frederick Sander; and a few orchids from 'Zulu country' consigned by the English plant hunter Robert Plant. The trade in orchids was truly international, with London at its heart.

A barometer to changing fashions, the prices achieved at auction reflected scarcity values and show how deep pockets were needed to acquire the choicest, rarest orchids. At her death in 1855, Mrs Lawrence's collection raised nearly £1,000 over two days; her whole estate of Ealing Park had cost just £9,000 less than twenty years earlier. Having inherited his mother's love of orchids, her son Sir Trevor Lawrence paid £235 in 1883 for a new Cat's tail orchid (*Aerides*) introduced by Frederick Sander, but most orchids sold for much less. If you were vigilant it was possible to pick up a bargain, according to advice from the prolific writer on orchids, Benjamin Samuel Williams, whose articles on 'Orchids for the Million' in the *Gardeners' Chronicle* expanded into the best-selling *The Orchid-Grower's Manual*, which went through seven editions between 1852 and 1894.

Stevens's orchid auctions long outlived their originator, George Ure Skinner, who became – like so many other plant hunters – a martyr to his passion. When past sixty, Skinner returned to Guatemala for one last visit to wind up his affairs. Delayed in Panama by overcrowding on the weekly boat to Guatemala, he went collecting with his usual enthusiasm, returning to the Caribbean coast for Sunday's divine service and dining that night on board the *Danube*. Here he is supposed to have caught yellow fever, reported James Bateman to the Royal Horticultural Society in February 1867, 'for on Monday he felt uncomfortable, was very ill on Tuesday, and died on Wednesday, the 9th of January'. The ship bringing news of his death also carried a last letter to his old friend James Veitch of the Royal Exotic Nursery at Chelsea, 'written in high spirits and full of plant gossip'.

SKINNER'S CORRESPONDENT WAS the son of the original James Veitch who had greatly expanded his father's nursery at Killerton in south Devon, buying additional land in Exeter in 1832. In 1853, the firm was offered the London nursery of Messrs Knight & Perry in the King's Road, Chelsea, and with the younger Veitch in charge it developed one of the most extensive and valuable stocks of exotic plants in the country. Loddiges had just closed on the expiry of their lease, leaving Veitch's Exotic Nursery as the undisputed king of the orchid nurseries, financing its own plant hunters – the Cornish brothers William and Thomas Lobb had collected for the company since the early 1840s, William in South America, and Thomas in India and South-East Asia – and displaying their plants in a 'plain yet elegant conservatory somewhat Grecian in its style'. The description comes from an occasional country correspondent to *Gardeners' Chronicle*, writing in 1859, who was plainly awed by the sheer variety and splendour of the orchids on display: after the temperate fern house he passed open-mouthed to a glasshouse devoted entirely to aerial orchids, 'all glowing with health, whilst the air is filled with a delicious perfume such as the beautiful wax-like flowers of these Orchids alone can give'. After another turn he landed in a swamp of pitcher plants, then crossed the nursery's central path to a house filled with *Cattleyas*, and two more devoted to 'parasitical natives' from tropical forests, temperate orchids and tree ferns. Here the correspondent picked out a blaze of *Odontoglossum grande*, 'a perfect bank of butterfly-like flowers, the finest of the kind I have ever seen', their success attributed to the nursery's skill in approximating the climate and growing habits of plants in their native lands, 'instead of jumbling them up together as is often done, to the utter ruin and destruction of many valuable plants'.

By the time the company published its history in 1906, it claimed to have introduced nearly 240 principal orchid species into cultivation, among them the beautiful blue *Vanda coerulea* from the Khasi hills of north-eastern India, whose story illuminates the joys and perils of orchid hunting but also the lasting damage inflicted on native habitats by overzealous collecting. First spotted by the explorer and botanist William Griffith in 1837, it was rediscovered in 1850 by Joseph Dalton Hooker on his Himalayan journey, after crossing unhealthy marshes where he and his party had the 'misfortune' to lose one of their servants to fever. In a curious sacred grove of fig and banyan trees they stumbled across 'an immense flowering tuft' of the flower he judged 'the rarest and most beautiful of Indian orchids', which they then found growing in great profusion in oak woods near the village of Lernai. They collected 'seven men's loads of this superb plant for the Royal Gardens at Kew', and a further 360 flower panicles as herbarium specimens, enough to form three piles on the veranda floor, each a yard high.

It was all in vain. Few of Hooker's specimens reached England alive, although a gentleman's gardener who accompanied them to acquaint himself with the locality was surely more successful:

he sent one man's load to England on commission, and though it arrived in a very poor state, it sold for 300*l.*, the individual plants fetching prices varying from 3*l.* to 10*l.* Had all arrived alive, they would have cleared 1000*l.* An active collector, with the facilities I possessed, might easily clear from 2000*l.* to 3000*l.*, in one season, by the sale of Khasia orchids.

T HAT 'GARDENER' WAS surely Thomas Lobb, who sent home plants from the Khasi Hills to Veitch's Killerton nursery – Chelsea had not yet opened – in the same year. One flowered in December 1850 and was exhibited at a meeting of the Horticultural Society of London where it was greeted with marked favour. 'The large flowers of soft light blue, tessellated with azure blue, are of great beauty,' wrote James Herbert Veitch of their prime specimen. So popular did this – and many other exotic orchids – prove to Victorian collectors that it became an endangered species, and was until recently given maximum protection under legislation drawn up by CITES, the Convention on International Trade in Endangered Species of Wild Fauna and Flora.

Exotics are not the only orchids at risk. Paxton reported, in 1837, that one of Britain's loveliest natives, the Lady's slipper orchid, *Cypripedium calceolus*, had fallen prey to the 'rapacity of the curious', who dug it up for their own gardens or for profit, and was fast disappearing from its northern haunts. He had heard of a Yorkshire gardener who boasted of taking all he could find, leaving just holes in the ground, and who showed no fear when threatened 'with an act of Parliament made expressly to hang him'. This orchid survives – but only just. In 2010, one of the last remaining Lady's slipper orchids in England was put under armed police guard after plant thieves had attacked and mutilated it twice in six years, despite its protected status. This partic-ular plant is now thought to be of European stock and Kew has thank-fully raised progeny from an English strain, but its continued survival remains precarious.

The Veitch nurseries could at least claim to have increased the total number of orchid varieties by creating 100 more orchid hybrids than the species orchids they took from the wild. By the turn of the last century they had bred 340 hybrids, a process first achieved success-fully by their Exeter foreman John Dominy, who crossed two *Calanthe* species to produce *Calanthe × dominyi*, which first flowered in October 1856. Fearing that many supposed 'species' from the wild might prove to be natural hybrids, John Lindley – who named it in Dominy's honour – is said to have remarked, 'You will drive the botanists mad!' A hybrid *Cattleya* followed, and an inter-generic cross in 1861. In all, Dominy's fifteen years of labour produced twenty-four successful hybrids – a trifling result but 'the foundation of all future work'; his successor John Seden added several hundred more before his retire-ment in 1905.

From the 1870s, Veitch's nurseries had a rival for sheer bravado and scale in the nursery of German-born Frederick Sander, who benefited from a crucial early encounter with the Bohemian explorer and orchid collector, Benedict Roezel. After making a good marriage, Sander used his wife's money to take over an old-established agricultural seed business in St Albans. Soon the consignments of orchids and other plants he received regularly from Roezel proved so profitable that he was able to concentrate on orchids, and by the early 1880s he had vastly expanded his operations. He would later launch orchid businesses in Summit, New Jersey and Bruges in Belgium.

Sander's example shows just how far orchids could take you: not only were many of Europe's crowned heads his patrons, but he is credited with having brought the orchid within reach of ordinary people. But he must also take responsibility for stripping some locations bare of their precious orchids, sending out upwards of twenty collectors to jungles around the world where they laid waste whole areas to reach the epiphytic orchids growing on the upper branches of trees. This destruction was plainly recorded by one of Sander's collectors, Carl Johannsen, writing to Sander in January 1896 from the Colombian city of Medellin. Johannsen promised to despatch in the morning thirty boxes of orchids, all collected from the spot where these grow mixed, and I shall clear them out. They are now nearly extinguished in this spot, and this will surely be the last season. I have finished all along the Rio Dagua, where there are no plants left; the last days I remained in that spot the people brought in two or three plants a day and some came back without a single plant.

Sander's more impressive legacy was his monumental work, *Reichenbachia*, named after the great German orchidologist Heinrich Gustav Reichenbach, who became the world's leading orchid expert after John Lindley's death in 1865. Published in two series of two volumes each from 1888 to 1894, and variously dedicated to Queen Victoria and the empresses or queens of Germany and Prussia, Russia and the Belgians, Sander's *Reichenbachia* set out to depict orchids life-sized (both species and hybrids), with text in English, French and German. As massive as Bateman's work on Guatemalan orchids, it is actually a bit of a brute but filled with fascinating detail about where the orchids were found or raised, the excitement they caused and how to grow them.

Naturally, it was Frederick Sander who by royal command supplied the great orchid bouquet of 1887 to celebrate Queen Victoria's Golden Jubilee, displayed at Buckingham Palace in a vase presented to Mr Sander by the empress of Germany. To call it a 'bouquet' is an understatement: it stood nearly four feet tall and five in diameter, its body formed by masses of *Cattleya mossiae* interspersed with plumes of *Odontoglossum*, *Oncidium*, *Vanda* – 'in short, all species of this lovely flower'. Picked out in the scarlet flowers of *Epidendrum vitellinum majus* were the letters VRI, and surmounting the whole was a golden crown of *Oncidium* and *Dendrobium* topped with a golden cross. News of its splendour spread around the globe, one local paper from New South Wales duly noting that many of the orchids came from the Queen's dominions.

Despite their gradual 'democratization', orchids remained a potent symbol of (largely male) power and prestige well into the twentieth century, as typified by the British politician Joseph Chamberlain with his trademark monocle and orchid buttonhole. The flower's admirers included wealthy amateurs such as Sir Jeremiah Colman of Gatton Park, who extolled his Gatton hybrids in a privately printed book in which he slyly declared his anti-democratic principles, believing that 'Noble parents are essential before noble offspring can be produced'. The orchid house at Kew presented a fitting target for the suffragettes, who attacked it in February 1913, although the damage was less severe than at first feared and most of the stock was expected to survive. The object was to shock people into taking notice of the suffragette cause. As Mrs Pankhurst told the weekly meeting of the Women's Social and Political Union:

We are not destroying Orchid Houses, breaking windows, cutting telegraph wires, injuring golf greens, in order to win the approval of the people who were attacked. If the general public were pleased with what we are doing, that would be a proof that our warfare is ineffective. We don't intend that you should be pleased.

Worldwide, interest in the orchid was spreading and, as the century progressed, America took the lead in fostering interest in orchids. After Lindley and Reichenbach, Professor Oakes Ames of Harvard University became the world's leading orchid scholar, especially renowned for his work on the orchids of the Philippines. The American Orchid Society, founded in 1921, sponsored the first World Orchid Conference in 1954, bringing together amateur enthusiasts, scientists and commercial interests from the main orchid-producing regions. Now co-sponsored by Britain's Royal Horticultural Society (RHS), the conference is held every three years in far-distant locations. London retains its place at the heart of the orchid world through research undertaken by the Royal Botanic Gardens at Kew and the RHS's role in maintaining the international register of orchid hybrids.

In common with the tulip and other flowers in this book, industrial production techniques have turned orchids into big business, with an estimated turnover worldwide of some £5.6 billion, and

transformed the way orchids are grown: many are now mass-produced
in sterile media, untouched by human hand, to achieve the ubiquitous supermarket orchid sold at bargain-basement prices. Global ac-
tion means, too, that orchids now enjoy more legal protection than
most other flowers under CITES. Established in 1972 to monitor and
control the international trade in threatened species, CITES is concerned with the movement of animals and plants, including herbarium specimens, across national borders; it requires import and export
licences for plants listed in three appendices, which establish varying degrees of control. A number of listed Orchidaceae – among them
Cypripedium calceolus, all *Paphiopedilum* and *Phragmipedium* species,
and all European orchids – are subject to the strictest controls, which
permit trade only for artificially propagated plants, subject to licences.
All remaining Orchidaceae appear in the second group; this requires
an export permit for plants collected directly from the wild, but allows
trade in artificially propagated plants subject to licensing.

Given such a turbulent history, the orchid has played a surprisingly modest role in western literature, its presence in
early writings largely medical rather than literary, although those are
surely Britain's native Early purple orchids, *Orchis mascula*, thrust
by Shakespeare into Ophelia's hands when she drowns herself in the
brook, wreathed in fantastic garlands

> Of crowflowers, nettles, daisies and long purples,
> That liberal shepherds give a grosser name
> But our cold maids do dead men's fingers call them.

We know some of those 'grosser names' from Shakespeare's
contemporary John Gerard, and can learn politer ones from the
Northamptonshire poet John Clare, who named an astonishing 370
plants in his poetry and prose, and was especially fond of orchids. He
called Shakespeare's Early purples 'gaping, speckled cuckoo flowers'
and the 'pouched-lipped cuckoo bud', marvelling at the way they could

be seen at noon in May 'just creeping from their hoods, / With the sweet season, like their bard, beguil'd'. The American writer and naturalist Henry David Thoreau was similarly enamoured of native orchids and their 'fair and delicate, nymph-like' flowers – a very un-western view – considering the Great purple fringed orchid a 'delicate belle of the swamp . . . A beauty reared in the shade of a convent, who has never strayed beyond the convent bell.'

A very different sort of orchid appeared in Joris-Karl Huysmans's defiantly decadent novel of 1884, *Against Nature* (*À Rebours*), in which the anti-hero Des Esseintes gratified his morbid sensibilities with grotesque hothouse blooms, 'vegetative follies' that looked more art-ificial than real and naturally included orchids. His *Cypripediums* come straight out of Ruskin: 'They resembled a clog, or a small oval bowl, with a human tongue curled back above it, its tendon stretched tight just as one sees tongues drawn in the illustrations to works deal-ing with diseases of the throat and mouth.' Two little wings, gumdrop red, completed this 'weird assemblage', and 'a shiny pouch, its lining oozing with a viscous glue'. Among his exotic purchases was a *Cattleya* from New Granada in a muted shade of lilac, which emitted a smell of varnished deal, like a toy chest, 'evoking the horrors of presents on New Year's Day'. Horticulturists who bred monstrous flowers like these were the only true artists, Des Esseintes concluded, nonethe-less succumbing to a horrifying vision of a syphilitic Woman-Flower, a blood-red bromeliad blossoming between her thighs, 'opening wide its sword-shaped petals above the bloody interior'.

Another European writer who equated the *Cattleya* orchid with sex was Marcel Proust, who introduced the flower into the private lan-guage between Charles Swann and the courtesan Odette de Crécy in the first of his seven-volume epic, *À la Recherche du Temps Perdu* (he would later liken a solitary homosexual to an orchid or sterile jellyfish cast onto the beach). 'To make Cattleya' [*faire catleya*] was shorthand between Swann and Odette for making love, ever since an episode in her carriage when her horse shied at an obstacle and Swann sought permission to restore the *Cattleyas* to her bodice (she was wearing more orchids in her hair, and carried them in a bouquet). That night he possessed her for the first time, and his habitual timidity led him to repeat the pretext ever afterwards.

The orchid's essential weirdness was perfectly captured by H. G. Wells in his cautionary tale 'The Flowering of the Strange Orchid', which poked gentle fun at the late Victorian craze for collecting hot-house orchids. It tells the story of the bachelor Winter-Wedderburn, who attends the London auction of tropical orchids collected by a young man who died in the attempt, his blood apparently sucked dry by jungle leeches. Among Wedderburn's purchases is an unidentified shrivelled rhizome found under the young man's body, which he plants in his hot-house, its aerial rootlets appearing to the housekeeper 'like little white fingers poking out of the brown'. Overcome by the orchid's sickeningly sweet scent when it finally flowers, Wedderburn is mercifully rescued by his housekeeper, who finds him lying face upwards under the strange orchid, its rootlets attached like a tangle of grey ropes to his neck. Heroically snapping off their tentacles, she smashes the glass with a flowerpot and drags his body outside. 'The next morning the strange orchid still lay there, black now and putrescent.' Wedderburn's other orchids are similarly moribund, but the man himself becomes bright and garrulous, exulting in the glory of his strange adventure.

British and American crime and detective fiction would also project orchids as a curious, often unhealthy passion: lovingly tended by Rex Stout's corpulent detective, Nero Wolfe; added to the title of James Hadley Chase's nasty low-life thriller, *No Orchids for Miss Blandish*, although the flower itself is never mentioned by name; and memorably introduced by Raymond Chandler at the start of *The Big Sleep* when Chandler's private eye Philip Marlowe calls at General Sternwood's mansion in West Hollywood. The butler shows him into the conservatory, its wet steamy air 'larded with the cloying smell of tropical orchids in bloom'.

'Do you like orchids?' asked the General.
'Not particularly,' Marlowe replied.

The General half closed his eyes. 'They are nasty things. Their flesh is too much like the flesh of men. And their perfume has the rotten sweetness of a prostitute.'

After horrors like these, it is refreshing to turn to writers who draw their orchids from remembered experience. In his 'greenhouse poems', the Michigan-born poet Theodore Roethke recalls his childhood explorations of the vast greenhouses owned by his nurseryman father and uncle, where the orchids swayed close to his face, mouths open like adders, delicate as the tongues of young birds.

I think, too, of the tropical orchids in *Wide Sargasso Sea* by Jean Rhys, which tells the back-story of the Jamaican heiress Antoinette Cosway, the mad Mrs Rochester in Charlotte Brontë's *Jane Eyre*. Like the ones from my own childhood, Antoinette's orchids are simply part of the given, growing in the beautiful but neglected garden of the family's Colibri Estate, where they flourish out of reach.

One was snaky looking, another like an octopus with long thin brown tentacles bare of leaves hanging from a twisted root. Twice a year the octopus orchid flowered – then not an inch of tentacle showed. It was a bell-shaped mass of white, mauve, deep purples, wonderful to see. The scent was very sweet and strong. I never went near it.

ORCHIDS STILL HAVE the power to lure plant collectors and enthusiasts into dangerous territory, where some tread a fine line between the legal and illegal pursuit of their passion – witness the popularity of books such as Susan Orlean's *The Orchid Thief*, based on the arrest of John Laroche and three Semiole men for stealing rare orchids from a Florida swamp, the Fakahatchee Strand State Preserve; and Eric Hansen's *Orchid Fever*, which embroiled the author in heated discussions with Kew. Intent on studying orchids in the wild rather than collecting them, the young British enthusiast Tom Hart Dyke travelled to the jungles of Central America; in Panama, while walking the Darién Gap with fellow backpacker Paul Winder, the pair were captured by

Marxist guerrillas and spent nine months in captivity, all for the love of this most unyielding of flowers.

There are those who claim that no flower has been quite so coveted, or so plundered, as the orchid. It even captured the heart of the curmudgeonly alpine specialist Reginald Farrer, who considered himself an 'innocent and happy gardener' until the ominous day he set eyes on a beautiful golden-yellow Indian Slipper orchid, *Paphiopedilum insigne* f. *sanderae*. His pained bewilderment speaks for all those orchid enthusiasts – and flower enthusiasts generally – who find themselves gripped by a passion they are powerless to resist.

In that instant I understood Romeo and Juliet better than I ever had before. But my doom was sealed; as cruel engines draw in, first one's coat-tail, and then by degrees the whole body, so the Orchids have now enveloped me densely in their web. I am engulfed in Orchids and their dreadful bills; nor do I see the slightest chance of ever tasting solvency or peace again.

Afterword

THE ORCHID IS the last of my seven flowers, and the one that surprised me the most. Here is a flower endowed with overwhelming powers of seduction, of man no less than of insects, one that highlights the gulf between East and West in the way we look at flowers, and what we take those flowers to 'mean'. Yet the Chinese sage consoling himself with the orchid's modest blooming, the Japanese *daimyo* inhaling the orchid's scent to lift his spirits on the tortuous journey to the capital, and Raymond Chandler's private eye squirming with disgust among the hothouse blooms of a Californian client all express the power of flowers to hold our attention.

So it is with each of my other flowers; their stories reveal surprising echoes and even more remarkable differences that tell us much about ourselves. I may not love them equally, but each has earned my respect. The lotus of eastern religions has been with me from the beginning; joined with the lotus of ancient Egypt, it was present at the moment when time, creation and human history revealed themselves as mysteries that man wanted — needed — to crack. I still find the sunflower creepy, and would not willingly plant it in my garden, but I love the hope it gave to van Gogh, and like Allen Ginsberg have regained a little of my optimism that flowers can help transform our futures, in life and in art. The lily and the rose are now for me forever joined, jostling for supremacy in Christianity's roll-call of flowers but also in other cultures; and I can honestly say that the rose retains its crown as the Queen of Flowers, revered almost universally as the ultimate flower of love. The opium poppy has, I believe, revealed its true colours: fair

without and foul within, the 'Joan Silver Pin' of old, yet the astonishing
beauty of both flower and seed-head can still stop me dead. For all its
wild beauty and the sumptuous sheen of the old feathered and flamed
varieties, the tulip continues to amaze me in the extremes of human
folly it has provoked, and in the contrast between its erstwhile beauty
and the banality of many modern cultivars. As I said of the rose, we get
the flowers we deserve, and I believe we deserve better than this.

And so I shall continue to track down my flowers, the ones I couldn't
find space for here and new ones that catch my eye. Increasingly, it is
the weeds and wild flowers to which I am drawn: a tiny but fantastically
camouflaged Bee orchid growing on an otherwise unremarkable grass
verge beside the estuary near Arnside on the Cumbrian coast; a creamy
Rosa arvensis, Shakespeare's Musk rose, sweetening the air of a Devon
lane; pungent stands of milkweed (*Asclepias syriaca*) lining the roadside of a Pennsylvanian wood. Painted by John White, the governor
of Virginia's Lost Colony in the late sixteenth century, and shown to
White's friend John Gerard, this last flower appeared in Gerard's great
Elizabethan *Herball*, together with the fervent hope that the colonists
were still alive, 'if neither untimely death by murdering, or pestilence,
or corrupt aire, bloodie flixes, or some other mortall sickness hath
not destroied them'. They were never found and to this day their fate
remains a mystery.

Soon after encountering the Bee orchid, I was taken to the spot where
one of England's last Lady's slipper orchids still blooms. It wasn't yet
in flower; only the leaves were poking through the earth and despite all
the media hullaballoo, there was no armed guard. For all its modesty,
this whorl of green leaves spoke to me of Aphrodite's birthplace, and
of those wildly divergent views expressed by Charles Darwin and John
Ruskin, about the origin of species and what flowers are for. Guard it
well: this slip of a flower contains our histories, yours and mine.

Acknowledgements

My thanks go first of all to the libraries and their staffs who made this book possible and turned the hard graft of research into a pleasure. I would like to single out especially Dr Brent Elliott, historian and archivist to the Royal Horticultural Society; Elizabeth Koper and Elizabeth Gilbert at the RHS Lindley Library in London; staffs of the Rare Books Reading Room of the British Library, and of the London Library, to whom I am indebted for the generous support of its Carlyle membership; the Wellcome Library; the RHS Lindley Library at Wisley; and the library and archives of the Royal Botanic Gardens, Kew. Julian Shaw, the International Orchid Hybrid Registrar, kept me abreast of the orchid hybrids, and once again, I am happy to record my debt to RBG Kew's Dr Mark Nesbitt for his perceptive comments on the manuscript, and for keeping me in touch with developments in ethnobotany.

Among the many people who suggested connections between flowers, literature and art, I would like to thank especially Christopher Bailes, Phil Baker, Professor Catherine Maxwell, Chris Petit, Camilla Swift, Richard Williams, and Robert Irwin for his help with Arabic names. I am particularly grateful to Barbara Latham and David Redmore for introducing me to orchids – to Barbara for her much enjoyed hospitality and to David for his patient and illuminating reading of the manuscript in its final stages. Special thanks go also to Pamela Wilson, a warm and generous host, who took me orchid-hunting around my grandfather's old home in Silverdale; and to other family and friends who sustained me during the writing of this book, particularly Ros

Franey, Chris Potter, Lynn Ritchie, Robert Petit, Catherine King, Louie Burghes, Philippa Campbell, Jude Harris, Andrea Jones, Michael Kerr, the late Roger Payton of the Worshipful Company of Gardeners, Bill Wilson, Judith Wilcox and fellow members of The Gardeners Club.

At Atlantic Books, my thanks go to my editor, Angus MacKinnon, and to James Nightingale; I also want to pay a warm tribute to my agent, Caroline Dawnay of United Agents, for her tireless and enthusiastic support, ably aided until recently by Olivia Hunt and Sophie Scard. Finally, I am grateful to the Hawthornden Trust for a writing fellow-ship, and to the Royal Literary Fund for my fellowship at King's College London. Without such help and support, this book could not have been written: thank you all.

Main Sources
and Select Bibliography

Principal sources are given for each chapter, and full references appear online – see www.atlantic-books.co.uk.

The following works provide the backbone for several chapters; subsequent mentions of listed works use short titles only.

Pedanius Dioscorides, *De Materia Medica*, trans. T. A. Osbaldeston and R. P. A. Wood (Johannesburg, Ibidis, 2000).

John Gerard, *The Herball or Generall Historie of Plantes* (London, 1597).

John Gerard, *The Herball or Generall Historie of Plantes*, amended and enlarged by Thomas Johnson (London, 1633).

Henry Hawkins, *Partheneia Sacra, or The Mysterious and Delicious Garden of the Sacred Parthenes* (Rouen, 1633).

Herodotus, *The Histories*, trans. Aubrey de Sélincourt (London, Penguin Books, 2003).

Philip Miller, *The Gardeners Dictionary*, especially the first edn (London, 1731) and the eighth edn, revised in accordance with Linnaean botany (London, 1768).

John Parkinson, *Paradisi in Sole Paradisus Terrestris* (London, 1629).

John Parkinson, *Theatrum Botanicum: The Theater of Plants* (London, 1640).

The Natural History of Pliny, trans. John Bostock and H. T. Riley (6 vols, London, 1855).

Theophrastus, *Enquiry into Plants and Minor Works on Odours and Weather Signs*, trans. Sir Arthur Hort (2 vols, London, William Heinemann, 1916).

Robert John Thornton, *Temple of Flora, or Garden of the Botanist, Poet, Painter and Philosopher* (London, 1812).

William Robinson, *The English Flower Garden* (London, John Murray, 1883).

Also frequently to hand were these works of criticism and commentary:

Wilfrid Blunt and William T. Stearn, *The Art of Botanical Illustration* (Woodbridge, Antique Collectors' Club, revised edn, 1994).

Jack Goody, *The Culture of Flowers* (Cambridge University Press, 1993).

Debra N. Mancoff, *Flora Symbolica: Flowers in Pre-Raphaelite Art* (Munich, Prestel, 2003).

Andrew Moore and Christopher Garibaldi, *Flower Power: The Meaning of Flowers in Art* (London, Philip Wilson Publishers, 2003).

Lotus

Among general works, these were especially helpful on ancient Egyptian and eastern lotuses: Perry D. Slocum, *Waterlilies and Lotuses: Species, Cultivars, and New Hybrids* (Portland, Timber Press, 2005); and Mark Griffiths, *The Lotus Quest* (London, Chatto & Windus, 2009).

Of the many works consulted on the cosmology, mythology and culture of ancient Egypt, I am indebted to Donald B. Redford (ed.), *The Oxford Encyclopedia of Ancient Egypt* (3 vols, Oxford University Press, 2001); John H. Taylor (ed.), *Journey Through the Afterlife: Ancient Egyptian Book of the Dead* (Cambridge, Mass., Harvard University Press, 2010); G. Maspero, *Histoire Ancienne des Peuples de l'Orient Classique* (3 vols, Paris, Librairie Hachette, 1895–9); *The Egyptian Book of the Dead: The Book of Going Forth by Day*, second revised edn (Chicago, KWS Publishers, 1998).

For Tutankhamun's flowers and artefacts I consulted Howard Carter and A. C. Mace, *The Tomb of Tut.ankh.Amen* (3 vols, London, Cassell & Co., 1923–33); F. Nigel Hepper, *Pharaoh's Flowers: The Botanical Treasures of Tutankhamun* (London, HMSO, 1990); John Bellinger, *Ancient Egyptian Gardens* (Sheffield, Amarna Publishing, 2008); and Lise Manniche, *An*

Ancient Egyptian Herbal (London, British Museum Press, 1999), pp. 27–31.

These works were helpful on lotuses in ancient Egyptian gardens, tomb decorations and everyday life: Nathalie Beaux, *Le Cabinet de Curiosités de Thoutmosis III: Plantes et Animaux du 'Jardin Botanique' de Karnak* (Leuven, Departement Oriëntalistick/Peeters, 1990); Alix Wilkinson, *The Garden in Ancient Egypt* (London, Rubicon Press, 1998); Tassilio Wengel, *The Art of Gardening Through the Ages*, trans. Leonard Goldman (Leipzig, Edition Leipzig, 1987); Percy E. Newberry, *El Bersheh: Part I (The Tomb of Tehuti-Hetep)* (London, Egyptian Exploration Fund, n.d.); and J. G. Wilkinson, *Manners and Customs of the Ancient Egyptians* (3 vols, London, John Murray, 1837).

On the narcotic properties of ancient Egyptian water lilies, see William A. Emboden, 'Transcultural use of narcotic water lilies in ancient Egyptian and Maya drug ritual', *Journal of Ethno-Pharmacology*, vol. 3, no. 1 (1981), pp. 39–83; David J. Counsell, 'Intoxicants in ancient Egypt? Opium, nymphaea, coca and tobacco', in Rosalie David (ed.), *Egyptian Mummies and Modern Science* (Cambridge University Press, 2008), pp. 195–215; and Joyce Tydesley, *The Private Lives of the Pharaohs* (London, Channel 4 Books, 2000), pp. 171–5.

For the lotuses of ancient Greece and Rome, see Herodotus, *The Histories*, pp. 129–30; *The Geography of Strabo*, trans. H. C. Hamilton and W. Falconer (3 vols, London, Henry G. Bohn, 1854), vol. 3, p. 88; Theophrastus, *Enquiry into Plants*, vol. 1, pp. 351–5 (from Book 4, Chapter 8); *The Natural History of Pliny*, vol. 3, pp. 198–200 (from Book 13, Chapter 32), and vol. 4, p. 45 (from Book 18, Chapter 30); Lucius Junius Moderatus Columella, trans. E. S. Forster and Edward H. Heffner, *On Agriculture [De Re Rustica]* (3 vols, London, William Heinemann, 1954), vol. 2, pp. 397–9; P. G. P. Meyboom, *The Nile Mosaic of Palestrina: Early Evidence of Egyptian Religion in Italy* (Leiden, E. J. Brill, 1994); and Wilhelmina Feemster Jashemski and Frederick G. Meyer, *The Natural History of Pompeii* (Cambridge University Press, 2002).

Napoleon's lotuses are portrayed in *Description de l'Égypte, ou Recueil des Observations et des Recherches qui ont été faites en Égypte pendant l'expédition de l'armée française* (20 vols, Paris, 1809–28), vol. 9, pp. 303–13, and *Planches, Histoire Naturelle*, vol. 2, 'Botanique'. Redouté's blue water lily appears in Pierre-Joseph Redouté, *Choix des Plus Belles Fleurs* (Paris, 1827); and see Martyn Rix and William T. Stearn, *Redouté's Fairest Flowers* (London,

The Herbert Press/British Museum, 1987). For Robert Thornton's lotuses, see Geoffrey Grigson's introduction to *Thornton's Temple of Flora* (London, Collins, 1951), pp. 1–13, and William T. Stearn's botanical notes, p. 20.

These are my main sources for the mythological history of the sacred lotus in India: Dr Raj Pandit Sharma, 'Flowers and plants in Hinduism', consulted 8 June 2011 on www.hinducounciluk.org; Heinrich Zimmer, *Myths and Symbols in Indian Art and Civilization*, ed. Joseph Campbell (Washington DC, Pantheon Books, 1947); Carol Radcliffe Bolon, *Forms of the Goddess Lajja Gauri in Indian Art* (University Park, Pa, Pennsylvania State University Press, 1992); and *Upanisads*, trans. from Sanskrit by Patrick Olivelle (Oxford University Press, 1996).

For the sacred lotus in Nepal, Buddhism and South-East Asia, I consulted Narayan P. Manadhar, *Plants and People of Nepal* (Portland, Oregon, Timber Press, 2002); Dr Sarla Khosla, *Lalitavistara and the Evolution of the Buddha Legend* (New Delhi, Galaxy Publications, 1991); S. K. Gupta, *Elephant in Indian Art and Mythology* (New Delhi, Abhinav Publications, 1983); *The Lalita-Vistara: Memoirs of the Early Life of Sakya Sinha*, trans. Rajendralala Mitra (Calcutta, 1881); Moore and Garibaldi, *Flower Power*, p. 25; Martin Lerner and Steven Kossak, *The Lotus Transcendent: Indian and Southeast Asian Art from the Samuel Eilenberg Collection* (New York, The Metropolitan Museum of Art, 1991); and W. Zwalf (ed.), *Buddhism: Art and Faith* (London, British Museum Publications, 1985).

For the history of the lotus in China and Japan, see Seizo Kashioka and Mikinori Ogisu, *Illustrated History and Principle of the Traditional Floriculture in Japan*, trans. Tetsuo Koyama et al. (Osaka, ABOC-sha Co. Ltd, 1997). On the lotus in Chinese literature, gardens, art, ornament and customs see: Maggie Keswick, *The Chinese Garden: History, Art and Architecture*, revised by Alison Hardie (London, Frances Lincoln, 2003); Arthur Waley, *The Book of Songs* (London, George Allen & Unwin, 1937); Hans H. Frankel, *The Flowering Plum and the Palace Lady: Interpretations of Chinese Poetry* (New Haven, Yale University Press, 1976); Loraine E. Kuck, *The Art of Japanese Gardens* (New York, The Japan Society, 1941); Alfred Koehn, *Chinese Flower Symbolism* (Tokyo, At the Lotus Court, 1954); Jessica Rawson, *Chinese Ornament: The Lotus and the Dragon* (London, British Museum Publications, 1984); H. A.

Lorentz, *A View of Chinese Rugs from the Seventeenth to the Twentieth Century* (London, Routledge & Kegan Paul, 1972); P. R. J. Ford, *Oriental Carpet Design: A Guide to Traditional Motifs, Patterns and Symbols* (London, Thames and Hudson, 1992); Howard S. Levy, *The Lotus Lovers: The Complete History of the Curious Erotic Custom of Footbinding in China* (Buffalo, NY, Prometheus Books, 1992); *The Secret of the Golden Flower: A Chinese Book of Life*, trans. Richard Wilhelm (London, Routledge & Kegan Paul, 1962); and C. G. Jung, *Psychology and Alchemy*, vol. 12 of the collected works of C. G. Jung, ed. Sir Herbert Read et al. (London, Routledge & Kegan Paul, second edn, 1968).

For the lotus in nineteenth- and twentieth-century Japan I consulted: *The Flowers and Gardens of Japan*, painted by Ella du Cane, described by Florence du Cane (London, Adam & Charles, 1908); Christopher Dresser, *Japan: Its Architecture, Art, and Art Manufactures* (London, Longmans Green & Co., 1882); Josiah Conder, *Landscape Gardening in Japan* (Tokyo, 1893); Josiah Conder, *The Flowers of Japan and the Art of Floral Arrangement* (Tokyo, 1891); Alfred Koehn, *Japanese Flower Symbolism* (Peiping, China, Lotus Court Publications, 1937); Alfred Parsons, *Notes in Japan* (London, Osgood, McIlvaine & Co., 1896); Ayako Ono, *Japonisme in Britain: Whistler, Menpes, Henry, Hornel and Nineteenth-Century Japan* (London, RoutledgeCurzon, 2003); and Pierre Loti (a pseudonym of the French novelist and naval officer Julien Viaud), *Japan, Madame Chrysanthemum*, trans. Laura Ensor (London, KPI, 1985).

These are some of the works I consulted for the lotus in poetry and art: Edward S. Forster, 'Trees and plants in Homer', *The Classical Review*, vol. 50, no. 3 (July 1936), pp. 97–104; Homer, *The Odyssey*, trans. Robert Fagles (New York, Penguin, 1996); Alfred Tennyson, *Oenone and Lotos-Eaters*, ed. F. A. Cavenagh (Oxford, Clarendon Press, 1915); Constance Classen, David Howes and Anthony Synnott, *Aroma: The Cultural History of Smell* (London, Routledge, 1994); Charles Baudelaire, 'Le Voyage', in *Les Fleurs du Mal et Autres Poèmes* (Paris, Garnier-Flammarion, 1964), pp. 150–5; Howard Hodgkin, *Indian Leaves* (London, Petersburg Press, c.1982); Michael Compton, *Howard Hodgkin's Indian Leaves* (London, Tate Gallery, 1982); T. S. Eliot, *Four Quartets* (London, Faber and Faber, 1956); Peter Harris (ed.), *Zen Poems* (London, Everyman's Library, 1999); and Fu Ji Tsang, *The Meaning of Flowers: A Chinese Painter's Perspective* (Paris, Flammarion, 2004).

Vivian Russell writes of Monet's water lilies in *Monet's Garden: Through the Seasons at Giverny* (London, Frances Lincoln, 1995). The RHS Lindley Library in London holds Latour-Marliac's nursery catalogue for 1996/7.

Lily

Keat's lily comes from 'La Belle Dame San Merci', Ballad, *The Poetical Works of John Keats* (London, Maccmillan, 1884), pp. 254–6. These are my main sources on the Minoan lilies of Crete and Thera (Santorini): Gisela Walberg, 'Minoan floral iconography' in *EikΩn, Aegean Bronze Age Iconography: Shaping a Methodology*, ed. Robert Laffineur and Janice L. Crowley (Liège, Université de Liège, 1992); Sir Arthur Evans, *The Palace of Minos* (6 vols, London, Macmillan, 1921–36); Hellmut Baumann, *Greek Wild Flowers and Plant Lore in Ancient Greece*, trans. William T. Stearn and Eldwyth Ruth Stearn (London, The Herbert Press, 1993); Maria C. Shaw, 'The "Priest-King" fresco from Knossos: man, woman, priest, king, or someone else?', in *Essays in Honor of Sara A. Immerwahr*, ed. Anne P. Chapin (Athens, The American School of Classical Studies at Athens, 2004), pp. 65–84; Christos Doumas, *The Wall-Paintings of Thera*, trans. Alex Doumas (Athens, The Thera Foundation, 1992); and Lyvia Morgan, *The Miniature Wall Paintings of Thera: A Study in Aegean Culture and Iconography* (Cambridge University Press, 1988).

For lilies in ancient Egypt and ancient Greece, see Hepper, *Pharaoh's Flowers*, p. 25; Alix Wilkinson, *The Garden in Ancient Egypt*, pp. 39–40; Lin Foxhall, 'Environments and landscapes of Greek culture', in Konrad H. Kinzl (ed.), *A Companion to the Classical Greek World* (Oxford, Blackwell, 2006), pp. 245–80; *Hesiod: The Homeric Hymns and Homerica*, trans. Hugh G. Evelyn-White (London, William Heinemann, 1914), p. 81; and H. B. D. Woodcock and W. T. Stearn, *Lilies of the World: Their Cultivation and Classification* (London, Country Life, 1950).

In his *Enquiry into Plants*, Theophrastus discusses lily flowers in vol. 2, pp. 37–9 and 45 (from Book 6, Chapter 6), and lily perfume in 'Concerning Odours', vol. 2, p. 365. Dioscorides' instructions for making lily ointment come from *De Materia Medica*, pp. 59–62. The Roman sources include *The*

Natural History of Pliny, vol. 4, pp. 314–16 and 366–7 (from Book 21, Chapters 11 and 74); Jashemski and Meyer (eds), *The Natural History of Pompeii*, pp. 121–2; John Henderson, *Hortus: The Roman Book of Gardening* (London, Routledge, 2004); *Ovid's Fasti*, trans. Sir James George Frazer (London, William Heinemann, 1931), p. 139; Ovid, *Metamorphoses*, trans. A. D. Melville (Oxford University Press, 1986), p. 231; and Marcel de Cleene and Marie Claire Lejeune, *Compendium of Symbolic and Ritual Plants in Europe* (2 vols, Ghent, Man and Culture, 2002), vol. 2, pp. 321–3. Nicander's description of the lily appears in Joris-Karl Huysmans, *Against Nature*, trans. Margaret Mauldon (Oxford University Press, 1998), p. 136.

The lily in early Christian and medieval Europe draws on Goody, *The Culture of Flowers*; John Harvey, *Mediaeval Gardens* (London, B. T. Batsford, 1981); Jennifer Potter, *The Rose: A True History* (London, Atlantic Books, 2010); Marilyn Stokstad and Jerry Stannard, *Gardens of the Middle Ages* (Kansas, Spencer Museum of Art, 1983); Walahfrid Strabo, *Hortulus*, trans. Raef Payne (Pittsburg, Hunt Botanical Library, 1966); Marilyn Stokstad, *Medieval Art*, second edn (Boulder, Westview Press, 2004); and Luigi Gambero, *Mary in the Middle Ages: The Blessed Virgin Mary in the Thought of Medieval Latin Theologians* (San Francisco, Ignatius Press, 2005). For the lily in Byzantium, see A. R. Littlewood, 'Gardens of Byzantium', *Journal of Garden History*, vol. 12, no. 2 (1992), pp. 126–53; Margaret H. Thomson (ed. and trans.), *The Symbolic Garden: Reflections Drawn from a Garden of Virtues, A XIIth century Greek manuscript* (North York, Ontario, Captus University Publications, 1989), p. 38; and for the lily in scenes of the Annunciation, see Helene E. Roberts (ed.), *Encyclopedia of Comparative Iconography: Themes Depicted in Works of Art* (2 vols, Chicago, Fitzroy Dearborn, 1998); and Mancoff, *Flora Symbolica*, pp. 32–3. Lily crucifixes are discussed by E. J. M. Duggan, 'Notes concerning the "Lily Crucifixion" in the Llanbelig Hours', *National Library of Wales Journal*, vol. 27, no. 1 (Summer 1991), pp. 39–48; W. L. Hildburgh, 'An alabaster table of the Annunciation with the crucifix: a study in English iconography', *Archaeologia*, vol. 74 (1925), pp. 203–32; and W. L. Hildburgh, 'Some further notes on the crucifix on the lily', *The Antiquaries Journal*, vol. 12 (1932), pp. 24–6. Henry Hawkins's lily meditation appears in *Partheneia Sacra*, pp. 28–37; and for biblical lilies see Ariel Bloch and Chana Bloch, *The Song of*

Songs: A New Translation (Berkeley, University of California Press, 1995), especially pp. 148–9.

Virtually all my information on the fleur-de-lis comes from the French medievalist, Michel Pastoureau. See especially his *Heraldry: Its Origins and Meaning*, trans. Francisca Garvie (London, Thames & Hudson, 1997), pp. 98–191, 'Do historians fear the fleur-de-lis?'

In addition to the works of John Gerard and John Parkinson, my sources on Elizabethan and Stuart lilies include B. D. Jackson, *A Catalogue of Plants Cultivated in the Garden of John Gerard in the Years 1596–99* (London, 1876); Prudence Leith-Ross, *The Florilegium of Alexander Marshal in the Collection of Her Majesty the Queen at Windsor Castle* (London, The Royal Collection, 2000); and Rev. Henry N. Ellacombe, *The Plant-Lore & Garden-Craft of Shakespeare* (London, W. Satchell & Co., second edn, 1884), pp. 140–6.

For early North American lilies, I turned to John Josselyn, *New-Englands Rarities Discovered* (London, 1672), pp. 42 and 54; Timothy Coffey, *The History and Folklore of North American Wildflowers* (New York, Facts on File, 1993), pp. 305–6; Patrick M. Synge, *Lilies: A Revision of Elwes' 'Monograph of the Genus Lilium' and its Supplements* (London, B. T. Batsford, 1980); Denis Dodart, *Mémoires pour servir à l'Histoire des Plantes* (Paris, 1676), p. 91; Mark Catesby, *The Natural History of Carolina, Florida and the Bahama Islands* (2 vols, London, 1731–43); André Michaux, *Flora Boreali-Americana* (2 vols, Paris, 1803); and *Curtis's Botanical Magazine*, vol. 108, third series (1882), tab. 6650.

Sources for Chinese lilies in gardens and pharmacology include: Hui-lin Li, *The Garden Flowers of China* (New York, Ronald Press, 1959), pp. 115–20; Dan Bensky and Andrew Gamble, *Chinese Herbal Medicine: Materia Medica*, revised edn (Seattle, Eastland Press, 1993); *Herbal Pharmacology in the People's Republic of China: A Trip Report of the American Herbal Pharmacology Delegation* (Washington, National Academy of Sciences, 1975), pp. 163–4; Jane Kilpatrick, *Gifts from the Gardens of China* (London, Frances Lincoln, 2007); Potter, *The Rose*, pp. 217–29; *Curtis's Botanical Magazine*, vol. 132 (1906), tab. 8102, for Wilson's *Lilium regale*; and E. H. Wilson, *The Lilies of Eastern Asia: A Monograph* (London, Dulau & Co., 1925), p. 8. The Tiger lily appears in Gertrude Jekyll, *Lilies for English Gardens: A Guide for Amateurs* (Woodbridge, Suffolk, Antique Collectors' Club, 1982, first published Country Life, 1901),

p. 6; and Lewis Carroll, *Through the Looking-glass, And What Alice Found There* (London, Macmillan, 1872), p. 28.

For Japanese lilies (including the early history of Deshima Island), see K. Vos, *Assignment Japan: Von Siebold, Pioneer and Collector* (The Hague, SDU, 1989); Reginald J. Farrer, *The Gardens of Asia: Impressions from Japan* (London, Methuen, 1904), p. 2; Dandra Knapp, *Potted Histories: An Artistic Voyage Through Plant Exploration* (London, Scriptum, 2003), pp. 272–5; Engelbert Kaempfer, *Amoenitatum exoticarum politico-physico-medicarum fasciculi V* (Lemgoviae, 1712), pp. 870–2; *Botanical Register*, vol. 23 (1837), tab. 2000; Richard Gorer, *The Growth of Gardens* (London, Faber & Faber, 1978), pp. 158–6; Philipp Franz von Siebold and J. G. Zuccarini, *Flora Japonica* (Lugduni Batavorum, 1835), pp. 31–5, 86–7; *Gardeners' Chronicle*, 5 July 1862, p. 623, and 12 July 1862, p. 644; and Du Cane, *The Flowers and Gardens of Japan*, pp. 95–100.

My sources on the lily in late nineteenth-century art and poetry include: Georgiana Burne-Jones, *Memorials of Edward Burne-Jones* (2 vols, London, Macmillan and Co., 1904), vol. 1, p. 225; Edward Burne-Jones, *The Flower Book* (London, The Fine Art Society, 1905); Ono, *Japonisme in Britain*; Richard Dorment and Margaret F. MacDonald, *James McNeill Whistler* (London, Tate Gallery Publications, 1995); H. C. Marillier, *Dante Gabriel Rossetti: An Illustrated Memorial of His Art and Life* (London, George Bell and Sons, 1899); Dresser, *Japan*, pp. 286–316; 'Love and sleep', in *The Poems of Algernon Charles Swinburne* (6 vols, London, Chatto & Windus, 1904), vol. 1, p. 272; Stéphane Mallarmé, *Les Noces d'Hérodiade* (Paris, Gallimard, 1959), p. 64 (author's translation); *Poems by Oscar Wilde, Together with his Lecture on the English Renaissance* (Paris, 1903), pp. 215–16; Peter Raby, *Oscar Wilde* (Cambridge University Press, 1988), p. 22; Sarah Bernhardt, *My Double Life: Memoirs of Sarah Bernhardt* (London, William Heinemann, 1907), pp. 297–8; Marina Henderson, 'Women and flowers', in Ann Bridges (ed.), *Alphonse Mucha: The Graphic Works* (London, Academy Editions, 1980), pp. 9–14; and David M. H. Kern (ed.), *The Art Nouveau Style Book of Alphonse Mucha* (New York, Dover, 1980).

The lily in the garden returns to Jekyll, *Lillies*, pp. 7, 96 and 103; Synge, *Lilies*, pp. 25–6; Helen Morgenthau Fox, *Garden Cinderellas: How to Grow Lilies in the Garden* (New York, Macmillan, 1928); and Henry John Elwes, *A Monograph of the Genus Lilium* (London, 1880) and later supplements.

Sunflower

Allen Ginsberg's 'Sunflower Sutra' appears in his *Collected Poems 1947–1980* (London, Penguin, 1987), pp. 138–9; Edward Burne-Jones's comment on sunflowers in Burne-Jones, *Memorials*, vol. 1, p. 225; and the 'creepy' sunflowers in the poem 'Fragment' by June English, *Sunflower Equations* (London, Hearing Eye, 2008), p. 66.

My sources on the origin and domestication of the sunflower include: Charles B. Heiser Jr, *The Sunflower* (Norman, Okla., University of Oklahoma Press, 1976); David L. Lentz et al., 'Sunflower (*Helianthus annuus* L.) as a pre-Columbian domesticate in Mexico', *Proceedings of the National Academy of Sciences of the United States of America* (*PNAS*), vol. 105, no. 17 (29 April 2008), pp. 6232–7; Charles B. Heiser Jr, 'Taxonomy of *Helianthus* and origin of domesticated sunflower', in Jack F. Carter (ed.), *Sunflower Science and Technology* (Madison, Wis., American Society of Agronomy, no. 19, 1978), pp. 31–53; David L. Lentz et al., 'Prehistoric sunflower (*Helianthus annuus* L.) domestication in Mexico', *Economic Botany*, vol. 55, no. 3 (July–Sept 2001), pp. 370–6; Jonathan W. Silvertown, *An Orchard Invisible: A Natural History of Seeds* (Chicago, University of Chicago Press, 2009), pp. 135–54; William W. Dunmire, *Gardens of New Spain: How Mediterranean Plants and Foods Changed America* (Austin, University of Texas Press, 2004), pp. 32–4; Charles B. Heiser, 'The sunflower (*Helianthus annuus*) in Mexico: further evidence for a North American domestication', *Genetic Resources and Crop Evolution*, no. 55, 2008, pp. 9–13; and David L. Lentz et al., 'Reply to Reiseberg and Burke, Heiser, Brown, and Smith: molecular, linguistic, and archaeological evidence for domesticated sunflower in pre-Columbian Mesoamerica, PNAS, vol. 105, no. 30, (29 July 2008), consulted online 3 April 2013.

On the search for Mayan, Inca and Aztec sunflowers, see V. S. Naipaul, *The Loss of El Dorado* (Harmondsworth, Penguin Books, 1973), pp. 38 and 18; Elizabeth H. Boone, 'Incarnations of the Aztec supernatural; the image of Huitzilopochtli in Mexico and Europe', *Transactions of the American Philosophical Society*, vol. 79, part 2 (1989), pp. 1–107; Alan R. Sandstrom, 'Sacred mountains and miniature worlds: altar design among the Nahua of northern Veracruz, Mexico', in Douglas Sharon (ed.), *Mesas & Cosmologies in Mesoamerica* (San Diego Museum Papers 42, 2003), pp. 51–70; Zelia Nuttall, 'Ancient Mexican superstitions', reprinted from the *Journal of American Folklore*, vol. 10, no. 39 (Boston, Mass., 1897), p. 271; Sabine MacCormack, *Religion in the Andes: Vision and Imagination in Early Colonial Peru* (Princeton, Princeton University Press, 1991); Zelia Nuttall, 'The gardens of ancient Mexico', in *Annual Report of the Board of Regents of the Smithsonian Institution, 1923* (Washington, 1925), pp. 453–64; Fray Bernardino de Sahagún, *Florentine Codex, General History of the Things of New Spain, Book 9 – The Merchants* (Santa Fe, The School of American Research and the University of Utah, 1959), no. 14, part X, pp. 33–5; *Codex Ixtlilxochitl, Bibliothèque Nationale, Paris (Ms. Mex. 65–71)* (Graz, Akademische Druck, 1976), 108r., and p. 31; and Joseph Acosta, *The Naturall and Morall Historie of the East and West Indies*, trans. E. G. (London, 1604), Book 4, Chapter 27, pp. 282–4.

My main sources on the sunflower's introduction to Europe are: Nicolas Monardes, *Joyfull Newes out of the Newe Founde Worlde ... Englished by John Frampton* (2 vols, London, Constable, 1925, from an original of 1577), vol. 2, p. 23; John Peacock, *The Look of Van Dyck: The Self-Portrait with a Sunflower and the Vision of the Painter* (Aldershot, Ashgate, 2006); Rembert Dodoens, *Florum et Coronariarum Odoratarumque Nonnullarum Herbarum Historia* (Antwerp, 1568); Gerard, *The Herball* (1597), pp. 612–13; Simon Varey et al. (eds), *Searching for the Secrets of Nature: The Life and Works of Dr Francisco Hernández* (Stanford, Calif., Stanford University Press, 2000), pp. 106–7; Simon Varey (ed.), *The Mexican Treasury: The Writings of Dr Franciso Hernández* (Stanford, Calif., Stanford University Press, c.2000); Parkinson, *Paradisi in Sole*, pp. 295–7. For more on Fibonacci spirals in the sunflower, see Ryuji Takaki et al., 'Simulations of sunflower spirals and Fibonacci numbers', *Forma*, vol. 18 (2003), pp. 295–305; and John A. Adam, *Mathematics in Nature: Moulding Patterns in the Natural World* (Princeton, Princeton University Press, 2003), pp. 216–21.

Here are my main sources for North American sunflowers: Thomas Hariot,

A Briefe and True Report of the New Found Land of Virginia, a facsimile edition of the 1588 Quarto (Ann Arbor, The Clements Library Associates, 1951); Kim Sloan, *A New World: England's First View of America* (London, British Museum Press, 2007), pp. 110–11; Theodore de Bry, *A Briefe and True Report of the New Found Land of Virginia* (Frankfurt, 1590), plate XX, 'The Towne of Secota'; Samuel de Champlain, *Voyages to New France*, trans. Michael Macklem (Ottawa, Oberon Press, n.d.), pp. 40–41; and Daniel E. Moerman, *Native American Medicinal Plants: An Ethnobotanical Dictionary* (Portland, Timber Press, 2009), pp. 228–9.

For the strange beauty of the sunflower to European eyes, see Blunt and Stearn, *The Art of Botanical Illustration*, pp. 102–6; Basilius Besler, *Hortus Eystettensis* (2 vols, Nürnberg, 1613), vol. 2, Quintus Ordo., fols 1 and 2; Crispin de Passe, *Hortus Floridus* (1614–17); Emanuel Sweert, *Florilegium* (Frankfurt, 1612); E. F. Bleiler (ed.), *Early Floral Engravings* (New York, Dover Publications, 1976); Leith-Ross, *The Florilegium of Alexander Marshal*, p. 137, 'Large Sun-flower – Liver-colord Dog in miniature'; and Gloria Cottesloe and Doris Hunt, *The Duchess of Beaufort's Flowers* (Exeter, Webb & Bower, 1983), pp. 54–7, plate 29.

To track the sunflower's emblematic power, I turned to Erika von Erhardt-Siebold, 'The heliotrope tradition', *Osiris*, vol. 3 (1937), pp. 22–46; Ovid, *Metamorphoses*, p. 82; Peacock, *The Look of Van Dyck*, p. 146; E. de Jongh, 'Bol vincit amorem', *Simiolus: Netherlands Quarterly for the History of Art*, vol. 12, no. 2/3 (1981–2), pp. 147–61; Hawkins, *Partheneia Sacra*, pp. 48–58; Sir Kenelm Digby, *A Late Discourse ... Touching the Cure of Wounds by the Powder of Sympathy* (London, 1658); Daniel de la Feuille, *Devises et Emblemes* (Amsterdam, 1691); and *Emblems for the Entertainment and Improvement of Youth* (London, 1750). For William Blake's sunflower, see Mary Lynn Johnson, 'Emblem and symbol in Blake', *The Huntington Library Quarterly*, vol. 37 (February 1974), pp. 151–70; William Blake, *Poems and Prophecies* (London, Everyman's Library, 1991), p. 29; Albert S. Roe, *Blake's Illustrations to the Divine Comedy* (Princeton, Princeton University Press, 1953), pp. 193–6, and plate 99; and Potter, *The Rose*, pp. 89–91.

My sources for the sunflower in British gardens through the eighteenth and nineteenth centuries include Philip Miller, *The Gardeners Dictionary*;

Thomas Fairchild, *The City Gardener* (London, 1722); Robert Furber, *Twelve Months of Flowers* (London, 1730); Jane Loudon, *Gardening for Ladies; and Companion to the Flower Garden*, first American edn, ed. A. J. Downing (New York, 1848); and William Robinson, *The English Flower Garden*, eighth edition (London, John Murray, 1900), pp. 583–5.

For the sunflower in the 'language of flowers', see Beverly Seaton, *The Language of Flowers* (Charlottesville, University Press of Virginia, 1995); Potter, *The Rose*, pp. 422–6; B. Delachénaye, *Abécédaire de Flore ou Langage des Fleurs* (Paris, 1811), pp. 154 and 95; Charlotte de Latour, *Le Langage des Fleurs, Nouvelle édition augmentée* (Brussels, 1854); and Taxile Delord, *Les Fleurs Animées* (Paris, 1847).

For the sunflower in nineteenth- and early twentieth-century art and decoration, see Walter Hamilton, *The Aesthetic Movement in England* (London, Reeves & Turner, 1882); Wilde, *Poems*, p. 215; William Morris, 'The story of the unknown church', *Oxford and Cambridge Magazine* (January 1856), pp. 28–33; Debra N. Mancoff, *Sunflowers* (Chicago, The Art Institute of Chicago, 2001); Burne-Jones, *Memorials*, vol. 1, p. 225; Elizabeth Aslin, *The Aesthetic Movement: Prelude to Art Nouveau* (London, Elek, 1969); Lillie Langtry (Lady De Bathe), *The Days that I Knew* (London, Futura, 1978), pp. 74–5; *Punch*, vol. 80 (25 June 1881), p. 298; and *The British Architect* (10 November 1882), p. 534.

My discussion of van Gogh's sunflowers draws on these main sources: Judith Bumpus, *Van Gogh's Flowers* (Oxford, Phaidon, 1989); the website vangoghletters.org/vg, letters 657, 665, 666, 668, 721, 739, 856, 881; *The Real Van Gogh: The Artist and His Letters* (London, Royal Academy of Arts, 2010); and Douglas W. Druick and Peter Kort Zegers, *Van Gogh and Gauguin: The Studio of the South* (New York, Thames and Hudson, 2001).

For the twentieth-century history of the sunflower, see Putt, 'History and present world status', in Carter (ed.), *Sunflower Science*; Norma Paniego et al., 'Sunflower', in C. Kole (ed.), *Genome Mapping and Molecular Breeding in Plants*, vol. 2, *Oilseeds* (Berlin, Springer-Verlag, 2007), pp. 153–77; Silvertown, *An Orchard Invisible*, pp. 135–54; Andrew Evans, *Ukraine* (Chalfont St Peter, Bradt Travel Guide, second edn, 2007), pp. 37–8; http://www.hort.purdue.edu/newcrop/afcm/sunflower.html; D. H. Putnam et al., 'Sunflower', in *Alternative Field Crops Manual* (University of Wisconsin-Madison,

WI 53706, November 1990), accessed 6 April 2011; http://www.netstate.com/ states/symb/flowers/ks_wild_native_sunflower.htm; *Kansas Statutes*, Chapter 73, Article 18, Sections 73–1801; Craig Miner, *The History of the Sunflower State, 1854–2000* (Lawrence, Kan., University Press of Kansas, 2002), pp. 13–15; and http://www.tate.org.uk/whats-on/tate-modern/exhibition/unilever-series-ai-weiwei-sunflower-seeds.

Opium Poppy

Othello's words are from The Arden Shakespeare's *Othello*, third edn, ed. E. A. J. Honigmann (Walton-on-Thames, Thomas Nelson & Sons, 1997), Act 3 Scene 3, lines 334–6, p. 230. Verdicts on the poppy are taken from John Ruskin, *Proserpina: Studies of Wayside Flowers* (2 vols, Orpington, George Allen, 1879–82), vol. 1, p. 86; Gerard, *The Herball* (1597), pp. 295–8; Parkinson, *Theatrum Botanicum*, pp. 365–9; and Friedrich A. Flückiger and Daniel Hanbury, *Pharmacographia: A History of the Principal Drugs of Vegetable Origin Met with in Great Britain and British India* (London, Macmillan, 1879), pp. 40–43.

My main sources for the domestication of the opium poppy are Sir Ghillean Prance and Mark Nesbitt (eds), *The Cultural History of Plants* (New York, Routledge, 2005), pp. 199–200; and Daniel Zohary and Maria Hopf, *Domestication of Plants in the Old World*, second edn (Oxford, Clarendon Press, 1993), pp. 128–31. Further detail can be found in Mark David Merlin, *On the Trail of the Ancient Opium Poppy* (Cranbury, NJ, Associated University Presses, 1984). For the opium poppy among the Sumerians, Assyrians and Egyptians, see R. Campbell Thompson, *A Dictionary of Assyrian Botany* (London, The British Academy, 1949); R. Campbell Thompson, *The Assyrian Herbal: A Monograph on the Assyrian Vegetable Drugs* (London, Luzac, 1924); Manniche, *An Egyptian Herbal*; Abraham D. Krikorian, 'Were the opium poppy and opium known in the ancient Near East?', *Journal of the History of Biology*, vol. 8, no. 1 (Spring 1975), pp. 95–114; Hepper, *Pharaoh's Flowers*, pp. 10 and 16; Professor Dr P. G. Kritikos and S. P. Papadaki, 'The history of the poppy and of opium and their expansion in antiquity in the eastern Mediterranean area', *Bulletin on*

Narcotics, vol. 19, no. 3 (July–September 1967), pp. 17–38.

For ancient Greek and Roman poppies, and opium use, see Homer, *The Iliad*, trans. E. V. Rieu, updated by Peter Jones with D. C. H. Rieu (London, Penguin, 2003); Homer, *The Odyssey*, p. 269; John Scarborough, 'The opium poppy in Hellenistic and Roman medicine', in Roy Porter and Mikulás Teich (eds), *Drugs and Narcotics in History* (Cambridge University Press, 1995), p. 4; Theophrastus, *Enquiry into Plants*, vol. 2, pp. 253, 279–81 and 289–91 (from Book 9, Chapters 5, 12, 15); Dioscorides, *De Materia Medica*, pp. 611–15 and 608–11; Robert T. Gunther (ed.), *The Greek Herbal of Dioscorides . . . Englished by John Goodyer* (Oxford, 1934), p. 460; *The Natural History of Pliny*, vol. 4, pp. 196–7 and pp. 275–7 (from Book 19, Chapter 53, and Book 20, Chapter 76); Giulia Caneva and Lorenza Bohuny, 'Botanic analysis of Livia's painted flora (Prima Porta, Rome)', *Journal of Cultural Heritage*, vol. 4 (2003), pp. 149–55; Wilhelmina Feemster Jashemski, *The Gardens of Pompeii, Herculaneum and the Villas Destroyed by Vesuvius*, vol. 2, *Appendices* (New York, Aristide D. Caratzas, 1993), pp. 349–53; Jashemski and Meyer (eds), *The Natural History of Pompeii*, pp. 139–40; H. Roux and L. Barré, *Herculaneum et Pompeii: Receuil Général des Peintures, Bronzes, Mosaiques etc.* (8 vols, Paris, Firmin Didot, 1875–7), vol. 1, plate 14; and Ovid, *Metamorphoses*, p. 267.

For a brief history of Demeter and her daughter Persephone (also known as 'Kore', the girl), see Simon Hornblower and Antony Spawforth (eds), *The Oxford Classical Dictionary* (Oxford University Press, 1996), pp. 447–8. For the poppy in German Romanticism, see Peter Wegmann, *Caspar David Friedrich to Ferdinand Hodler: A Romantic Tradition* (Frankfurt, Insel, 1993), pp. 72–5; and Novalis (Friedrich von Hardenberg), *Hymns to the Night*, trans. Mabel Cotterell (London, Phoenix Press, 1948), pp. 23–5. Lieutenant Colonel John McCrae's poem 'In Flanders Fields' was first published anonymously in *Punch* (8 December 1915), p. 468.

These are my main sources for the poppy in medieval Europe: Pierre-Arnaud Chouvy, *Opium: Uncovering the Politics of the Poppy* (London, I. B. Tauris, 2009); Harvey, *Mediaeval Gardens*, pp. 29–35; John Harvey, 'Westminster Abbey: the infirmarer's garden', *Garden History*, vol. 20, no. 2 (1992), pp. 97–115; H. R. Loyn and J. Percival, *The Reign of Charlemagne: Documents on Carolingian Government and Administration* (London, Edward Arnold, 1975), pp. 64–73; Potter, *The Rose*, pp. 85–7; and Strabo, *Hortulus*, pp. 48–9.

For Elizabethan and Stuart poppies, see Gerard's *Herball*, pp. 295–8 and pp. 368-72 in the revised (1633) edn; Jackson, *A Catalogue of Plants*; Edmund Spenser, *The Faerie Queene*, taken from Edwin Greenlaw et al. (eds), *The Works of Edmund Spenser: A Variorum Edition* (11 vols, Baltimore, The Johns Hopkins University Press, 1932–57), vol. 2, pp. 90–91; Parkinson, *Paradisi in Sole*, pp. 284–7; Aymonin, *The Besler Florilegium*, p. 404; Crispin de Passe, *Hortus Floridus* (Utrecht, 1614); Sweert, *Florilegium*; and Besler, *Hortus Eystettensis*, Book 2, summer plants of the twelfth order [*duodecimus ordo*], fols 7–10.

For garden poppies from the eighteenth century onwards, see Miller, *The Gardeners Dictionary*; Henry Phillips, *History of Cultivated Vegetables*, second edn (2 vols, London, Henry Colburn, 1822), vol. 2, pp. 57–77; Henry Phillips, *Flora Historica: or the Three Seasons of the British Parterre Historically and Botanically Treated*, second edn revised (2 vols, London, 1829), vol. 2, pp. 188–97; Mrs Loudon, *The Ladies' Flower-Garden of Ornamental Annuals* (London, William Smith, 1840), pp. 18–23; Robinson, *The English Flower Garden*, pp. 206–7; and Nori and Sandra Pope, *Colour by Design: Planting the Contemporary Garden* (London, Conran Octopus, 1998), pp. 100–103.

The story of the opium poppy's use in pharmacology draws on many sources, including Parkinson, *Theatrum Botanicum*, pp. 365–9; C. E. Dubler, 'Afyun', *Encyclopedia of Islam*, second edn, ed. P. Bearman et al. (Brill, 2011), *Brill Online*, British Library, consulted 19 August 2011; John Scarborough, 'Herbs of the field and herbs of the garden in Byzantine medicinal pharmacy', in Antony Littlewood et al. (eds), *Byzantine Garden Culture* (Washington DC, Dumbarton Oaks Research Library & Collection, 2002), pp. 182–3; Martin Booth, *Opium: A History* (New York, St Martin's Press, 1998), p. 104; Luis Gogliati Arano, *The Medieval Health Handbook* (London, Barrie & Jenkins, 1976); Gilbert Watson, *Theriac and Mithridatium: A Study in Therapeutics* (London, The Wellcome Historical Medical Library, 1966); Flückiger and Hanbury, *Pharmacographia*, pp. 40–42; 'Paracelsus', Encyclopaedia Britannica Online Academic Edition, 2011, consulted 19 August 2011; Henry E. Sigerist (ed.), *Paracelsus: Four Treatises*, trans. C. L. Temkin et al. (Baltimore, Johns Hopkins University Press, 1941); William Langham, *The Garden of Health* (London, 1597), pp. 506–9; William Turner, *A New Herball Parts II and III*, ed. George

T. L. Chapman, Frank McCombie, Anne Wesencraft (Cambridge University Press, 1995), pp. 486–9; Gervase Markham, *The English House-wife* (London, 1637), pp. 6–12; David E. Allen and Gabrielle Hatfield, *Medicinal Plants in Folk Tradition: An Ethnobotany of Britain and Ireland* (Portland, Timber Press, 2004), pp. 77–8; Donald Watts, *Dictionary of Plant Lore* (Oxford, Academic Press, 2007), p. 278; Roy Vickery, *A Dictionary of Plant-Lore* (Oxford University Press, 1997), p. 268; and *Pharmacopoeia Londinensis* (London, 1618), p. 112. For Thomas Sydenham, see C. G. Meynell, *Thomas Sydenham's Observationes Medicae and Medical Observations* (Folkestone, Winterdown Books, 1991), p. 172; and John D. Comrie, *Selected Works of Thomas Sydenham, M. D., with a short biography and explanatory notes* (London, John Bale, 1922), p. 1. Dr John Jones lists his recommended opiates in *The Mysteries of Opium Reveal'd* (London, 1700), pp. 294 and 295; and see Alethea Hayter, *Opium and the Romantic Imagination* (London, Faber and Faber, 1968), p. 31.

Travellers' tales about opium habits are taken from Jean Chardin, *Voyages du Chevalier Chardin en Perse, et Autres Lieux de l'Orient* (4 vols, Amsterdam, 1735), vol. 3, pp. 14–15; Baron François de Tott, *Memoirs of Baron de Tott*, trans. from the French (2 vols, London, 1785), vol. 1, pp. 141–3; Edward G. Browne, *A Year Amongst the Persians* (London, Adam and Charles Black, 1893); and *Memoirs of ****. Commonly known by the Name of George Psalmanazar; A Reputed Native of Formosa* (London, 1764), pp. 56–63.

My quotations from Thomas de Quincey come from the second edition of *Confessions of an English Opium-Eater* (London, Taylor and Hessey, 1823); and for Mike Jay's perceptive essay on Berlioz, first broadcast on BBC Radio 3 in 2002, see http://mikejay.net/articles/opium-and-the-symphonie-fantastique/. See also Ernest Hartley Coleridge (ed.), *Letters of Samuel Taylor Coleridge* (2 vols, William Heinemann, 1895), vol. 1, pp. 229 and 240; M. H. Abrams, *The Milk of Paradise: The Effect of Opium Visions on the Work of de Quincey, Crabbe, Francis Thompson and Coleridge* (New York, Harper & Row, 1970); and Robert F. Fleissner, *Sources, Meaning, and Influences of Coleridge's Kubla Khan* (Lewiston, The Edwin Mellen Press, 2000). The two French translations of de Quincey's *Confessions* are: Thomas de Quincey, *L'Anglais Mangeur d'Opium*, trans. Alfred de Musset (Paris, 1828); and Charles Baudelaire, *Les Paradis Artificiels: Opium et Haschisch* (Paris, 1860).

See also 'Le Poison', in Baudelaire, *Les Fleurs du Mal*, p. 73. For individuals known to have taken opium or laudanum, see Hayter, *Opium and the Romantic Imagination*, and Barbara Hodgson, *In the Arms of Morpheus: The Tragic History of Laudanum, Morphine and Patent Medicines* (Vancouver, Greystone Books, 2001). Cocteau's comment appears in Jean Cocteau, *Opium: The Diary of an Addict*, trans. Ernest Boyd (London, Longmans, Green & Co., 1932), p. 16; and Dorothy Wordsworth's in *The Grasmere Journal*, revised by Jonathan Wordsworth (New York, Henry Holt and Company, 1987), p. 64. For opium production in Britain, see Loudon, *The Ladies' Flower-Garden*, pp. 18–23; and for Fenland poppies, Allen and Hatfield, *Medicinal Plants in Folk Tradition*, pp. 77–8.

These works were helpful on the poppy in western art: Celia Fisher, *Flowers of the Renaissance* (London, Frances Lincoln, 2011); Roberts (ed.), *Encyclopedia of Comparative Iconography*; and Mancoff, *Flora Symbolica*. For the 'language of flowers' see Potter, *The Rose*; *Le Langage des fleurs, ou les Selams de l'Orient* (Paris, 1819); de Latour, *Le Langage des Fleurs*, pp. 275 and 225; John Ingram, *Flora Symbolica; Or, the Language and Sentiment of Flowers* (London, Frederick Warne & Co., 1870), pp. 140–1; Mrs E. W. Wirt of Virginia, *Flora's Dictionary* (Baltimore, Lucas Brothers, 1855), p. 102; and Delord, *Les Fleurs Animées*, pp. 242–4 (author's translation).

My main background sources to the Opium Wars were Peter Ward Fay, *The Opium War, 1840–1842* (Chapel Hill, University of North Carolina Press, 1975), and Hsin-pao Chang, *Commissioner Lin and the Opium War* (Cambridge, Mass., Harvard University Press, 1964), supplemented by Toby and Will Musgrave, *An Empire of Plants: People and Plants that Changed the World* (London, Cassell, 2000). For points of detail, I have also drawn on J. F. B. Tinling, *The Poppy-Plague and England's Crime* (London, Elliot Stock, 1876); Duarte Barbosa, *A Description of the Coasts of East Africa and Malabar in the Beginning of the Sixteenth Century*, trans. Hon. Henry E. J. Stanley (London, Hakluyt Society, 1866), pp. 221–3; Flückiger and Hanbury, *Pharmacographia*, p. 41; Booth, *Opium*; and Nathan Allen, *An Essay on the Opium Trade* (Boston, 1850). For American involvement, see Diana L. Ahmad, *The Opium Debate and Chinese Exclusion Laws* (Reno and Las Vegas, University of Nevada Press, 2007), especially pp. 20–21; and for drug trafficking today, see Tom Kramer et al., *Withdrawal Symptoms in the Golden Triangle: A Drug Market in Disarray* (Amsterdam, Transnational Institute, 2009). Mark Twain's opium den appears in *Roughing It* (Berkeley, University of California Press, 1972), pp. 353–5; Michael Pollan's report, 'Opium, made easy, one gardener's encounter with the war on drugs', in *Harper's Magazine*, vol. 294, no. 1763 (April 1997), pp. 35–58; and the innocent poppy field in L. Frank Baum, *The Wizard of Oz* (Chicago, George M. Hill, 1900), Chapter 8. Conan Doyle's story, *The Man with the Twisted Lip*, was published by George Newnes.

On the chemistry and pharmacology of opium, see Rudolf Schmitz, 'Friedrich Wilhelm Sertürner and the discovery of morphine', *Pharmacy in History*, vol. 27, no. 2 (1985), pp. 61–74; Scarborough, 'The opium poppy in Hellenistic and Roman medicine', p. 12; Flückiger and Hanbury, *Pharmacographia*, pp. 53–4; Hodgson, *In the Arms of Morpheus*; Ryan J. Huxtable and Stephen K. W. Schwartz, 'The isolation of morphine – first principles in science and ethics', *Molecular Interventions*, vol. 1, no. 4 (October 2001), pp. 189–91; Susanna Fürst and Sándor Hosztafi, 'Pharmacology of poppy alkaloids', in Jeno Bernáth (ed.), *Poppy: The Genus Papaver* (Amsterdam, Harwood Academic Publishers, 1998), pp. 291–318; and James A. Duke, 'Utilization of papaver', *Economic Botany*, vol. 27 (October–December 1973), pp. 390–400. For the drugs trade today, see Jeno Bernáth, 'Overview of world tendencies on cultivation, processing and trade of raw [opium] and opiates', in Bernáth (ed.), *Poppy*, pp. 319–35; United Nations Office on Drugs and Crime, *World Drug Report 2011* (New York, United Nations, 2011), pp. 45–86; and *Herbal Pharmacology in the People's Republic of China*. Amitav Ghosh's novel, *Sea of Poppies*, was published by John Murray (London, 2009), and Camilla Swift's article 'The romance of Midland Farm' appeared in *The Garden*, vol. 136, no. 6 (June 2011), pp. 384–7.

Rose

Rilke's poem comes from 'Les Roses II' in *The Complete French Poems of Rainer Maria Rilke*, trans. A. Poulin Jr (Saint Paul, Minn., Graywolf, 2002), p. 3. For full sources on the rose, see Jennifer Potter, *The Rose: A True History* (London,

Atlantic Books, 2010). Sir Arthur Evans described his excavations in *The Palace of Minos*, vol. 2, part 2, pp. 454–9; and see Arthur O. Tucker, 'Identification of the rose, sage, iris, and lily in the "Blue Bird Fresco" from Knossos, Crete (ca. 1450 B.C.E.)', *Economic Botany*, vol. 58, no. 4 (Winter 2004), pp. 733–5. Other sources on the rose's early history include: Herodotus, *The Histories*, p. 550; A. S. Hoey, 'Rosaliae Signorum', *The Harvard Theological Review*, vol. 30 (1937), pp. 13–35; and R. D. Fink, A. S. Hoey and W. F Snyder, 'The Feriale Duranum', *Yale Classical Studies*, vol. 7 (1940), pp. 115–20; *The Natural History of Pliny*, especially vol. 4, pp. 310–14 (from Book 21, Chapter 10); Naphtali Lewis, *Life in Egypt under Roman Rule* (Oxford, Clarendon Press, 1985); Jashemski and Meyer, *The Natural History of Pompeii*; and Annamaria Ciarallo, *Gardens of Pompeii* (Los Angeles, J. Paul Getty Museum, 2001).

For roses in Charlemagne's time, see Loyn and Percival (eds), *The Reign of Charlemagne*, p. 73; and for roses in Byzantium, Costas N. Constantinides, 'Byzantine gardens and horticulture in the late Byzantine period, 1204–1453: the secular sources', in Littlewood et al. (eds), *Byzantine Garden Culture*, pp. 87–103. My sources for roses in Moorish Spain include *Le Livre de l'Agriculture d'Ibn-al-Awwam*, trans. J.-J. Clément-Mullet (2 vols, Paris, 1864), pp. 281–3; and John Harvey, 'Gardening books and plant lists of Moorish Spain', *Garden History*, vol. 21, no. 1 (1993), pp. 118–20. Jerry Stannard names medieval roses in 'Identification of the plants described by Albertus Magnus, *De Vegetabilibus*', *Res Publica Litterarum, Studies in the Classical Tradition*, vol. 2 (1979), pp. 281–318. For Martin Schongauer's *The Madonna of The Rose Bower*, see Fisher, *Flowers of the Renaissance*, pp. 20–21 and 94–5.

Charles Joret explored the Persian origins of the rose in *La Rose dans l'Antiquité et au Moyen Age* (Paris, 1892). For the Damask rose's parentage, see Hikaru Iwata et al., 'Triparental origin of Damask roses', *Gene*, vol. 259 (2000), pp. 53–9. These sources were helpful on the rose's gradual diffusion: Zohary and Hopf, *Domestication of Plants*, pp. 248–9; and Andrew M. Watson, *Agricultural Innovation in the Early Islamic World: The Diffusion of Crops and Farming Techniques 700–1100* (Cambridge University Press, 1983). Jekyll's comments on the Centifolia's smell come from Gertrude Jekyll and Edward Mawley, *Roses for English Gardens* (London, Country Life, 1902), p. 12.

Two good sources on Chinese roses are Guoliang Wang, 'Ancient Chinese roses', in Andrew V. Roberts (ed.), *Encyclopedia of Rose Science* (3 vols, Amsterdam, Elsevier Academic Press, 2003), vol. 1, pp. 387–96; and 'A study on the history of Chinese roses from ancient works and images', *Acta Horticulturae*, no. 751 (2007), pp. 347–56. The report on Chinese nursery gardens is taken from Sir George Staunton Bt, *An Authentic Account of an Embassy from the King of Great Britain to the Emperor of China* (2 vols, London, 1797).

For a re-evaluation of the Empress Josephine's reputation as France's greatest rose lover, see Potter, *The Rose*, pp.178–204, and pp. 363–90 for nineteenth-century rose mania. Dean Hole's comments come from Samuel Reynolds Hole, *A Book about Roses* (Edinburgh, William Blackwood & Sons, 1869 and many subsequent editions). Among many later sources on rose breeding, I consulted Pat Shanley and Peter Kukielski (eds), *The Sustainable Rose Garden: Exploring 21st Century Environmental Rose Gardening* (New York, Manhattan Rose Society, 2008), pp. 57–66; and David Austin, *The Rose* (Woodbridge, Garden Art Press, 2009).

Here are some of my sources for the rose in perfumery: Theophrastus, 'Concerning odours', in his *Enquiry into Plants*, vol. 2, pp. 323–89; R. J. Forbes, *Short History of the Art of Distillation* (Leiden, E. J. Brill, 1948); J. Ch. Sawer, *Rhodologia: A Discourse on Roses and the Odour of Rose* (Brighton, W. J. Smith, 1894), see p. 23 for Engelbert Kaempfer's remarks on Persian roses, and p. 25 for Geronimo Rossi; Wheeler M. Thackston (ed. and trans.), *The Jahangirnama: Memoirs of Jahangir, Emperor of India* (New York, Oxford University Press, 1999); Eugene Rimmel, *The Book of Perfumes* (London, Chapman & Hall, 1865); and Georges Vigarello, *Concepts of Cleanliness: Changing Attitudes in France since the Middle Ages*, trans. Jean Birrell (Cambridge University Press, 1988).

The literature on the healing rose is extensive: see Potter, *The Rose*, pp. 293–331 and 492–6. My principal sources include: Dioscorides, *De Materia Medica*; Turner, *A New Herball: Parts II and III*, p. 545; Langham, *The Garden of Health*, pp. 532–40; *Herbal Pharmacology in the People's Republic of China*, p. 206; Josselyn, *New Englands Rarities Discovered*, p. 58; Gerard, *The Herball*, pp. 1082–4; Nicholas Culpeper, *Pharmacopoeia Londinensis: Or the London Dispensatory* (London, 1653); Benjamin Woolley, *The Herbalist: Nicholas Culpeper and the Fight for Medical Freedom* (London, HarperCollins, 2005), especially pp. 174–6; John Evelyn, *Fumifugium: Or The Inconvenience of the Aer and Smoak of London Dissipated* (London, 1661), pp. 24–5; Robert Boyle, *Medicinal Experiments: Or, A Collection of Choice and Safe Remedies* (London, 1731); *Herbal Drugs and Phytopharmaceuticals on a Scientific Basis*, second edn (Stuttgart, Medfarm, 2001), pp. 424–6; and *Nursing Practice*, 22 September 2008.

My discussion of the rose as the flower of love begins with Paul Jellinek, *The Psychological Basis of Perfumery*, ed. and trans. J. Stephan Jellinek (London, Blackie Academic & Professional, 1997). Among many other sources, these stand out: Anne Carson, *If Not, Winter: Fragments of Sappho* (London, Virago, 2003); Ovid's *Fasti*; Guillaume de Lorris and Jean de Meun, *The Romance of the Rose*, trans. Charles Dahlberg (Princeton, NJ, Princeton University Press, 1971); Thelma S. Fenster and Mary Carpenter Erler, *Poems of Cupid, God of Love* (Leiden, E. J. Brill, 1990); Joseph L. Baird and John R. Kane, *La Querelle de la Rose: Letters and Documents* (Chapel Hill, North Carolina Studies in the Romance Languages and Literature, no. 199, 1978); 'The Parliament of Fowls', in Geoffrey Chaucer, *The Riverside Chaucer*, ed. Larry D. Benson (Boston, Mass., Houghton Mifflin, *c*.1987), p. 389; Jack B. Oruch, 'St Valentine, Chaucer, and Spring in February'; in *Speculum*, vol. 56 no.3 (1981), pp. 534–65; Gordon Williams, *A Dictionary of Sexual Language and Imagery in Shakespearean and Stuart Literature* (3 vols, London, The Arthouse Press, 1994), see entries for bud, flower, garland, rose, velvet; Eric Partridge, *A Dictionary of Slang and Unconventional English*, second edn (London, George Routledge & Sons, 1938); and Helkiah Crooke, *Mikrokosmographica: A Description of the Body of Man* (London, 1615). Rilke's poem, *Les Roses IX*, appears in Rilke, *The Complete French Poems*, pp. 6–7; and Jo Shapcott's 'Rosa Sancta' is from *Tender Taxes* (London, Faber and Faber, 2001), p. 67.

Potter, *The Rose*, examines the gradual emergence of the Christian rose in Chapter 5, 'The Virgin's Bower', pp. 73–91. St Cecilia's story is taken from Jacobus de Voragine, *The Golden Legend: Selections*, trans. Christopher Stace (London, Penguin Books, 1998); and Dorothy's story from David Farmer, *The Oxford Dictionary of Saints*, fifth edn (Oxford University Press, 2003). Other sources include Goody, *The Culture of Flowers*; Beverly Seaton, 'Towards a Historical Semiotics of Literary Flower Personification' in *Poetics Today*, vol. 10, no. 4 (Winter 1989), pp. 679–701; Eithne Wilkins, *The Rose-Garden*

Game, The Symbolic Background to the European Prayer-beads (London, Victor Gollancz, 1969); Harvey, *Mediaeval Gardens*; Eliza Allen Starr, *Patron Saints* (1871, republished 2003 by Kessinger Publishing, Whitefish, Montana), p. 100; Alcuin, 'Farewell to his cell', in Frederick Brittain, *The Penguin Book of Latin Verse* (Harmondsworth, Penguin, 1962), pp. 137–8; Strabo, *Hortulus*, pp. 61–3; and Barbara Seward, *The Symbolic Rose* (New York, Columbia University Press, 1960), pp. 43 and 51.

For sources on the rose in Islam, see Annemarie Schimmel, *And Muhammad is His Messenger: The Veneration of the Prophet in Islamic Piety* (Lahore, Vanguard, 1987), pp. 159–75; and for roses in Persian poetry, Annemarie Schimmel, *A Two-Colored Brocade: The Imagery of Persian Poetry* (Chapel Hill, University of North Carolina Press, 1992), pp. 169–76.

Illuminating my discussion of the Tudor rose is S. B. Chrimes, *Lancastrians, Yorkists and Henry VII*, second edn (London, Macmillan, 1966), pp. xi–xiv. See also Mortimer Levine, *Tudor Dynastic Problems 1460–1571* (London, George Allen & Unwin, 1973); and W. J. Petchey, *Armorial Bearings of the Sovereigns of England* (London, Bedford Square Press, 1977), pp. 18–19. The Gerard quotations are taken from Thomas Johnson's revised edition of his *Herball*; and see Potter, *The Rose*, pp. 139–43, for more on Robert Devereux and Queen Elizabeth I's Eglantine. Sources for other political roses include US President Ronald Reagan's Proclamation 5574, filed with the Office of Federal Register 21 November 1986 (see Pub.L.99-449, Oct 7, 1986, 100 Stat.1128); http://www.lours.org, 'le poing et la rose'; and for New Labour's red rose, see Bob Franklin, *Packaging Politics, Political Communications in Britain's Media Democracy* (London, Edward Arnold, 1994), pp. 132–3.

My sources on the dark rose include Homer, *Iliad*, trans. A. T. Murray and revised by William F. Wyatt (2 vols, Cambridge, Mass., Harvard University Press, 1999), vol. 2, p. 507; Percy E. Newberry, 'On the vegetable remains discovered in the Cemetery of Hawara', in W. M. Flinders Petrie, *Hawara, Biahmu, and Arsinoe* (London, Field & Tuer, 1889), pp. 46–53; Frederick Stuart Church's painting of 'Silence', in David Bernard Dearinger (ed.), *Paintings and Sculpture in the Collection of the National Academy of Design*, vol. 1, *1826–1925* (Manchester, Vermont, Hudson Hills Press, 2004), pp. 104–5; C. G. Jung, *Mysterium Coniuncionis*, vol. 14 of *The Collected Works of C. G. Jung*, trans. R. F. C Hull, second edn (London, Routledge & Kegan Paul, 1970), pp. 305–7; and C. G. Jung, *The Practice of Psychotherapy*, in *The Collected Works*, vol. 16, pp. 244–5; William Blake, 'The sick rose' from Songs of Experience, in Blake, *Poems and Prophecies*, p. 27; Huysmans, *Against Nature*, p. 72; Georges Bataille, 'The Language of Flowers', in *Visions of Excess: Selected Writings, 1927–1939*, ed. Allan Stoekl, trans. Stoekl et al., in *Theory and History of Literature*, vol. 14 (Manchester, Manchester University Press, 1985), pp. 10–14; Gertrude Stein, 'Sacred Emily', in *Geography and Plays* (Boston, Mass., Four Seas Co, 1922), p. 187; and Umberto Eco, *Reflections on the Name of the Rose*, trans. William Weaver (London, Secker & Warburg, 1985), pp. 1–3.

For the Rosicrucian rose, see Potter, *The Rose*, pp. 112–28 and pp. 474–6. Much of the background comes from Frances A. Yates, *The Rosicrucian Enlightenment* (London, Routledge & Kegan Paul, 1972), supplemented by Christopher McIntosh, *The Rosicrucians: The History, Mythology, and Rituals of an Esoteric Order* (San Francisco, Weiser Books, 1998). See also Johann Valentin Andreae, *The Chymical Wedding of Christian Rosenkreutz*, trans. Edward Foxcroft (London, Minerva Books, n.d.); and Richard Ellmann, *Yeats: The Man and the Masks* (London, Faber & Faber, 1961).

Peter Harkness summarized research on the spread of the Cherokee rose in 'Ancestry & Kinship of the Rose', Royal National Rose Society, *Rose Annual 2005*, pp. 72–3; and Gerd Krüssmann discussed the Cherokee rose in *Roses*, trans. Gerd Krüssmann and Nigel Raban (London, B. T. Batsford, 1982), p. 46. Rilke's epitaph comes from George C. Schoolfield, *Rilke's Last Year* (Lawrence, University of Kansas Libraries, 1966), pp. 16–17.

Tulip

The chapter's epigraph comes from Zbigniew Herbert, 'The Bitter Smell of Tulips' in *Still Life with a Bridle, Essays and Apocryphas* (London, Jonathan Cape, 1993), pp. 41–65. Michael Pollan writes about tulips in *The Botany of Desire: A Plant's-Eye View of the World* (New York, Random House, 2001), pp. 59–110. In addition to more modern works on the tulip, I went back to these early authors: Pierre Belon, *Les Observations de Plusieurs Singular-*

itez et Choses Memorables (Paris, 1553), pp. 206v.–7r.; *A Treatise on Tulips by Carolus Clusius of Arras*, trans. W. Van Dijk (Haarlem, Associated Bulb Growers of Holland, 1951); Gerard, *The Herball*, pp. 116–20; Charles de la Chesnée Monstereul, *Le Floriste François: traittant de l'origine des tulippes* (Caen, 1654), pp. 13–14; and Alexandre Dumas, *The Black Tulip*, trans. Robin Buss (London, Penguin, 2003), p. 43. For the number and distribution of species, I consulted Richard Wilford, *Tulips: Species and Hybrids for the Gardener* (Oregon, Timber Press, 2006), pp. 13–14; J. Esteban Hernandez Bermajo and Expiracion Garcia Sanchez, 'Tulips: an ornamental crop in the Andalusian Middle Ages', *Economic Botany*, vol. 63, no. 1 (2009), pp. 60–6; L. W. D. Van Raamsdonk et al., 'The systematics of the genus *Tulipa* L.', *Acta Horticulturae*, vol. 430, no. 2 (1997), pp. 821–8; and Dr Mark Nesbitt at the Royal Botanic Gardens, Kew.

Much of the background to the Ottoman tulip comes from Turhan Baytop, 'The tulip in Istanbul during the Ottoman period', in Michiel Roding and Hans Theunissen, *The Tulip: A Symbol of Two Nations* (Utrecht and Istanbul, M. Th. Houtsma Stichting and Turco-Dutch Friendship Association, 1993), pp. 51–6. See also: Yanni Petsopoulos (ed.), *Tulips, Arabesques & Turbans: Decorative Arts from the Ottoman Empire* (London, Alexandria Press, 1982); Nurhan Atasoy and Julian Raby, *Iznik: The Pottery of Ottoman Turkey* (London, Alexandria Press/Thames and Hudson, 1989); John Harvey, 'Turkey as a source of garden plants', *Garden History*, vol. 4, no. 3 (Autumn 1976), pp. 21–42; Walter G. Andrews, Najaat Black and Mehmet Kalpakli, *Ottoman Lyric Poetry: An Anthology* (Austin, University of Texas Press, 1997); and C.-H. de Fouchécour, *La Description de la Nature dans la Poésie Lyrique Persane du XIe Siècle* (Paris, Librairie D. Klincksieck, 1969), pp. 73–6. The story of the dervish preacher comes from Yildiz Demiriz, 'Tulips in Ottoman Turkish culture and art', in Roding and Theunissen, *The Tulip*, p. 57. For a discussion of the tulip's religious significance, see Annemarie Schimmel, 'The celestial garden in Islam', in Elizabeth B. Macdougall and Richard Ettinghausen (eds), *The Islamic Garden* (Washington DC, Dumbarton Oaks, 1976), p. 25; and for Süleyman the Magnificent's tulip embroidery, see Anna Pavord, *The Tulip* (London, Bloomsbury, 1999), p. 35; her source is possibly Arthur Baker, 'The cult of the tulip in Turkey', *Journal of the Royal Horticultural Society*, vol. 56 (1931), pp. 234–44.

De Busbecq's tulip letter appears in *The Turkish Letters of Ogier Ghiselin de Busbecq*, trans. Edward Seymour Forster (Oxford, Clarendon Press, 1927), pp. 24–5; and the description of Councillor Herwart's red tulip in Valerius Cordius, *Annotationes in Pedaci Dioscorides* (Strasbourg, 1561), fol. 213, r. and v. A partial translation of the latter appears in W. S. Murray, 'The introduction of the tulip, and the tulipomania', *Journal of the Royal Horticultural Society*, vol. 35 (1909), Part I, pp. 18–30. See also Sam Segal, 'Tulips portrayed: the tulip trade in Holland in the 17th century', in Roding and Theunissen, *The Tulip*, pp. 9–24; and Anne Goldgar's painstaking cataloguing of early botanical writings on the tulip, in *Tulipmania: Money, Honor, and Knowledge in the Dutch Golden Age* (Chicago, University of Chicago Press, 2007). Clusius's *A Treatise on Tulips* usefully brings together all his writings on the tulip, which helped me to track their introduction into Europe.

John Rea writes of breaking tulips in *Flora: seu, De Florum Cultura. Or, a Complete Florilege* (London, 1665), p. 51. For the causes of their breaking, see Elise L. Dekker, 'Characterization of potyviruses from tulip and lily which cause flower-breaking', *Journal of General Virology*, vol. 74 (1993), pp. 881–7; other authors writing on the phenomenon include: Philip Miller, *The Gardeners and Florists Dictionary, or a Complete System of Horticulture* (2 vols, London, 1724), and *The Gardeners Dictionary*; Parkinson, *Paradisi in Sole*, pp. 62–3; and Henry van Oosten, *The Dutch Gardner: or, the Compleat Florist*, trans. from the Dutch (London, 1703), pp. 65–6. Richard Hakluyt's reference to Clusius's tulip appears in *The Principal Navigations, Voyages, Traffiques and Discoveries of the English Nation*, collected by Richard Hakluyt, Preacher, and edited by Edmund Goldsmid, vol. 5, *Central and Southern Europe* (Edinburgh, E. & G. Goldsmid, 1887), pp. 300–301. For Clusius's distress at the commercialization of the tulip trade, see Goldgar, *Tulipmania*, pp. 58–9.

For tulips in seventeenth-century florilegia, I consulted these works: Lee Hendrix and Thea Vignau-Wilberg, *Nature Illuminated: Flora and Fauna from the Court of the Emperor Rudolf II* (London, Thames and Hudson, c.1997); Blunt and Stearn, *The Art of Botanical Illustration*; Aymonin, *The Besler Florilegium*, pp. 114–17; Pierre Vallet, *Le Jardin du Roy Tres Chrestien Henry IV* (Paris, 1608), revised for King Louis XIII in 1623; Crispin de Passe, *Hortus Floridus, A Garden of Flowers* (Utrecht, 1615).

The works by Gerard, Parkinson and Thomas Johnson listed under general sources describe the growing number of tulips coming to Britain. For more on the Lime Street community, see Margaret Willes, *The Making of the English Gardener* (New Haven, Yale University Press, 2011), pp. 88–9 and *passim*. The Tradescants' tulips appear in Jennifer Potter, *Strange Blooms: The Curious Lives and Adventures of the John Tradescants* (London, Atlantic Books, 2006), especially p. 304; for their full plant lists, see Prudence Leith-Ross, *The John Tradescants: Gardeners to the Rose and Lily Queen* (London, Peter Owen, revised edn 2006), pp. 213–17, 235 and 304–5; and for Alexander Marshal's painted tulips, see Leith-Ross, *The Florilegium of Alexander Marshal*. My sources on Sir Thomas Hanmer include Willes, *The Making of the English Gardener*, pp. 256–9; *The Garden Book of Sir Thomas Hanmer Bart* (London, Gerald Howe, 1933); John Evelyn, 'Elysium Britannicum', f. 286, quoted by Leith-Ross, *The Florilegium of Alexander Marshal*, pp. 96–7; and John Rea's *Flora*.

For French tulip mania, see Pavord, *The Tulip*, pp. 82–101; La Chesnée Monstereul, *Le Floriste François*, pp. 18–19; Potter, *Strange Blooms*, pp. 159–60; E. S. de Beer (ed.), *The Diary of John Evelyn* (London, Everyman's Library, 2006), pp. 72–3 (1–6 April 1644) and pp. 269–70 (21 May 1651); and Pierre Morin, *Remarques Necessaires pour la Culture des Fleurs* (Paris, 1658), pp. 181–98.

General accounts of Dutch tulip fever appear in Pavord, *The Tulip*; Mike Dash, *Tulipomania: The Story of the World's Most Coveted Flower and the Extraordinary Passions it Aroused* (London, Victor Gollancz, 1999); Deborah Moggach, *Tulip Fever: A Novel* (London, Heinemann, 1999); Sam Segal, 'Tulips Portrayed', in Roding and Theunissen, *The Tulip*; and most exhaustively in Goldgar, *Tulipmania*. The first (exaggerated but entertaining) English account of tulip fever appeared in Charles Mackay's *Memoirs of Extraordinary Popular Delusions* (3 vols, London, Richard Bentley, 1841), vol. 1, pp. 139–53. Other works consulted include Peter Mundy, *The Travels of Peter Mundy*, vol. 4, ed. Lieut. Col. Sir Richard Carnac Temple (London, Hakluyt Society, 1925), 2nd series, no. 55, pp. 60–81; Roland Barthes, 'The world as object', in Norman Bryson (ed.), *Calligram: Essays in New Art History from France* (Cambridge University Press, 1988), pp. 106–15; Roemer Visscher, *Sinnenpoppen* (The Hague, 1949), from an original of 1614; Paul Taylor, *Dutch*

Flower Painting 1600–1720 (New Haven, Yale University Press, 1995); Dr Frans Willemse, *The Mystery of the Tulip Painter* (Lisse, Museum de Zwarte Tulp, 2005); and James Sowerby, *Flora Luxurians; or, The Florist's Delight No. 3* (London, 1791).

In addition to the general works cited, my principal sources on Turkey's 'Tulip Era' were these: I. Mélikoff, 'Lâle Devri', *Encyclopaedia of Islam*, second edn, ed. P. Bearman et al., Brill Online, accessed British Library, 30 September 2011; Salzmann, 'The age of tulips'; Baytop, 'The tulip in Istanbul'; Tahsin Öz, 'Ciraghan', *Encyclopaedia of Islam*, second edn, ed. P. Bearman et al., Brill Online, accessed British Library, 30 September 2011; Philip Mansel, *Constantinople: City of the World's Desire 1453–1924* (London, John Murray, 1995), p. 182; and Baker, 'The cult of the tulip in Turkey', p. 244.

Thomas Johnson's praise of the tulip appears in his revised edition of Gerard's *Herball*, pp. 137–46; the biblical reference is from Matthew 6: 28–9. The discussion between the flowers comes from *Antheologia, or The Speech of Flowers* (London, 1655), pp. 5–13. For the story of florists' societies, see Ruth Duthie, *Florists' Flowers and Societies* (Princes Risborough, Shire, 1988). Also consulted were A. D. Hall, 'The English or florist's tulip', *Journal of the Royal Horticultural Society*, vol. 27 (1902), Part I, pp. 142–62; J. W. Bentley, *The English Tulip and its History*, lecture delivered at the Great Tulip Conference of the Royal National Tulip Society, 12 May 1897 (London, Barr & Sons, 1897); James Douglas, *Hardy Florists' Flowers: Their Cultivation and Management* (London, 1880), pp. 44–55; *Gardeners' Chronicle* (15 May 1897), p. 327; Miller, *The Gardeners and Florists Dictionary*; George Glenny, *The Standard of Perfection for the Properties of Flowers and Plants*, second edn (London, Houlston and Stoneman, 1847); The Wakefield and North of England Tulip Society, *The English Florists' Tulip* (Bradford, 1997); Robinson, *The English Flower Garden*; and Sacheverell Sitwell, *Old Fashioned Flowers* (London, Country Life, 1939), pp. 73–88.

The tulip poems quoted are: 'La Tulipe', in Théophile Gautier, *Poésies Complètes* (3 vols, Paris, A. G. Nizet, 1970), vol. 3, p. 189; 'Tulips', in Sylvia Plath, *Ariel* (London, Faber and Faber, 1965), pp. 20–3; and James Fenton, *Yellow Tulips: Poems 1968–2011* (London, Faber and Faber, 2012), p. 140. My information on the tulip trade today comes from Maarten Benschop et al.,

'The Global Flower Bulb Industry: Production, Utilization, Research', Wiley Online Library (accessed 28 October 2011), pp. 7–8, and 30–33; and J. C. M. Buschman, 'Globalisation – flower – flower bulbs – bulb flowers', *Acta Horticulturae*, vol. 1, no. 673 (2005), pp. 27–33.

Orchid

The chapter's epigraph comes from Raymond Chandler, *The Big Sleep* (London, Hamish Hamilton, 1939), p. 16. The most comprehensive orchid history is Merle A. Reinikka, *A History of the Orchid* (Portland, Oregon, Timber Press, 1995). Other sources consulted for the introduction include John Lindley, *Sertum Orchidaceum: A Wreath of the Most Beautiful Orchidaceous Flowers* (London, James Ridgway & Sons, 1838), plate XXXIII; Shiu-ying Hu, 'Orchids in the life and culture of the Chinese people', *The Chung Chi Journal*, vol. 10, nos 1 & 2 (October 1971), pp. 1–26; and Oakes Ames, 'The origin of the term orchis', *American Orchid Society Bulletin*, vol. 11 (1942–3), pp. 146–7.

Much of my botanical information about orchids comes from Wilma and Brian Rittershausen, *The Amazing World of Orchids* (London, Quadrille, 2009). For the newly discovered night-flowering orchid, see Ian Sample, 'Found in the forest, the only nocturnal orchid', *Guardian*, 22 November 2011, and orchid numbers from http://www.kew.org/science-research-data/directory/teams/monocots-III-orchids/index.htm, accessed 11 April 2013. For more detail on orchid classification, see Mark W. Chase, 'Classification of Orchidaceae in the Age of DNA data', *Curtis's Botanical Magazine*, vol. 22, no. 1, pp. 2–7 (2005); and see K. W. Dixon et al., 'The Western Australian fully subterranean orchid *Rhizanthella gardneri*', in *Orchid Biology, Reviews and Perspectives, V*, ed. Joseph Arditti (Portland, Timber Press, 1990), pp. 37–62.

These sources were helpful on Chinese orchids: Hu, 'Orchids', p. 19; Hui-Lin Li, *The Garden Flowers of China* (New York, Ronald Press, 1959); Sing-chi Chen and Tsin Tang, 'A general review of the orchid flora of China', *Orchid Biology, Reviews and Perspectives, II*, ed. Joseph Arditti (Ithaca, Comstock Pub. Associates, 1982), pp. 59–67; Catherine Paganini, 'Perfect men and true friends, the orchid in Chinese culture', *American Orchid Society Bulletin*

(December 1991), pp. 1176–83; and Helmut Brinker, *Zen in the Art of Painting*, trans. George Campbell (London, Arkana, 1987), pp. 117–22. The poems of Su Shih and Huang T'ing-chien are quoted in Richard M. Barnhart, *Peach Blossom Spring: Gardens and Flowers in Chinese Paintings* (New York, Metropolitan Museum of Art, *c.*1983), pp. 55–6. Also illuminating on Chinese art were Ching-I Tu (ed.), *Classics and Interpretations: The Hermeneutic Traditions in Chinese Culture* (New Brunswick, NJ, Transaction Publishers, 2000), pp. 283–4, consulted online; and *The Mustard Seed Garden Manual of Painting*, a facsimile of the 1887–8 Shanghai edn, trans. Mai-mai Sze (Princeton, NJ, Bollingen Foundation/Princeton University Press, 1977).

My information on Japanese orchids comes principally from Kashioka and Ogisu, *Illustrated History*, pp. 85–94. I also drew on Alfred Koehn, *The Art of Japanese Flower Arrangement* (Japan, J. L. Thomson & Co., 1933); and Conder, *The Flowers of Japan*, pp. 133–4.

For western views of the orchid, see Theophrastus, *Enquiry into Plants*, vol. 2, pp. 309–11 (from Book 9, Chapter 18); Jerry Stannard, 'The herbal as medical document', *Bulletin of the History of Medicine*, vol. 43, no. 3 (1969), pp. 212–20; and Chalmers L. Gemmill, MD, 'The missing passage in Hort's translation of Theophrastus', *Bulletin of the New York Academy of Medicine*, vol. 49, no. 2 (February 1973), pp. 127–9. John Goodyer's translation appears in Gunther (ed.), *The Greek Herbal of Dioscorides*, p. 373. Other sources on the orchid's medical uses include: Langham, *The Garden of Health*, pp. 450–1; and Gerard, *The Herball*, pp. 156–76; Luigi Berliocchi, *The Orchid in Lore and Legend*, trans. Leonore Rosen and Anita Weston, ed. Mark Griffiths (Portland, Timber Press, 2004); Dioscorides, *De Materia Medica*, pp. 522–4; Li, *The Garden Flowers of China*, pp. 14–15; Chen and Tang, 'Orchid flora of China', p. 43; and Hu, 'Orchids', p. 15.

Western perceptions of the orchid are explored more fully in Martha W. Hoffman Lewis, 'Power and passion: the orchid in literature', in *Orchid Biology V*, pp. 207–49; Margaret B. Freeman, *The Unicorn Tapestries* (New York, The Metropolitan Museum of Art, 1976), pp. 143–53; Reinikka, *A History of the Orchid*, p. 5; and Leonard J. Lawler, 'Ethnobotany of the Orchidaceae', *Orchid Biology, Reviews and Perspectives, III*, ed. Joseph Arditti (Ithaca, New York, Comstock Pub. Associates, 1984), pp. 27–149. See also

Geoffrey Hadley, 'Orchid Mycorrhiza', *Orchid Biology, II*, pp. 83–118; Parkinson, *Theatrum Botanicum*, pp. 1341–62; Miller, *The Gardeners Dictionary*, entry for 'Orchis'; Caroli Linnaei, *Species Plantarum* (2 vols, Stockholm, 1753), vol. 2, pp. 939–54; and Erasmus Darwin, *The Botanic Garden; A Poem, in Two Parts. Part II, containing the Loves of the Plants* (London, 1791).

Charles Darwin wrote about orchids in *On the Various Contrivances by which British and Foreign Orchids are Fertilised by Insects, and on the Good Effects of Intercrossing* (London, John Murray, 1862); and John Ruskin, in *Proserpina*, vol. 1, pp. 202–205. See also M. M. Mahood, 'Ruskin's flowers of evil', in *The Poet as Botanist* (Cambridge University Press, 2008), pp. 147–82; and Michael Pollan's introduction to Christian Ziegler, *Deceptive Beauties: The World of Wild Orchids* (Chicago, University of Chicago Press, c.2011), p. 22.

For a full ethnobotany of Orchidaceae, see Lawler, 'Ethnobotany of the Orchidaceae', in *Orchid Biology III*, pp. 27–149; and for vanilla and the Aztecs, see *The Badianus Manuscript (Codex Barberini, Latin 241)*, ed. and trans. Emily Walcott Emmart (Baltimore, The Johns Hopkins University Press, 1940); vanilla appears in plate 104. Also on vanilla, see Michael Lorant, 'The story of vanilla', *Orchid Review*, vol. 92, no. 1094 (December 1984), pp. 404–5; Javier De la Cruz et al., 'Vanilla: Post-Harvest Operations, 16.6.2009', from www.fao.org (Food and Agriculture Organization of the United Nations), accessed 7 March 2012; Flückiger and Hanbury, *Pharmacographia*, pp. 595–8; *The Voyages and Adventures of Capt. William Dampier* (2 vols, London, 1776), vol. 1, pp. 368–70; and Miller, *The Gardeners Dictionary* (1768 edn).

My discussion of other exotic orchids draws on these sources: Reinikka, *A History of the Orchid*, pp. 16–18; Dan H. Nicolson et al., *An Interpretation of Van Rheede's Hortus Malabaricus* (Königstein, Koeltz Scientific Books, 1988), pp. 297–303; E. M. Beekman (ed. and trans.), *Rumphius' Orchids: Orchid Texts from the Ambonese Herbal by Georgius Everhardus Rumphius* (New Haven, Yale University Press, 2003); Paulus Hermannus, *Paradisus Batavus* (Lugduni Batavorum, 1698), p. 207 (misnumbered 187); J. Martyn's *Historia Plantarum Rariorum* (London, 1728–37); John Hill, *Hortus Kewensis* (London, 1768), pp. 346–8; William Aiton, *Hortus Kewensis; or, a Catalogue of the Plants Cultivated in the Royal Botanic Garden at Kew* (3 vols, London, George Nicol, 1789), vol. 3, pp. 294–304; William Townsend Aiton, *Hortus Kewensis* (5 vols, London,

1810–13), vol. 5, pp. 188–220; and *Gardeners' Chronicle* (8 October 1859), p. 807.

For the story of Swainson's *Cattleya*, see Sir William Jackson Hooker, *Exotic Flora* (3 vols, Edinburgh, William Blackwood, 1812–27), vol. 2 (1825), tab. 157; John Lindley, *Collectanea Botanica* (London, 1821), no. 7, plate 33; other versions of the story are told by Frederick Boyle, *About Orchids: A Chat* (London, Chapman & Hall, 1893), and Reinikka, *A History of the Orchid*, pp. 23–5.

Among my sources on Europe's growing fascination with orchids are: John Lindley's 'History, introduction, natural habitats, and cultivation of orchideous epiphytes', *Paxton's Magazine of Botany and Register of Flowering Plants*, vol. 1 (London, 1834), see Paxton's footnote about orchid numbers on p. 263; John Lindley, *The Genera and Species of Orchidaceous Plants* (London, Ridgways, 1830–40); the Duke of Devonshire's death notice in *Gardeners' Chronicle* (23 January 1858), pp. 51–2; *Paxton's Magazine of Botany*, vol. 1, pp. 14–15; Lindley, *Sertum Orchidaceum*, especially plates I, III, VIII and XXXIII; 'New and beautiful orchideae', in *Paxton's Magazine of Botany*, vol. 1, pp. 14–15; Reinikka, *A History of Orchids*, pp. 169–73; Brent Elliott, 'The Royal Horticultural Society and its orchids: a social history', *Occasional Papers from the RHS Lindley Library*, no. 2, 2010; and James Bateman, *The Orchidaceae of Mexico and Guatemala* (London, 1837–43). See also James Bateman's much more manageable *A Second Century of Orchidaceous Plants* (London, L. Reeve & Co., 1867). On orchid auctions, I consulted R. M. Hamilton (ed.), *Orchid Auction Sales in England 1842–1850* (Richmond, British Columbia, 1999); Donal P. McCracken, 'Robert Plant (1818–1858): a Victorian plant hunter in Natal, Zululand, Mauritius and the Seychelles', *South African Journal of Science*, vol. 107, no. 3–4 (March/April 2011); and Benjamin Samuel Williams, *The Orchid-Grower's Manual* (London, Chapman and Hall, 1852). See also James Bateman, *Address on George Skinner 1867*, Orchid History Reference Papers no. 7. ed. R. M. Hamilton (Richmond, British Columbia, 1992).

A good source on the Veitch family nurseries is James H. Veitch, *Hortus Veitchii: A History* (London, James Veitch & Sons, Chelsea, 1906); see also 'Royal Exotic Nursery, King's Road, Chelsea', *Gardeners' Chronicle* (15 October 1859), pp. 831–2. Joseph Dalton Hooker tells the story of *Vanda coerulea* in *Himalayan Journals* (2 vols, London, 1854), vol. 2, pp. 319–23. For the endangered Lady's slipper orchid, see *Paxton's Magazine of Botany*, vol.

4 (1837), pp. 247–8; and 'Police on petal patrol to protect UK's rarest wild flower', *Daily Mail*, 7 May 2010.

An excellent contemporary source on Sander's orchid nursery is Frederick Boyle, *The Woodlands Orchids* (London, Macmillan and Co., 1901); see also Arthur Swinson, *Frederick Sander: The Orchid King, The Record of a Passion* (London, Hodder and Stoughton, 1970); and Henry Frederick Conrad Sander, *Reichenbachia. Orchids Illustrated and Described* (2 vols, London, H. Sotheran & Co., 1888–90), and the *Second Series* (2 vols, London, H. Sotheran & Co., 1892–4). Sander's bouquet for Queen Victoria is reported in *London Illustrated News* (25 June 1887), p. 711, and in 'The Queen's jubilee bouquet', *Maitland Mercury & Hunter River General Advertiser* of New South Wales (4 August 1887).

On the orchid's social power, I consulted Sir Jeremiah Colman, *Hybridization of Orchids: The Experience of an Amateur* (printed for private circulation [1932]); and 'Mrs Pankhurst on Recent Developments', *Morning Post* (11 February 1913) for news of the suffragettes at Kew. For the orchid's current protection, see Royal Horticultural Society, *Conservation and Environment Guidelines, Bringing Plants in from the Wild* (Wisley, RHS Science Departments, January 2002). For *Vanda coerulea*'s removal from CITES Appendix 1, see www.kew.org/plants-fungi/Vanda-coerulea.htm, consulted 4 April 2013.

Here are my sources for the orchid in western literature: William Shakespeare, *Hamlet*, Act IV, Scene 7; Ellacombe, *The Plant-Lore and Garden-Craft of Shakespeare*, pp. 157–9, entry for 'Long Purples'; Mahood, *The Poet as Botanist*, pp. 112–46; Lewis, 'Power and passion' in *Orchid Biology V*, pp. 207–49; Huysmans, *Against Nature*, pp. 72–81; Marcel Proust, 'Un amour de Swann', in *Du Coté de Chez Swann: À la Recherche du Temps Perdu* (Paris, Le Livre de Poche, 1966), p. 277; Goody, *The Culture of Flowers*, p. 298; H. G. Wells, 'The Flowering of the Strange Orchid', in *The Time Machine and the Wonderful Visit and Other Stories, The Works of H. G. Wells*, Atlantic Edition, vol. 1 (London, T. Fisher Unwin, 1924), pp. 308–19; 'The League of Frightened Men', in Rex Stout, *Full House: A Nero Wolfe Omnibus* (New York, Viking Press, 1955), pp. 3–212; James Hadley Chase, *No Orchids for Miss Blandish* (Berne, Alfred Scherz, 1946); 'Orchids', in *The Collected Poems of Theodore Roethke* (Garden City, NY, Doubleday, 1966), p. 39; and Jean Rhys, *Wide Sargasso Sea* (London, Penguin, 1968), p. 17.

Finally, on the orchid's continuing fascination, I turned to Susan Orlean, *The Orchid Thief* (London, Vintage, 2000); Eric Hansen, *Orchid Fever* (London, Methuen, 2000); Tom Hart Dyke and Paul Winder, *The Cloud Garden* (London, Bantam Press, 2003); and Reginald Farrer, *My Rock-Garden* (London, Edward Arnold, 1907), p. 279.

Illustrations

p. 39 Bronze-Age Minoan wall painting of red lilies and swallows from a townhouse at Akrotiri on the Aegean island of Thera (*DEA/G. Nimatallah/ Getty Images*)

p. 55 John Tenniel's engraving of Alice's encounter with the Tiger-lily in Lewis Carroll's *Through the Looking-glass*, 1872 (*Morphart Creation/Shutter-stock.com*)

p. 65 Sunflowers, drawn and engraved by Crispin de Passe the Younger, *Hortus Floridus*, 1614 (*Courtesy of Dover Publications, Inc.*)

p. 72 The Aztec ruler Nezahualpilli (d. 1515) holding in his left hand a stylized sunflower. From the late sixteenth-century *Codex Ixtlilxochitl* (*Bibliothèque nationale de France*)

p. 89 Cartoon by Edward Linley Sambourne for *Punch*, 25 June 1881, depict-ing the Irish writer and aesthete Oscar Wilde as a sunflower (*Universal Images Group/Getty Images*)

p. 97 Poppies from a late printing (1790) of Nicholas Culpeper's *The English Physitian Enlarged* (*Image provided by Peter H. Raven Library, Missouri Botanical Garden, http://www.missouribotanicalgarden.org/*)

p. 105 An opium poppy from the 'Vienna Dioscorides', an early sixth-century Byzantine copy of Dioscorides' *De Materia Medica* (*SSPL via Getty Images*)

p. 127 Gustave Doré's illustration of the Lascar's room in Charles Dickens's *The Mystery of Edwin Drood*, for *London: A Pilgrimage*, 1872 (© *Lebrecht Music & Arts/Corbis*)

p. 131 Roses, drawn and engraved by Crispin de Passe the Younger, *Hortus Floridus*, 1614 (*Courtesy of Dover Publications, Inc.*)

p. 138 A double yellow rose from the Levant, described by Carolus Clusius in *Curae Posteriores*, Leiden, 1611 (*Image provided by Peter H. Raven Library, Missouri Botanical Garden, http://www.missouribotanicalgarden.org/*)

p. 158 Frederick Stuart Church, *Silence*, c.1880 (© *2013. Photo: Smithsonian American Art Museum/Art Resource/Scala, Florence*)

p. 163 Tulips, drawn and engraved by Crispin de Passe the Younger, *Hortus Floridus*, 1614 (*Courtesy of Dover Publications, Inc.*)

p. 170 Europe's first garden tulip, Conrad Gesner, 1559 (*Universitätsbibliothek Erlangen-Nürnberg, MS 2386, folio 220v*)

p. 182 John Lambert depicted on a playing card (*Bridgeman Art Library/English School/Getty Images*)

p. 199 Title page to John Lindley's *Sertum Orchidaceum*, 1838 (*Image provided by Peter H. Raven Library, Missouri Botanical Garden, http://www.missouri botanicalgarden.org/*)

p. 207 Orchid in the traditional style, Chen Banding (*© Artkey/Corbis*)

p. 221 The librarian's nightmare: woodcut from a drawing by George Cruikshank in James Bateman's *The Orchidaceae of Mexico and Guatemala*, 1837–43 (*Image provided by Peter H. Raven Library, Missouri Botanical Garden, http://www.missouribotanicalgarden.org/*)

COLOUR ILLUSTRATIONS

SECTION ONE

June's flowers in Robert Furber's *Twelve Months of Flowers*, 1730 (*© Historical Picture Archive/Corbis*)

Yun Shou-p'ing, *Lotuses on a Summer Evening*, 1684 (*© 2013. Photo: The Metropolitan Museum of Art/Art Resource/Scala, Florence*)

Pierre-Joseph Redouté's blue Nile 'lotus' (*Nymphaea caerulea*) from *Choix des Plus Belles Fleurs*, Paris, 1827–33 (*Image provided by Peter H. Raven Library, Missouri Botanical Garden, http://www.missouribotanicalgarden.org/*)

The Hindu god Krishna removes the clothes of cowgirls who are bathing in a lotus pool, c.1820–30 (*Pahari School/Bridgeman Art Library/Getty Images*)

SECTION TWO

Sandro Botticelli, *The Annunciation*, c.1490 (© *Summerfield Press/Corbis*)

Hog-nose snake with Martagon lily by Mark Catesby for *The Natural History of Carolina, Florida and the Bahama Islands*, London, 1731–43 (*Image provided by Peter H. Raven Library, Missouri Botanical Garden, http://www.missouri botanicalgarden.org/*)

Hand-coloured engraved sunflower from Basilius Besler's *Hortus Eystettensis* of 1613 (© *Corbis*)

Vincent van Gogh, *Sunflowers*, 1887 (*DEA Picture Library/Getty Images*)

SECTION THREE

An opium poppy (*Papaver somniferum*) from *British Phaenogamous Botany* on British flowering plants, 1834–43, by William Baxter (*Florilegius/SSPL via Getty Images*)

Dante Gabriel Rossetti, *Beata Beatrix*, c.1864–1870 (*Universal Images Group/ Getty Images*)

Detail of Martin Schongauer's *Madonna of the Rose Bower*, 1473 (*DEA/G. Dagli Orti/Getty Images*)

A bouquet of roses (1805) painted by Dr Robert John Thornton and engraved by Richard Earlom, from *Temple of Flora, or Garden of Nature* (*Image provided by Peter H. Raven Library, Missouri Botanical Garden, http://www.missouri botanicalgarden.org/*)

A lady holds a bowl of rose flowers in a Mughal miniature, c.1700–40 (© *Stapleton Collection/Corbis*)

SECTION FOUR

Five tulips from Basilius Besler's *Hortus Eystettensis* of 1613 (*British Library/ Robana via Getty Images*)

An 'Istanbul tulip' from an Ottoman tulip album of 1725 (*© Christie's Images/ The Bridgeman Art Library*)

Pierre-Joseph Redouté's Lady's slipper orchid (*Cypripedium calceoleus*) from *Les Liliacées*, 1802–16 (*Image provided by Peter H. Raven Library, Missouri Botanical Garden, http://www.missouribotanicalgarden.org/*)

Martin Johnson Heade, *Cattleya Orchid and Three Brazilian Hummingbirds*, 1871 (*National Gallery of Art, Washington, DC*)

Edouard Manet, *Olympia*, 1865 (*© Corbis*)

Note on the Author

Celebrated for her fiction and non-fiction, Jennifer Potter writes about the history and culture of plants, plantsmen and gardens. She reviews for the *Times Literary Supplement*, and has been variously a Royal Literary Fund Fellow, a Hawthornden Fellow and an Honorary Teaching Fellow on the Warwick Writing Programme. Her most recent books include *Strange Blooms* and *The Rose, A True History*, both published by Atlantic Books.

Index

Note: you will find common flower names in the general alphabetical listing; Latin names are grouped together either under the main genus ('*Rosa*', for instance) or under a separate listing for varieties (e.g. 'Orchid varieties').

Page numbers in **bold** refer to illustrations.